TExES Social Studies 4-8
118 Teacher Certification Exam

By: Sharon A. Wynne, M.S.

XAMonline, Inc.
Boston

XAMonline, Inc.
21 Orient Avenue
Melrose, MA 02176
Toll Free 1-800-301-4647
Email: info@xamonline.com
Web www.xamonline.com

Library of Congress Cataloging-in-Publication Data
Wynne, Sharon A.

    TExES Social Studies 4-8 (118): Teacher Certification / Sharon A. Wynne.
    ISBN 978-1-60787-976-3

1. Social Studies 4-8   2. Study Guides.   3. TExES
4. Teachers' Certification & Licensure.   5. Careers

Disclaimer:
The opinions expressed in this publication are the sole works of XAMonline and were created independently from the National Education Association, Educational Testing Service, or any State Department of Education, National Evaluation Systems or other testing affiliates.

Between the time of publication and printing, state specific standards as well as testing formats and website information may change that is not included in part or in whole within this product. XAMonline developed the sample test questions and the questions reflect similar content as on real tests; however, they are not former tests. XAMonline assembles content that aligns with state standards but makes no claims nor guarantees teacher candidates a passing score. Numerical scores are determined by testing companies such as NES or ETS and then are compared with individual state standards. A passing score varies from state to state.

Printed in the United States of America
TExES: Social Studies 4-8 (118)
ISBN: 978-1-60787-976-3

Table of Contents

DOMAIN I.   SOCIAL STUDIES CONTENT

COMPETENCY 1.0   HISTORY 1

Skill 1.1   Understand traditional historical points of reference in the history of Texas, the United States, and the world 1

Skill 1.2   Analyze how individuals, events, and issues shaped the history of Texas, the United States, and the world 16

Skill 1.3   Analyze the influence of various factors on the development of societies 36

Skill 1.4   Know common characteristics of communities, past and present 37

Skill 1.5   Apply knowledge of the concept of chronology and its use in understanding history and historical events 38

Skill 1.6   Apply different methods of interpreting the past to understand, evaluate, and support multiple points of view, frames of reference, and the historical context of events and issues 39

Skill 1.7   Understands similarities and differences among Native American groups in Texas, the United States, and the Western Hemisphere before European colonization 39

Skill 1.8   Understand the causes and effects of European exploration and colonization of Texas, the United States, and the Western Hemisphere 42

Skill 1.9   Understand the foundations of representative government in the United States, significant issues of the revolutionary era, and challenges confronting the U.S. Government in the early years of the republic 46

Skill 1.10   Understand westward expansion and analyzes its effects on the political, economic, and social development of the United States 50

Skill 1.11   Analyze ways in which political, economic, and social factors led to the growth of sectionalism and the Civil War 52

Skill 1.12   Know individuals, issues, and events of the Civil War and analyzes the effects of Reconstruction on the political, economic, and social life of the nation 52

Skill 1.13   Demonstrate knowledge of major U.S. reform movements of the nineteenth century..61

Skill 1.14   Understand important issues, events, and individuals of the twentieth century in Texas, the United States, and the world 63

Skill 1.15   Understand the contributions of people of various racial, ethnic, and religious groups in Texas, the United States, and the world...68

Skill 1.16   Analyze ways in which particular contemporary societies reflect historical events..74

COMPETENCY 2.0   GEOGRAPHY **76**

Skill 2.1   Understand and apply the geographic concept of region 76

Skill 2.2   Know the location and the human and physical characteristics of places and regions in Texas, the United States, and the world 76

Skill 2.3   Analyze ways in which humans adapt to, use, and modify the physical Environment 78

Skill 2.4   Know how regional physical characteristics and human modifications to the environment affect people's activities and settlement patterns 79

Skill 2.5   Analyze ways in which location affects people, places, and environments 79

Skill 2.6   Demonstrate knowledge of physical processes and their effects on environmental patterns 80

Skill 2.7   Understand the characteristics, distribution, and migration of populations in Texas, the United States, and the world 81

Skill 2.8   Understand the physical environmental characteristics of Texas, the United States, and the world, past and present, and how humans have adapted to and modified the environment 82

Skill 2.9   Analyze how geographic factors have influenced the settlement patterns, economic development, political relationships, and policies of societies and regions in Texas, the United States, and the world 84

Skill 2.10   Analyze interactions between people and the physical environment and the effects of these interactions on the development of places and regions 85

COMPETENCY 3.0   ECONOMICS..**87**

Skill 3.1   Understand that basic human needs are met in many ways 87

Skill 3.2   Understand and apply knowledge of basic economic concepts 87

Skill 3.3   Demonstrate knowledge of the ways in which people organize economic systems, and similarities and differences among various economic systems around the world 88

Skill 3.4   Understand the value and importance of work and purposes for spending and saving money 88

Skill 3.5   Demonstrate knowledge of patterns of work and economic activities in Texas, the United States, and the world, past and present 89

Skill 3.6   Understand the characteristics, benefits, and development of the free-enterprise system in Texas and the United States 90

Skill 3.7   Analyze the roles of producers and consumers in the production of goods and services 91

Skill 3.8   Demonstrate knowledge of how businesses operate in the U.S. free-enterprise system 91

Skill 3.9   Apply knowledge of the effects of supply and demand on consumers and producers in a free-enterprise system 92

Skill 3.10   Demonstrate knowledge of categories of economic activities and methods used to measure a society's economic level 92

Skill 3.11   Use economic indicators to describe and measure levels of economic activity 93

Skill 3.12   Understand major events and trends in economic history 93

Skill 3.13   Analyze the interdependence of the Texas economy with the United States and the world 95

Skill 3.14   Apply knowledge of significant economic events and issues and their effects in Texas, the United States, and the world 95

COMPETENCY 4.0   GOVERNMENT AND CITIZENSHIP **97**

Skill 4.1 ☐   Understand the purpose of rules and laws; the relationship between rules, rights, and responsibilities; and the individual's role in making and enforcing rules and ensuring the welfare of society 97

Skill 4.2   Know the basic structure and functions of the U.S. government, the Texas government, and local governments and relationships among national, state, and local governments 99

Skill 4.3   Demonstrate knowledge of key principles and ideas in major political documents of Texas and the United States 101

Skill 4.4   Know how people organized governments in colonial America and during the early development of Texas 105

Skill 4.5   Understand the political process in the United States and Texas and how the U.S. political system works 106

Skill 4.6   Demonstrate knowledge of types of government and their effectiveness in meeting citizens' needs 106

Skill 4.7   Know the formal and informal process of changing the U.S. and Texas constitutions and the impact of changes on society 107

Skill 4.8   Understand the impact of landmark Supreme Court cases 108

Skill 4.9   Understand components of the democratic process and their significance in a democratic society 109

Skill 4.10   Demonstrate knowledge of important customs, symbols, and celebrations that represent American beliefs and principles and contribute to national unity 110

Skill 4.11   Analyze the relationship among individual rights, responsibilities, and freedoms in democratic societies 110

Skill 4.12   Apply knowledge of the rights and responsibilities of citizens in Texas and the United States, past and present 111

Skill 4.13   Understand how the nature, rights, and responsibilities of citizenship vary among societies 112

COMPETENCY 5.0   CULTURE, SCIENCE, TECHNOLOGY, AND SOCIETY 113

Skill 5.1   Understand basic concepts of culture and the processes of cultural adaptation, diffusion, and exchange 113

Skill 5.2   Analyze similarities and differences in the ways various peoples at different times in history have lived and met basic human needs 114

Skill 5.3   Apply knowledge of the role of families in meeting basic human needs and how families and cultures develop and use customs, traditions, and beliefs to define themselves 115

Skill 5.4   Demonstrate knowledge of institutions that exist in all societies and how characteristics of these institutions may vary among societies 115

Skill 5.5   Understand how people use oral tradition, stories, real and mythical heroes, music, paintings, and sculpture to create and represent culture in communities in Texas, the United States, and the world 116

Skill 5.6   Understand the contributions of people of various racial, ethnic, and religious groups in Texas, the United States, and the world 117

Skill 5.7   Demonstrate knowledge of relationships among world cultures and relationships between and among people from various groups, including racial, ethnic, and religious groups, in the United States and throughout the world 117

Skill 5.8   Analyze relationships among religion, philosophy, and culture, and the impact of religion on ways of life in the United States and world areas 118

Skill 5.9   Understand the concept of diversity within unity 118

Skill 5.10   Analyze the effects of race, gender, and socioeconomic class on ways of life in the United States and throughout the world 119

Skill 5.11   Understand the various roles of men, women, children, and families in cultures past and present 119

Skill 5.12   Understand how the self develops and the dynamic relationship between self and social context 120

Skill 5.13   Apply knowledge of the effects of scientific discoveries and technological innovations on political, economic, social, and environmental developments and on everyday life in Texas, the United States, and the world 120

Skill 5.14   Analyze how science and technology relate to political, economic, social, and cultural issues and events 121

Skill 5.15   Demonstrate knowledge of the origins, diffusion, and effects of major scientific, mathematical, and technological discoveries throughout history 122

Skill 5.16   Know how developments in science and technology have affected the physical environment; the growth of economies and societies; and definitions of, access to, and use of physical and human resources 123

Skill 5.17   Know how changes in science and technology affect moral and ethical issues 124

DOMAIN II.   **SOCIAL STUDIES FOUNDATIONS, SKILLS, AND INSTRUCTION**

COMPETENCY 6   SOCIAL STUDIES FOUNDATIONS AND SKILLS 125

Skill 6.1   Understand the philosophical foundations of the social science disciplines and knows how knowledge generated by the social sciences affects society and people's lives 125

Skill 6.2   Understand how social science disciplines relate to each other . 125

Skill 6.3   Understand practical applications of social studies education 127

Skill 6.4   Relate philosophical assumptions and ideas to issues and trends in the social sciences 127

Skill 6.5   Know characteristics and uses of various primary and secondary sources and uses information from a variety of sources to acquire social science information and answer social science questions 128

Skill 6.6   Know how to formulate research questions and use appropriate procedures to reach supportable judgments and conclusions in the social sciences 129

Skill 6.7   Understand social science research and knows how social scientists locate, gather, organize, analyze, and report information using standard research methodologies 130

Skill 6.8   Evaluate the validity of social science information from primary and secondary sources regarding bias issues, propaganda, point of view, and frame of reference 131

Skill 6.9   Understand and evaluates multiple points of view and frames of reference relating to issues in the social sciences 132

Skill 6.10   Know how to analyze social science information 134

Skill 6.11   Communicate and interpret social science information in written, oral, and visual forms and translates information from one medium to another 134

Skill 6.12   Know how to use problem-solving processes to identify problems, gather information, list and consider options, consider advantages and disadvantages, choose and implement solutions, and evaluate the effectiveness of solutions 135

Skill 6.13   Know how to use decision-making processes to identify situations that require decisions, gather information, identify options, predict consequences, and take action to implement decisions 136

Skill 6.14   Know how to create maps and other graphics to present geographic, political, historical, economic, and cultural features, distributions, and relationships 136

Skill 6.15   Analyze social science data by using basic mathematical and statistical concepts and analytical methods 140

Skill 6.16   Know how to apply skills for resolving conflict, including persuasion, compromise, debate, and negotiation 141

Skill 6.17   Understand and use social studies terminology correctly 141

COMPETENCY 7.0   **SOCIAL STUDIES INSTRUCTION AND ASSESSMENT** **142**

Skill 7.1   Know state content and performance standards for social studies that comprise the Texas Essential Knowledge and Skills (TEKS) 142

Skill 7.2   Understand the vertical alignment of the social sciences in the Texas Essential Knowledge and Skills (TEKS) from grade level to grade level, including prerequisite knowledge and skills 142

Skill 7.3   Understand the implications of stages of child growth and development for designing and implementing effective learning experiences in the social sciences 142

Skill 7.4   Understand the appropriate use of technology as a tool for learning and communicating social studies concepts 144

Skill 7.5   Select and use effective instructional practices, activities, technologies, and materials to promote students' knowledge and skills in the social sciences 145

Skill 7.6   Know how to promote students' use of social science skills, vocabulary, and research tools, including technological tools 145

Skill 7.7   Know how to communicate the value of social studies education to students, parents/caregivers, colleagues, and the community ... 147

Skill 7.8   Know how to provide instruction that relates skills, concepts, and ideas in different social science disciplines 147

Skill 7.9   Provide instruction that makes connections between knowledge and methods in the social sciences and in other content areas 147

Skill 7.10   Demonstrate knowledge of forms of assessment appropriate for evaluating students' progress and needs in the social sciences 148

Skill 7.11   Use multiple forms of assessment and knowledge of the Texas Essential Knowledge and Skills (TEKS) to determine students' progress and needs and to help plan instruction that addresses the strengths, needs, and interests of all students, including English Language Learners 148

Bibliography 153

Sample Test 155

Answer Key 171

Rigor Table 172

Rationales with Sample Questions 173

Great Study and Testing Tips!

What to study in order to prepare for the subject assessments is the focus of this study guide but equally important is *how* you study.

You can increase your chances of truly mastering the information by taking some simple, but effective steps.

Study Tips:

1. Some foods aid the learning process. Foods such as milk, nuts, seeds, rice, and oats help your study efforts by releasing natural memory enhancers called CCKs (*cholecystokinin*) composed of *tryptophan, choline* and *phenylalanine*. All of these chemicals enhance the neurotransmitters associated with memory. Before studying, try a light, protein-rich meal of eggs, turkey, and fish. All of these foods release the memory enhancing chemicals. The better the connections, the more you comprehend.

Likewise, before you take a test, stick to a light snack of energy boosting and relaxing foods. A glass of milk, a piece of fruit, or some peanuts all release various memory-boosting chemicals and help you to relax and focus on the subject at hand.

2. Learn to take great notes. A by-product of our modern culture is that we have grown accustomed to getting our information in short doses (i.e., TV news sound bites or USA Today style newspaper articles.)

Consequently, we've subconsciously trained ourselves to assimilate information better in neat little packages. If your notes are scrawled all over the paper, it fragments the flow of the information. Strive for clarity. Newspapers use a standard format to achieve clarity. Your notes can be much clearer through use of proper formatting. A very effective format is called the *"Cornell Method."*

> Take a sheet of loose-leaf lined notebook paper and draw a line all the way down the paper about 1-2" from the left-hand edge.
>
> Draw another line across the width of the paper about 1-2" up from the bottom. Repeat this process on the reverse side of the page.

Look at the highly effective result. You have ample room for notes, a left hand margin for special emphasis items or inserting supplementary data from the textbook, a large area at the bottom for a brief summary, and a little rectangular space for just about anything you want.

3. Get the concept then the details. Too often we focus on the details and don't gather an understanding of the concept. However, if you simply memorize only dates, places, or names, you may well miss the whole point of the subject.

A key way to understand things is to put them in your own words. If you are working from a textbook, automatically summarize each paragraph in your mind. If you are outlining text, don't simply copy the author's words.

Rephrase them in your own words. You remember your own thoughts and words much better than someone else's, and subconsciously tend to associate the important details to the core concepts.

4. Ask Why? Pull apart written material paragraph by paragraph and don't forget the captions under the illustrations.

Example: If the heading is "Stream Erosion", flip it around to read "Why do streams erode?" Then answer the questions.

If you train your mind to think in a series of questions and answers, not only will you learn more, but it also helps to lessen the test anxiety because you are used to answering questions.

5. Read for reinforcement and future needs. Even if you only have 10 minutes, put your notes or a book in your hand. Your mind is similar to a computer; you have to input data in order to have it processed. *By reading, you are creating the neural connections for future retrieval.* The more times you read something, the more you reinforce the learning of ideas.

Even if you don't fully understand something on the first pass, *your mind stores much of the material for later recall.*

6. Relax to learn so go into exile. Our bodies respond to an inner clock called biorhythms. Burning the midnight oil works well for some people, but not everyone.

If possible, set aside a particular place to study that is free of distractions. Shut off the television, cell phone, and pager and exile your friends and family during your study period.

If you really are bothered by silence, try background music. Light classical music at a low volume has been shown to aid in concentration over other types. Music that evokes pleasant emotions without lyrics is highly suggested. Try just about anything by Mozart. It relaxes you.

7. Use arrows not highlighters. At best, it's difficult to read a page full of yellow, pink, blue, and green streaks. Try staring at a neon sign for a while and you'll soon see that the horde of colors obscure the message.

A quick note, a brief dash of color, an underline, and an arrow pointing to a particular passage is much clearer than a horde of highlighted words.

8. Budget your study time. Although you shouldn't ignore any of the material, *allocate your available study time in the same ratio that topics may appear on the test.*

Testing Tips:

1. Get smart, play dumb. Don't read anything into the question. Don't make an assumption that the test writer is looking for something else than what is asked. Stick to the question as written and don't read extra things into it.

2. Read the question and all the choices *twice* before answering the question. You may miss something by not carefully reading, and then re-reading both the question and the answers.

If you really don't have a clue as to the right answer, leave it blank on the first time through. Go on to the other questions, as they may provide a clue as to how to answer the skipped questions.

If later on, you still can't answer the skipped ones. . . ***Guess.*** The only penalty for guessing is that you *might* get it wrong. Only one thing is certain; if you don't put anything down, you will get it wrong!

3. Turn the question into a statement. Look at the way the questions are worded. The syntax of the question usually provides a clue. Does it seem more familiar as a statement rather than as a question? Does it sound strange?

By turning a question into a statement, you may be able to spot if an answer sounds right, and it may also trigger memories of material you have read.

4. Look for hidden clues. It's actually very difficult to compose multiple-foil (choice) questions without giving away part of the answer in the options presented.

In most multiple-choice questions you can often readily eliminate one or two of the potential answers. This leaves you with only two real possibilities and automatically your odds go to Fifty-Fifty for very little work.

5. Trust your instincts. For every fact that you have read, you subconsciously retain something of that knowledge. On questions that you aren't really certain about, go with your basic instincts. **Your first impression on how to answer a question is usually correct.**

6. Mark your answers directly on the test booklet. Don't bother trying to fill in the optical scan sheet on the first pass through the test.

Just be very careful not to miss-mark your answers when you eventually transcribe them to the scan sheet.

7. Watch the clock! You have a set amount of time to answer the questions. Don't get bogged down trying to answer a single question at the expense of 10 questions you can more readily answer.

DOMAIN I.	SOCIAL STUDIES CONTENT

COMPETENCY 1.0   HISTORY

Skill 1.1   Understand traditional historical points of reference in the history of Texas, the United States, and the world.

Ancient civilizations were those cultures that developed faster and were considered advanced for their time. The following is an overview of some such civilizations with their major accomplishments.

The land of **Mesopotamia** (covering roughly the same territory as modern Iraq) is a good example of the various civilizations that crisscrossed the Fertile Crescent. The most ancient Mesopotamia civilizations were autocratic societies, with a single ruler at the head of the government and often the religion, as well. The people followed his strict instructions or faced the consequences, which were harsh and often deadly.

The civilizations of the Sumerians, Amorites, Hittites, Assyrians, Chaldeans, and Persians controlled various areas of Mesopotamia. With few exceptions, tyrants and military leaders controlled most aspects of society, including trade, religion, and law. Each of the numerous Sumerian city-states had its own god, with the city-state's leader doubling as the high priest of worship of that local god. Subsequent cultures had a handful of gods as well, although they had more of a national worship structure, with high priests centered in the capital city as advisers to the tyrant.

Trade was vital to these civilizations, since they had access to some but not all of the things that they needed to survive. Some trading agreements led to occupation, as was the case with the Sumerians. Egypt and the Phoenician cities were powerful and regular trading partners of the various Mesopotamian cultures.

Mesopotamian cultures gave us the following:

The first writing system, the wheel, and the first banking system (Sumeria);
The first written set of laws (Code of Hammurabi);
The first epic story (*Gilgamesh*);
The first library dedicated to preserving knowledge (instituted by the Assyrian leader Ashurbanipal);
The Hanging Gardens of Babylon (built by the Chaldean Nebuchadnezzar)

Sumerians also developed irrigation through use of canals, dikes, and devices for raising water; learned to divide time into twelve-month years using the lunar calendar; and built large boats for trade. The Babylonians devised the famous Code of Hammurabi, the first known law code.

Egypt made many significant contributions, including the construction of the great pyramids; the development of hieroglyphic writing; the practice of mummification; the creation of paper from papyrus; the advancement of arithmetic and geometry; the establishment of the decimal system (counting in groups of 1–10); the completion of a solar calendar; and laying the foundation for science and astronomy.

Egyptians also provided the earliest historical records of the civilization of **Kush**, also known as **Nubia**. They describe a region upstream (south) of the first cataract of the Nile as "wretched." The Kush civilization was characterized by a settled way of life in fortified mud-brick villages. They subsisted on hunting and fishing, herding cattle, and gathering grain. Skeletal remains suggest that the people were a blend of Negroid and Mediterranean peoples. This civilization appears to be the second oldest in Africa after Egypt.

In government, the king ruled through a law of custom that was interpreted by priests. The king was elected from the royal family. Descent was determined through the mother's line (as in Egypt). But in an unparalleled innovation, the Kushites were also ruled by a series of female monarchs.

The Kushite religion was polytheistic and included all of the primary Egyptian gods. There were, however, regional gods that were the principal gods of their regions. Derived from other African cultures, there was also a lion warrior god. This civilization remained vital through the last half of the first millennium BC, but it suffered about 300 years of gradual decline.

The ancient **Assyrians** were warlike and aggressive due to a highly organized military and use of horse drawn chariots.

The **Minoans** had a system of writing using symbols to represent syllables in words. They built palaces with multiple levels containing many rooms, water and sewage systems with flush toilets, bathtubs, hot and cold running water, and bright paintings on the walls. The **Mycenaeans** changed the Minoan writing system to aid their own language and used symbols to represent syllables.

The **Phoenicians** were sea traders well known for their manufacturing skills in glass and metals and the development of their famous purple dye. They became so proficient in navigation that they were able to sail by the stars at night. They also devised an alphabet using symbols to represent single sounds, which was an improved extension of the Egyptian principle and writing system.

The ancient **Israelites** (or Hebrews) and **Christians** created a powerful legacy of political and philosophical traditions, much of which survives to this day. The **Hebrews** were among the earliest major groups to practice monotheism, or the worship of one god. Monotheism had more of a personal nature to it, as believers thought they were able to communicate directly to their god. Conversely, polytheistic gods of Mesopotamia and Egypt were thought to be distant and unapproachable.

The Hebrew people created important scriptures that have been collected as the 24 books of the Hebrew Bible and which compose the Christian Old Testament. An important part of these scriptures was the Ten Commandments, a series of religious laws reportedly given to the Israelites directly by their deity. Such commandments as the ones that prohibit stealing and killing were revolutionary in their day because they applied to everyone, not just the disadvantaged. In many ancient cultures, the rich and powerful were above the law because they could buy their way out of trouble.

The ancient **Persians** developed an alphabet; contributed the religions and philosophies of Zoroastrianism, Mithraism, and Gnosticism; and allowed conquered peoples to retain their own customs, laws, and religions.

The classical civilization of **Greece** reached the pinnacle of the humanities, owing much to the ground work already laid by the Egyptians, Phoenicians, Minoans, and Mycenaeans. Among the more important Greek contributions were the Greek alphabet, which was derived from the Phoenician alphabetic system and formed the basis for the later Roman alphabet used with minor modifications today. Extensive trading and colonization resulted in the spread of the Greek civilization. The love of sports, with emphasis on a sound body, led to the tradition of the Olympic Games.

Greece was responsible for the rise of independent, strong city-states. Each of these city-states had distinctive characteristics. Athens, typically considered the cradle of democracy, made numerous political and cultural advances. Its primary rival, Sparta, relied on an oligarchic government and fostered a culture of strong militarism. Greek influences on modern society include drama, epic and lyric poetry, fables, myths centered on the many gods and goddesses, science, astronomy, medicine, mathematics, philosophy, art, architecture, and the recording of historical events.

The Greeks united to defend their peninsula from invading Persians, but also experienced internal warring and conflict. Greece eventually fell to the Macedonian ruler Philip. His son, Alexander the Great, was one of the most successful conquerors of classical times. The conquests of Alexander the Great spread Greek ideas to the areas he conquered and brought to the Greek world many Asian influences. Above all, the value of ideas, wisdom, curiosity, and the desire to learn as much about the world as possible satisfied Alexander's thirst for knowledge.

The ancient civilization of **Rome** lasted approximately 1,000 years from the time of its founding as a kingdom through the period of the republic and later empire. However, its influence on Europe and the West lasted much longer. There was a sharp contrast between the imaginative, inquisitive Greeks and the practical, no-nonsense Romans, who nonetheless spread and preserved ancient Greek ideas. The contributions and accomplishments of the Romans are numerous, but their greatest included language, engineering, building, law, government, roads, trade, and the **Pax Romana**. The Pax Romana was a long period of peace that enabled free travel and trade, which spread people, cultures, goods, and ideas all over the world.

In **India**, the caste system was developed, the principle of zero in mathematics was discovered, and the major religion of Hinduism was founded. In India, Hinduism and Buddhism grew in influence. Industry and commerce developed along with extensive trading with the Near East. Rapid developments in science and medicine were made, and Indian was one of the first civilizations to navigate and sail the oceans and seas.

Some historians consider **China** the oldest continuous civilization in the world. It existed around the same time as the Egyptian, Mesopotamian, and Indus Valley civilizations. The Chinese studied nature and weather; stressed the importance of education, family, and a strong central government; followed the religions of Buddhism, Confucianism, and Taoism; and invented such things as gunpowder, paper, printing, paper money, and the magnetic compass.

The Chinese built the Great Wall, practiced crop rotation and terrace farming, increased the silk industry, and developed caravan routes across Central Asia for extensive trade. They advanced rice cultivation and developed a written language based on drawings or pictographs; no alphabet symbolizing sounds emerged as each word or character had a form different from all others.

Ancient China was a land in constant turmoil. Tribes warred with one another almost from the first, with the Great Wall of China being a consolidation of walls built to keep out invaders. The Great Wall was built at the direction of China's emperor, and the idea of an emperor or very strong "government of one" was the rule of law until the twentieth century. The Chinese became very proficient at producing beautiful art and silk, and then exporting them via the Silk Road.

The civilization in **Japan** appeared during this time having borrowed much of their culture from China. It was the last of these classical civilizations to develop. Although they accepted and copied Chinese art, law, architecture, dress, and writing, the Japanese put their own unique "spin" on them. Early Japanese society focused on the emperor and the farm, in that order. However, the emperor's power declined as it was usurped the Shogun, the feudal Daimyo lords, and their loyal soldiers, the Samurai. Japan flourished economically and culturally during many of these years, although the policy of isolation the country developed kept it from experiencing much cultural exchange with the rest of the world. Buddhism and local religions were joined by Christianity in the sixteenth century, but it wasn't until the mid-nineteenth century that Japan rejoined the world community.

During the first millennium A.D., Sub-Sahara African civilizations were learning how to shape and use iron, first as farm implements and later for weapons. Trading was conducted overland using camels and at important seaports. The Arab influence was extremely important, as was their later contact with Indians, Christian Nubians, and Persians. In fact, their trading activities were probably the most important factor in the spread and assimilation of foreign influences and stimulation of growth.

During this time, African civilizations were few and far between. Most of northern Africa had been conquered by Moslem armies. The preponderance of deserts and other inhospitable lands restricted African settlements to a few select areas. The city of Zimbabwe became a trading center in south-central Africa in the 5th century but did not last long. Ghana was more successful: it was a Muslim-influenced kingdom that arose in the 9th century and lasted for nearly 300 years. Ghanaians had large farming areas, raised cattle and elephants, and traded with people from Europe and the Middle East. Ghana was eventually overrun by **Mali,** whose cultural center of Timbuktu survived its own empire's demise and blossomed into one of the world's trading and caravan destinations.

Mali produced a great deal of iron, tin, and leather. The succeeding civilization of the **Songhai**, for the most part, maintained the success of their predecessors and further expanded the role of the city of Timbuktu. Religion in Ghana, Mali, and other North African lands was largely Muslim; and even after extended contact with other cultures, technological advancements were relatively scarce.

The Pre-Columbian people of the Americas had a thriving, connected society. The civilizations in North America tended to be more spread out. Despite occasional conflict, they largely maintained their sovereignty. Native Americans in North America had a spiritual and personal relationship with the various Spirits of Nature and a keen appreciation of the ways of woodworking and metalworking. Various tribes dotted the landscape of what is now the United States. They struggled against one another for control of resources such as food and water but had no concept of ownership of land; they believed that they were living on the land with the permission of the Great Spirit.

Some Native American groups developed settled agricultural societies centered around permanent settlements. The Mississippian people, for example, built the large city of Cahokia. Crops and techniques developed by Native Americans. Artwork made of hides, beads, and jewels were popular at this time.

The South American civilizations, in contrast, tended to colonize one another, with the strongest city or tribe assuming control of the people and resources of conquered civilizations. The most well known South American societies were the Aztec, Inca, and Maya. Each had a central capital in which lived the emperor, who controlled all aspects of the lives of his subjects. The societies traded with other peoples. If trading relations soured, the results were usually absorption of the trading partners into the society. These societies, especially the Aztecs, had access to large amounts of metals and jewels, and they created impressively crafted weapons and artwork. The Inca Empire stretched across a vast period of territory down the western coast of South America and was connected by a series of roads. The Mayans are known for their pyramids and calendar, and developed a complex written language that remains not entirely understood.

The word **Renaissance** literally means "rebirth." This period signaled the rebirth of interest in ancient classical Greek and Roman civilizations. It marked the start of many ideas and innovations leading to our modern age. The Renaissance began in Italy with many of its ideas starting in Florence, controlled by the infamous Medici family. Renaissance education, especially for some of the merchants, required the study of reading, writing, math, law, and the works of classical Greek and Roman writers.

Several Italian artists, including Leonardo da Vinci, Michelangelo, Raphael, Titian, and Donatello, made significant contributions during this era. All of these men pioneered a new method of painting and sculpture based more closely on realism and classical form than that of its predecessors. Literature was also a focus during the Renaissance. Humanists, such as Petrarch, Boccaccio, Erasmus, and Sir Thomas More advanced the idea of being interested in life on Earth and the opportunities it can bring, rather than constantly focusing on the afterlife and its rewards. The works of Shakespeare, Dante, Machiavelli, and Cervantes found their origins in these ideas, as well as the ones that drove the painters and sculptors. All of these works, of course, owe much of their existence to the invention of the printing press, which occurred during the Renaissance.

The Renaissance also changed music. No longer just a religious experience, music could be fun and composed for its own sake to be enjoyed in fuller and more humanistic ways than it had been in the Middle Ages. Musicians worked for themselves rather than working for churches so that they can earn more money for their work, which increased their prestige.

Science also advanced considerably during the Renaissance, especially in the area of physics and astronomy. Copernicus, Kepler, and Galileo led a **Scientific Revolution** by proving that Earth and other planets in the solar system orbited the Sun, a shocking revelation to those who clung to medieval ideas of a geocentric existence. The Scientific Revolution and the **Enlightenment** were two of the most important movements in the history of civilization. They changed the way people viewed themselves and the world. The Scientific Revolution was, above all, a shift in focus from belief based on faith to belief based on evidence. Scientists and philosophers wanted to see the proof, not just believe what other people told them. Nevertheless, the Church still wielded tremendous power at this time, including the power to banish people or sentence them to prison or even death.

A Polish astronomer, **Nicolaus Copernicus**, began the Scientific Revolution. He crystallized a lifetime of observations into a book that was published about the time of his death. In this book, Copernicus argued that the Sun, not Earth, was the center of a solar system and that other planets revolved around it (and not the Earth). This contradicted established, Church-mandated doctrine.

The Danish astronomer **Tycho Brahe** was the first to catalog his observations of the night sky, of which he made thousands. Building on Brahe's data, German scientist Johannes Kepler instituted his theory of planetary movement, embodied in his famous Laws of Planetary Movement. Using Brahe's data, Kepler also confirmed Copernicus's observations and argument that the Earth revolved around the Sun.

The most famous defender of this idea was Italian scientist **Galileo Galilei**. He wrote a book comparing the two theories, but most readers could easily tell that he favored the heliocentric (sun-centered) theory. He had used the relatively new invention of the telescope to see four moons of Jupiter. When they did not revolve around the Earth, he wondered why everything else should. His ideas were ill-received by the Church, which asserted its authority over science and placed Galileo under house arrest.

Galileo died under house arrest, but his theory was advanced by the English scientist, **Isaac Newton**. Newton went on to discover gravity, and was a pioneering voice in the study of optics (light), calculus, and physics.

More than any other scientist, Newton argued form—and proved—the idea of a rational view of the world: You can see and prove how the world works through observation; if you can see these things with your own eyes, they must be so (**empiricism**). Up to this time, people believed what other people told them based on faith (**dogmatism**). Newton, following in the footsteps of Copernicus and Galileo, changed all that.

This subsequently led to the Enlightenment, a period of intense self-study that focused on ethics and logic. More than ever, scientists and philosophers questioned widely held beliefs in an attempt to discover why the world worked—from within. "I think, therefore I am" was one of the famous sayings of that or any day. It was uttered by **Rene Descartes,** a French scientist-philosopher whose dedication to logic and the rigid rules of observation were a blueprint for the thinkers who came after him.

One of the giants of the era was England's **David Hume**. A pioneer of empiricism, Hume was also a strong believer in the value of skepticism. In other words, he was naturally suspicious of things that other people told him to be true and constantly set out to discover the truth for himself. These two related ideas influenced many thinkers after Hume, and his many writings continue to inspire philosophers today.

One of the most famous philosophers of the Enlightenment was **Immanuel Kant** of Germany. He was both a philosopher and a scientist, and he took a definite scientific view of the world. He wrote the Age's most renowned essay, "Answering the Question: What Is Enlightenment?" and he answered his famous question with the motto "Dare to Know." For Kant, the human being was a rational being capable of very creative thought and intense self-evaluation. He encouraged all to examine themselves and the world around them. He believed that the source of morality laid neither in nature nor in the grace of God, but in the soul, itself. He believed that man believed in God for practical, rather than religious or mystical, reasons.

Also devised during the Enlightenment was the notion of the "social contract." Under this notion, people agreed to submit to the government so long as it was wanted by the people, protected the people, and did not infringe upon their basic human rights. This idea was first heralded by France's Jean-Jacques Rousseau, but was later adopted by England's John Locke and the United States' Thomas Jefferson. Locke was one of the most influential political writers of the seventeenth century. He emphasized human rights and proposed that when governments violate those rights, people should rebel. Locke 1690 work **Two Treatises of Government** had significant influence on political thought in the American colonies and helped shaped the U.S. Constitution and Declaration of Independence. The Founders used Locke's social contract a part of the basis for their decision to revolt against the British government.

American colonists believed that the British government infringed upon their taxes by levying increasingly harsh taxes without permitting the colonists to have a substantial say in the administration of the colonies. As a result, a number of colonial leaders met in the First and Second Continental Congress. These events led to the writing of the Declaration of Independence in 1776 and the ensuing American Revolution. The new nation of the United States came into being following the close of the American Revolution in 1787.

The success of the American Revolution encouraged the growth of other revolts. In 1789, the French Revolution began in Paris. By the end of the nineteenth century, both Germany and Italy had united into roughly their modern forms.

One of the major political movements of the twentieth century was **communism**. Communism has a rigid ideology based on the Marxist work *Das Capital* that sees Communism emerging as a result of almost cosmic laws. Proponents of communism are sure that it will achieve the perfect state; however, in practice it has sometimes been exercised in a ruthless way.

Communism reached its largest incarnation in Russia. Until the early years of the twentieth century, **Russia** was ruled by a succession of Czars. They ruled as autocrats, and sometimes as despots. Society was essentially feudalistic and was structured in three levels. The Czar held the top level. The rich nobles who held government positions and owned vast tracts of land held the second level. Finally, those who lived in poverty as peasants or serfs were at the third level. There was discontent among the peasants. There were several unsuccessful attempts to revolt during the nineteenth century, but they were quickly suppressed. The revolutions of 1905 and 1917, however, were quite different.

The causes of the 1905 Revolution were:

- Discontent with the social structure
- Discontent with the living conditions of the peasants
- Discontent with working conditions, despite industrialization
- The Russo-Japanese War (1904-1905)

The war caused rapid inflation. As a result, peasants who had previously made ends meet began to starve. This brewed further discontent. On the battle front of the increasingly unpopular Russo-Japanese War, many Russian troops were killed because of poor leadership, lack of training, and inferior weaponry. But despite these setbacks, Czar Nicholas II refused to end the war. In January 1905, Port Arthur fell.

A trade union leader, Father Gapon, organized a protest to demand an end to the war, industrial reform, more civil liberties, and a constituent assembly. Over 150,000 peasants joined a demonstration outside the Czar's Winter Palace. Before the demonstrators even spoke, the palace guards opened fire on the crowd, destroying any semblance of trust in the Czar. Illegal trade unions and political parties formed and organized strikes to gain power. The strikes eventually brought the Russian economy to a halt. This led Czar Nicholas II to sign the October Manifesto that created a constitutional monarchy, extended some civil rights, and gave the parliament limited legislative power. In a very short period of time, the Czar disbanded the parliament and violated the promised civil liberties. This violation contributed to the 1917 Revolution.

The causes of the 1917 Revolution were:

- The violation of the October Manifesto
- Defeats on the battlefields during WWI, which caused discontent, loss of life, and a popular desire to withdraw from the war

- The Czar's continued appointment of unqualified people to government posts, who handled the war and the economy incompetently
- The influence on the Czar by his wife Alexandra, who had been strongly influenced by Rasputin
- Further inflation and shortages of goods, as caused by WWI

The most significant differences between the 1905 and 1917 revolutions were that in 1917, political parties formed; they used propaganda; and they were supported by the military and some of the nobles.

Communist states controlled nearly every aspect of society, including religion and economics. The government owned factories and ports, machines and ships; thus, profits earned from goods produced therein went into the state-controlled coffers. This kind of economic system stood in stark contrast to the famous *laissez faire* (literally, "leave to do") free enterprise system that most Western nations practiced during the 1700s, 1800s, and 1900s.

The first organized **genocide** in the 1900s was the **Armenian genocide**. The Young Turks, who had inherited Turkey from the Ottoman Empire, attempted to exterminate the Armenians within their newly established borders. As a result, more than one million Armenian people— nearly half of their population—were slaughtered between 1915 and 1917. The government blamed the Armenians for early defeats at the hands of Russia and its allies. However, the Armenians were forcibly moved and kept in harsh conditions elsewhere. A total of 25 concentration camps are believed to have existed. Turkish authorities claimed that the Armenian people had attempted to separate from the Ottoman Empire and that the relocation was pursuant to the goals of both peoples. Others disagree. Some sources blame other causes for these deaths. Most scholars, however, agree that it was a determined attempt to exterminate an entire group of people.

The United States grew up significantly after the close of the Civil War in 1865. Under the administration of Theodore Roosevelt, the U.S. Armed Forces were built up. Roosevelt summed up his foreign policy with the slogan, "Speak softly and carry a big stick," that is, backing up diplomacy with a strong military. During the years before the outbreak of World War I, evidence of the United States' emergence as a world power could be seen in a number of actions. The **Monroe Doctrine** declared that the Western Hemisphere was off-limits to European colonization and intervention because it fell under the United States' "sphere of influence," and the nation had the right to protect that influence. Under this doctrine, President Roosevelt orchestrated several power-moves. He forced Italy, Germany, and Great Britain to remove their blockade of Venezuela; gained the rights to construct the Panama Canal by threatening the use of force; and assumed the finances of the Dominican Republic to stabilize it and prevent any intervention by Europeans. In 1916, President Woodrow Wilson followed on what became known as the "Roosevelt Corollary" and sent U.S. troops to the Dominican Republic to keep order there.

World War I ■ 1914 to 1918

During the late 1800s and 1900s, great changes had taken place around the world. In Europe, Italy and Germany had united into one nation from many smaller states. There were revolutions in Austria and Hungary, the Franco-Prussian War, the dividing of Africa among the strong European nations, interference and intervention of Western nations in Asia, and the breakup of Turkish dominance in the Balkans. In Africa, France, Great Britain, Italy, Portugal, Spain, Germany, and Belgium colonized and controlled the entire continent except Liberia and Ethiopia. In Asia and the Pacific Islands, only China, Japan, and present-day Thailand (Siam) remained independent. The others were colonized and controlled by the major European nations.

In 1914, war broke out in Europe. By war's end in 1918, nearly 30 nations had been involved. One of its major causes was the tremendous surge of national-ism during the late 1800s and early 1900s. People of the same nationality, ethnicity, or those sharing a common history, language or culture began uniting politically, or demanding the right of political unification. This was especially apparent in Eastern Europe empires, notably the Russian, Ottoman, and Austro-Hungarian Empires. Peoples' beliefs and loyalty toward common political, social, and economic goals were getting stronger and more hostile to other nations and peoples. Other causes included rapid militarization, wholesale colonization for the extraction of badly needed raw materials, and military and diplomatic alliances. The initial spark that started the conflagration was the assassination of Austrian Archduke Francis Ferdinand and his wife in the Balkan city of Sarajevo, where rising nationalist feeling was particularly strong.

World War I saw the introduction of tanks, combat airplanes, machine guns, submarines, poison gas, and flamethrowers. Fighting on the Western front was characterized by the use of a series of trenches that were used throughout the war until 1918. U.S. involvement in the war did not occur until 1916. When it began in 1914, President Woodrow Wilson declared that the U.S. was neutral, and most Americans opposed any involvement. British propaganda efforts and the German attack on the passenger ship *Lusitania,* which killed a number of Americans, swayed public support toward the Allied cause. In 1916, Wilson was elected to a second term based on his promise to keep America out of the war. For a few months after the election, he kept the United States out of the war, but by then, German submarines, or **U-Boats**, began conducting **"unrestricted submarine warfare"** against American merchant shipping. As a result, the United States entered the war.

There were 28 nations involved in the war, not including colonies and territories. It began July 28, 1914 and ended November 11, 1918 with the signing of the Treaty of Versailles. Economically, the war cost a total of $337 billion. It resulted in increased inflation, crushing war debts, and a loss of markets, goods, jobs, and factories.

Politically, old empires collapsed; many monarchies disappeared; smaller countries gained temporary independence; Communists seized power in Russia; and, in some cases, nationalism increased. Socially, total populations decreased because of war casualties and low birth rates. There were millions of displaced persons, while villages and farms were destroyed. However, cities grew while women made significant gains in the work force and the ballot box. There was less social distinction and classes. Attitudes completely changed and old beliefs and values were questioned. The peace settlement established the League of Nations to ensure peace, but as we will see, it failed to do so.

In the United States, President Wilson lost his bid in the U.S. Senate to approve the Treaty of Versailles. The Senate at the time was a reflection of American public opinion and its rejection of the Treaty was a rejection of Wilson. The approval of the Treaty would have made the U.S. a member of the League of Nations. However, America had just emerged from a bloody war to ensure that democracy would exist throughout the world. Americans did not want to accept the responsibility that resulted from its new position of power and were afraid that membership in the League of Nations would drag the United States into future conflicts in Europe. The nation eventually signed a separate agreement formally ending the conflict with opposing powers.

Pre-war empires lost tremendous amounts of territories as well as the wealth of natural resources in them. New, independent nations were formed and some predominately ethnic areas came under control of nations of different cultural backgrounds. Some national boundary changes overlapped, creating tensions, animosity, and political and economic confusion. The wishes and desires of every national or cultural group could not be realized or satisfied, resulting in disappointments for both; those who were victorious and those who were defeated. Germany received harsher terms than expected from the treaty that weakened its post-war government and, along with the worldwide depression of the 1930s, set the stage for the rise of Adolf Hitler and his Nationalist Socialist Party and **World War II**.

The most well known genocide of the twentieth century is the **Holocaust**, which took place before and during World War II. Much of it occurred in Germany, although the atrocities occurred throughout German-occupied countries and through the duration of the war. German authorities capitalized on hundreds of years of distrust of Jewish people and implemented what they saw as "the Final Solution of the Jewish Question": the extermination of the Jewish people. Germans in charge of the "Final Solution" constructed a vast, complicated network of transport systems and concentration camps, where Jews were imprisoned, forced to work, and killed by the millions.

The Holocaust was marked by its efficiency and its extensive record-keeping. Thousands of pages of documents describe in excruciating detail how thorough and determined Nazi authorities were in pursuing their goals. The number of Jews killed during the Holocaust is generally estimated at six million. This figure includes people from all over Europe. The Holocaust did not only target Jews, however. Gypsies, communists, homosexuals, Jehovah's Witnesses, Catholics, psychiatric patients, and even common criminals were systematically incarcerated and, in many cases, killed for being "enemies of the state." The number of concentration camps in Nazi-controlled lands during World War II reached the hundreds. Not all of them were death camps. The most infamous ones, including Auschwitz, were. The Holocaust ended with Germany's defeat in World War II. The liberating troops of the West and East uncovered the concentration camps and the Nazis' war-crimes. Much of the meticulous record keeping was intact, preserving the horrors that the Nazis had wrought.

The post-World War II world was a complicated place. The Axis powers were defeated, but the Cold War had sprung up. Many countries struggled to get out of the debt and devastation that the war had wrought. The American Marshall Plan helped the nations of Western Europe get back on their feet. The Soviet Union helped the Eastern European nations recover, with Communist governments at the helm. Asian nations were also rebuilt, with Communism taking over China and Americanization taking over Japan and Taiwan. East and West struggled for control in this arena, especially in Korea and Southeast Asia.

The kind of nationalism that Europe saw in the late-nineteenth and early twentieth centuries continued into the mid-twentieth century, with former European colonies declaring independence, especially in Africa. India, a longtime British protectorate, also achieved independence at this time. With independence, the number of sovereign countries worldwide continued to grow.

The **United Nations**, the follow-on to the defunct League of Nations, began in the waning days of World War II. It brought the nations of the world together to discuss their problems, rather than fight about them. UNICEF, a worldwide children's fund, has been able to achieve great things in just a few decades of existence. Other peace-based organizations like the International Red Cross and Medicines sans Frontiers (Doctors Without Borders) have seen their membership and their efficacy rise during this time as well.

The Cold War was, more than anything else, an ideological struggle between proponents of democracy and those of communism. The two major players were the United States and the Soviet Union, but other countries were involved as well.

It was a "cold" war because no direct fighting took place between the two, yet the two sides remained poised to engage each other.

The Soviet Union kept a tight grip on its territories, which included all of Eastern Europe. It established the Warsaw Pact, a military alliance which included all of the nations of Eastern Europe, and was controlled by the Soviet Union. For their part, Western Europe, the United States, and Canada established their own military alliance, the North Atlantic Treaty Organization (NATO).

Another contested region was Asia. There, the Soviet Union had allies in China, North Korea, and North Vietnam, while the U.S. had allies in Japan, South Korea, Taiwan, and South Vietnam. The Korean War and Vietnam War were major conflicts in which both superpowers were, in one way or another, involved but did not engage each other directly.

The enduring legacy of the Cold War was the arms race, a continual buildup of conventional arms and nuclear, biological, and chemical weapons that left each side with enough firepower to destroy each other several times. Defense spending on both sides sent national budgets skyrocketing. Many economists, historians, and political scientists argue that the Soviet Union collapsed in the late 1980s while trying to keep up with President Ronald Reagan's record defense spending.

The war was a cultural struggle, as well. Adults raised their children to fear "the other," whether they were American or Russian. Cold War tensions spilled over into everyday aspects of life across the world. Life in countries east and west of the "Iron Curtain" was so different that they seemed entirely foreign to outsiders.

Although historians disagree on the exact date of the end of the Cold War, many agree on December 31, 1991, when Premier Mikhail Gorbachev stepped down and the Soviet Union collapsed. By then, other Eastern European countries had had their communist puppet-regimes over-thrown, as well. The "Iron Curtain" had finally closed.

Native Americans inhabited Texas long before Europeans came. Some of those groups were migratory, while others stayed in one place, in some cases for many years. Among the major settled tribes were the Caddo, Cherokee, Chickasaw, Choctaw, Comanche, Karankawa, Kickapoo, and Tonkawa.

The Caddo, in the east, were good at farming, trading, and making pottery. The Cherokee and Choctaw had advanced political structures, with an elected chief. The Chickasaw did not stay in Texas long but were known as good hunters and farmers. The Choctaw were also good farmers, hunters, toolmakers, and house-builders. The Comanche were famous horsemen and hunters. The Karankawa were good jewelers and shell-makers. The Tonkawa were renowned for hunting bison and gathering fruits and nuts.

French and Spanish explorers reached Texas in the sixteenth century, and settlers soon followed. The first important Frenchman to arrive was La Salle, as part of his overall exploration of what became the Mississippi Territory. Other French explorers and settlers came to Texas, but a combination of meager resources and a surge in Spanish explorers eliminated the French from further influence across much of Texas. The Spanish were far more successful in colonizing Texas. Spain established the colony of Tejas, which was administered by forces of varying sizes. Conflict erupted over Louisiana, but the Spanish missions provided a strong base for settlement and defense. Ultimately, French influence ended with the Louisiana Purchase.

Spanish influence continued into the nineteenth century but ended with Mexican independence in 1821. Texas was under Mexican control until the end of the Texas Revolution in 1836. Texas became an independent nation with Sam Houston as its president.

One major result of the European occupation was a passage of Spanish culture into Texas culture, especially in the names of towns and foods. This legacy is still reflected in the state's culture, while French influence has largely disappeared.

Key points of reference in Texas history include the following:

Settlement and culture of Native American Tribes before European contact

- 1519: Spanish explorer Alonso Alvarez de Pineda maps the Texas coast
- 1528-34: Alvar Nunez Cabeza de Vaca (Spanish explorer) explores Texas for trade
- 1685: LaSalle established Fort St. Louis at Matagorda Bay, providing the basis of the French claim to Texas territory
  1689: With Fort St. Louis abandoned, Mexican explorer Alonso de Leon begins to reestablish Spanish control of the region
- 1690: Franciscan priests establish San Francisco de los Tejas Mission in East Texas, opening the Old San Antonio Road portion of the Camino Real
- 1716–1789: Spain established Catholic missions throughout Texas
- 1762: the French give up their claims to Texas and cede Louisiana to Spain until 1800
- 1800: Much of north Texas is returned to France and later sold to the U.S. in the Louisiana Purchase
- 1823: Stephen Austin begins a colony known as the Old Three Hundred along the Brazos River
- 1832: Battle of Velasco—first casualties of the Texas Revolution
- 1832–33: Two Conventions responded to unrest over the policies of the Mexican government

- 1835: The Texas Revolution officially began in an effort to obtain freedom from Mexico
- 1836: The Convention of 1836 signed the Texas Declaration of Independence; The Battle of the Alamo takes place; Santa Anna executed nearly 400 Texans in the Goliad Massacre; Santa Anna is believed to have crushed the Texas rebellion but Sam Houston leads an army of 800 to victory by routing Santa Anna's forces at Battle of San Jacinto; The Treaty of Velasco is signed by Santa Anna and Republic of Texas officials
- 1839: Austin becomes the capital of the Republic of Texas
- 1842: Mexican forces twice capture San Antonio and retreat
- 1845: Texas admitted to the Union as a state
- 1850: The Compromise of 1850 adjusts the state boundary and assumes Texas' debts
- 1861: Texas secedes from the Union and joins the Confederacy
- A government is organized, replacing Houston because he refused to swear allegiance to the Confederacy
- 1865: Union troops landed in Galveston and put the Emancipation Proclamation into effect in Texas, thus ending slavery
- 1870: Texas is readmitted to the Union
- 1900: Galveston is destroyed and 8000 people are killed by a category 4 hurricane
- 1901: The Lucas Gusher comes in, starting the Texas oil boom

Skill 1.2   Analyze how individuals, events, and issues shaped the history of Texas, the United States, and the world.

Native American settlement of the region that is now Texas began during the Upper Paleolithic period approximately 10,000 years ago. Some of the Native tribes that have inhabited the area include the Apache, Comanche, Cherokee and Wichita tribes, among others. In 1529, the Spanish explorer Alonso Alvarez de Pineda first mapped the coast of Texas, while Alvar Nunez Cabeza de Vaca explored inland for potential trade opportunities. It was the French, over 150 years later, who first attempted to establish a colony in the Texas territory. **Fort St. Louis** was founded by La Salle at Matagorda Bay in 1685, establishing France's claim on the region. Through mutiny and massacre at the hands of native peoples, the colony was destroyed in 1688. France continued to claim Texas for decades following the massacre, even though they had no physical presence in the region.

Meanwhile, Spanish priests began to build missions throughout Texas, beginning in 1690 with the San Francisco de los Tejas Mission in East Texas. Spain continued to populate the area with missions through the eighteenth century. France relinquished its claim on Texas in 1762, turning it over to Spain. France also turned over the Louisiana Territory, which included northern Texas, until 1800, when it was given back to France and sold to the United States in the

Louisiana Purchase.

Spain's effective control over Texas lasted from 1690 until 1821, when Mexico gained independence from Spain. During this time, it had mainly been a thinly populated buffer region between the territories claimed by France and Spain. Mexico, wanting to encourage settlement in the area, invited American settlers to the region. In 1823, Stephen Austin began a colony called the Old Three Hundred on the Brazos River, opening the way for further settlement.

As the young nation of Mexico sought to establish its influence over Texas and the new settlers, unrest developed over government policies. Mexico was officially a Catholic country, and expected its citizens to also be Catholic. However, many of the white American settlers were Protestant. Mexico also banned slavery, which was widespread in the southern U.S. at the time. Unrest eventually erupted into conflict in 1832 at the **Battle of Velasco** between a small Mexican force and a militia of Texas colonists. Following the battle, Texans held conventions to outline their disagreement with Mexican polices, culminating in the signing of a Texas Declaration of Independence on March 2, 1836. Four days later, a Mexican force of an estimated 1,800 to 6,000 attacked a small force of Texans at the Alamo in San Antonio following several days of siege. Although some civilians who had taken refuge in the Alamo survived, all of the Texan military defenders were killed, and the Alamo defeat became a battle cry for Texan independence.

Texans continued to battle against Mexican **General Santa Anna** and his forces. They suffered more setbacks, but eventually emerged victorious at the **Battle of San Jacinto**, where Texan troops led by Sam Houston captured the entire Mexican Army, including Santa Anna. Texas became an independent country with the signing of the Treaty of Velasco on May 15, 1836. Sam Houston was named the first President of the Republic of Texas.

After being moved six times, the capital of the **Republic of Texas** was established at Austin in 1839. Texas' decade as an independent country was marked by division between those who wished to remain independent and expand Texas' borders, and those, like Houston, who wished to become part of the United States. Houston's vision won out, and in 1845, Texas was annexed to the U.S. and concurrently made a state. In 1850, as part of the Compromise of 1850 that addressed the delicate issue of slavery, Texas' borders were adjusted to the present boundaries, and the United States assumed many of Texas' debts incurred while fighting against Mexico.

Approximately a decade later, in 1861, Texas seceded from the United States as part of the Confederacy. **Sam Houston**, then governor of the State of Texas, refused to swear allegiance to the Confederacy and was replaced. The final battle of the Civil War was fought in Texas at Palmito Ranch on May 12, 1865, some time after hostilities had formally ended at Appomattox Courthouse. One month later, Federal troops landed at Galveston to enforce the Emancipation Proclamation, which abolished slavery. Texas was readmitted into the Union in 1870.

The twentieth century began with disaster for Texas when, in 1900, a category 4 hurricane struck the coast at Galveston, devastating the city and killing at least 6,000 people. The century also started with prosperity, however, when the Spindletop oil range was discovered in early 1901. The discovery marked the Texas oil boom and its transformation into an oil-rich state.

The following is a partial list of well-known Americans who contributed their leadership and talents in various fields and reforms:

- Lucretia Mott and Elizabeth Cady Stanton for **women's rights**
- Emma Hart Willard, Catharine Esther Beecher, and Mary Lyon for **education for women**
- Dr. Elizabeth Blackwell, the **first woman doctor**
- Antoinette Louisa Blackwell, the **first female minister**
- Dorothea Lynde Dix for **reforms in prisons and insane asylums**
- Elihu Burritt and William Ladd for **peace movements**
- Robert Owen for a **Utopian society**
- Horace Mann, Henry Barmard, Calvin E. Stowe, Caleb Mills, and John Swett for **public education**
- Benjamin Lundy, David Walker, William Lloyd Garrison, Isaac Hooper, Arthur and Lewis Tappan, Theodore Weld, Frederick Douglass, Harriet Tubman, James G. Birney, Henry Highland Garnet, James Forten, Robert Purvis, Harriet Beecher Stowe, Wendell Phillips, and John Brown for the **abolition of slavery and the Underground Railroad**
- Louisa Mae Alcott, James Fennimore Cooper, Washington Irving, Walt Whitman, Henry David Thoreau, Ralph Waldo Emerson, Herman Melville, Richard Henry Dana, Nathaniel Hawthorne, Henry Wadsworth Longfellow, John Greenleaf Whittier, Edgar Allan Poe, Oliver Wendell Holmes: **famous writers**
- John C. Fremont, Zebulon Pike, Kit Carson: **explorers**
- Henry Clay, Daniel Webster, Stephen Douglas, John C. Calhoun: **American statesmen**
- Robert Fulton, Cyrus McCormick, and Eli Whitney: **inventors**

The U.S. as a World Power

Spain's colonial policy led to a revolt on the island of Cuba (1895-98). The U.S. intervened after claiming that its ship the *USS Maine* had been attacked and defeated Spain. The result of the war was that for the sum of $20 million, Spain gave up all claims to Cuba, Puerto Rico, the Philippine Islands, and Guam. This acquisition was part of the dramatic growth of the United States.

When Great Britain finally acknowledged American independence in 1783, the country claimed about 900,000 square miles of territory. By 1899, the purchase of the Louisiana Territory from France and Florida from Spain, the addition of Texas, California, the southwest, the Oregon Country, and the purchase of Alaska from Russia had more than quadrupled the size of the nation. The American "Empire" was now the fifth largest in the world.

Until the middle of the nineteenth century, American foreign policy and expansionism were essentially restricted to the North American continent. The nation had shown little interest in establishing colonies in other lands, aside from the establishment of the African colony of Liberia, which had been founded by freed African American slaves in the years before the Civil War. McKinley- and Roosevelt-era imperialism were not exactly comparable to European imperialism. American foreign policy sought to use military power in territories and other lands in the interest of the spread of democratic principles. Much of the concern and involvement in Central and South America, as well as the Caribbean, was also to link the two coasts of the nation and to protect America's economy from European encroachment.

The nation's power grew as its economy and population grew in the late nineteenth century and early twentieth centuries. New immigrants flocked to the country and took industrial jobs. Polish immigrants became steelworkers in Pittsburgh; Serbian immigrants became meatpackers in Chicago; Russian Jewish immigrants became tailors in New York City; Slovaks assembled cars in Detroit; Italians worked in the factories of Baltimore. Many people, both immigrant and native-born, migrated to cities. Throughout the nineteenth century, city populations grew faster than rural populations.

Urbanization requires many public utilities, including: adequate water supply, the management of sewage and the collection of garbage. It requires other public services, such as fire and police departments, road construction and maintenance, the building of bridges to connect parts of cities, and taller buildings to accommodate the swelling population. The latter led to the invention of steel-framed buildings and of the elevator. In addition, electricity and telephone lines were needed; department stores and supermarkets grew, as well as the demand for additional schools. With the large migration and low wages came overcrowding and sanitation issues. Slums began to appear. Soon, public health issues began to arise. During the Progressive Era in the early twentieth century, reformers sought to improve living conditions in cities, help the impoverished, and reform corrupt political machines, among other goals.

When the war of independence began in Cuba, it aroused the interest and concern of Americans who were aware of what was happening at their doorstep. Spanish attempts to end the revolt were often harsh, including a policy of "re-concentration" that forced much of the civilian populace into crowded, unsanitary towns. Much of the food that kept them alive came from supplies sent by the U.S. Americans were already concerned over years of anarchy and misrule by the Spanish. When reports of gross atrocities reached America, public sentiment clearly favored the Cuban people. President McKinley had refused to recognize the rebellion, but had affirmed the possibility of American intervention, which Spain resented. In February 1898, the American battleship *Maine* was blown up in Havana harbor. Although there was no evidence that the Spanish were responsible—in fact, the cause of the explosion still remains unknown—popular sentiment accused Spanish agents of sabotage and war became inevitable. Two months later, Congress declared war on Spain and the United States quickly defeated the Spanish in Cuba. The peace treaty gave the United States possession of Puerto Rico, the Philippines, and Guam. At about the same time, the United States also annexed the Pacific islands of Hawaii.

Although the idea of a canal in Panama goes back to the early sixteenth century, work did not begin until 1880 by the French. The French effort was eventually abandoned, but the United States restarted the project and opened the **Panama Canal** in 1914. Construction was an enormous task of complex engineering. The significance of the canal is that it connects the Gulf of Panama in the Pacific Ocean with the Caribbean Sea and the Atlantic Ocean. It eliminated the need for ships to skirt the southern boundary of South America, effectively reducing the sailing distance from New York to San Francisco by 8,000 miles (over half of the distance). The Canal results in a shorter and faster voyage, thus reducing shipping time and cost. The United States helped Panama win independence from Colombia in exchange for control of the Panama Canal Zone. A large investment was made in eliminating disease from the area, particularly yellow fever and malaria. After WWII, control of the canal became a contentious issue between the United States and Panama. Negotiations toward a settlement began in 1974, resulting in the **Torrijos-Carter Treaties** of 1977. Thus began the process of handing the canal over to Panama. On December 31, 1999, control of the canal was handed over to the Panama Canal Authority. Tolls for the use of the canal have ranged from $0.36, when Richard Halliburton swam the canal, to about $226,000.

The **Open Door Policy** was a policy granting all countries equal trading status with China and supporting Chinese territorial and administration integrity. The policy was first suggested by the United States, but its basis is the typical nation clause of the treaties made with China after the Opium War (1829–1842). This policy was in effect from about 1900 until the end of WWII. After the war, China was recognized as a sovereign state. When the Communist Party came to power in China in 1949, the policy was rejected. This continued until the late 1970s, when China began to adopt a policy of encouraging foreign trade.

Big Stick Diplomacy was a term adopted to describe President Theodore Roosevelt's foreign policy. Roosevelt supported the role of the United States assuming international police power in the Western Hemisphere. The intention was to safeguard American economic interests in Latin America, but it ultimately led to the expansion of the U.S. Navy and to greater involvement in world affairs. Should any nation in the Western Hemisphere become vulnerable to European control because of political or economic instability, the United States had both the right and the obligation to intervene.

Dollar Diplomacy describes U.S. efforts under President Taft to extend its foreign policy goals in Latin America and East Asia via economic power. The designation derives from Taft's claim that U.S. interests in Latin America had changed from "warlike and political" to "peaceful and economic." Taft justified this policy in terms of protecting the Panama Canal. The practice of dollar diplomacy was from time to time anything but peaceful, particularly in Nicaragua. When revolts or revolutions occurred, the U.S. sent troops to resolve the situation. Immediately upon resolution, bankers were sent in to loan money to the new regimes. The policy persisted until the election of Woodrow Wilson to the Presidency in 1913.

Wilson repudiated Dollar Diplomacy within weeks of his inauguration, preferring a policy of **Moral Diplomacy**. Under moral diplomacy, the United States supported only those nations that themselves supported democratic principles or the larger interests of the United States. Moral diplomacy relied largely on economic, rather than military, means to achieve its goals.

The United States war effort for WWI included over four million men who served in the military. The cost of the war up to April 30, 1919 was over 22.5 billion dollars. Over 116,000 Americans were killed in battle and over 200,000 wounded. On the home front, people energetically supported the war effort in every way necessary. The menace of German submarines was causing the loss of ships faster than new ships could be built. Scores of shipyards were quickly constructed to build both wooden and steel ships. At the end of the war the United States had more than 2,000 ships.

Herbert Hoover had previously chaired the Belgian Relief Commission. He was named "food commissioner" to the U.S. Food Administration Board. His function was to manage conservation and distribution of the food supply to ensure that there was adequate food to supply every American both at home and overseas. Rationing of other goods, particularly energy sources, also took places.

In December of 1917, the government assumed control of all of the railroads in the nation and consolidated them into a single system with regional directors. The goal of this action was to increase efficiency and enable the rail system to meet the needs of both commerce and military transportation. This was done with the understanding that private ownership would be restored after the war; it occurred in 1920. In 1918, telegraph, telephone and cable services were also taken over by the federal government; they were returned to original management and ownership in 1919.

To secure the huge sums of money needed to finance the war, the government sold "Liberty Bonds" to the people. Nearly $25 billion worth of bonds were sold, and in four series. After the war, "Victory Bonds" were sold. The first Liberty loan was issues at 3.5%, the second at 4%, and the remaining ones at 4.25%. A strong appeal was made to the people to buy bonds. The total response meant that more than 1/5 of all Americans bought bonds.

The war effort required massive production of weapons, ammunition, radios, and other military equipment. To achieve this goal, manufacturers began hiring women for industrial jobs normally filled by men. They also recruited African Americans from the South to fill Northern factory jobs, creating the first Great Migration.

To deter anti-war messages during the conflict, the U.S. government approved the Espionage Act and the Sedition Act. These made it illegal to publically speak out against the war, curtailing civil rights but keeping opposition to the war quiet. Socialist leader Eugene V. Debs was famously imprisoned under these acts. After the war, the return of millions of men to the workforce coupled with reduced production as the demand of war goods dropped caused tumultuous time throughout the country. Race riots took place throughout the country and opposition to radicals and socialists led to the first Red Scare.

Americans feared a Bolshevik-type revolution in America. As a result, people were jailed for expressing views that were considered anarchist, communist or socialist. In an attempt to control the potential for revolution, civil liberties were ignored and thousands were deported. The Socialist Party also came to be viewed as a group of anarchist radicals. Several state and local governments passed a variety of laws designed to reduce radical speech and activity. Congress considered more than 70 anti-sedition bills, though none was passed. Soon, however, the Red Scare had essentially run its course.

The 1920s were a period of relative prosperity, under the leadership of Warren G. Harding and Calvin Coolidge. Harding had promised a return to "normalcy" in the aftermath of World War I and the radical reactions of labor. During most of the decade, the output of industry boomed and the automobile industry put nearly 27 million cars on the road. Per capita income rose for almost everyone except farmers, and the availability of easy credit contributed to a boom in consumer goods.

Marcus Garvey, an English-educated Jamaican, established an organization called the *Universal Negro Improvement and Conservation Association and African Communities League* (usually called the Universal Negro Improvement

Association). In 1919, this "Black Moses" claimed followers numbering about two million. He spoke of a "new Negro" who was proud to be black. He published a newspaper in which he taught about the heroes of the race and the strengths of African culture. He told African Americans that they would be respected only when they were economically strong. He created a number of businesses by which he hoped to achieve this goal. He then called blacks to work with him to build an all-black nation in Africa. His belief in racial purity and black separatism was not shared by a number of black leaders. In 1922, he and other members of the organization were jailed for mail fraud. His sentence was commuted and he was deported to Jamaica as an undesirable alien.

The **Ku Klux Klan** (KKK) was established in 1866 by veterans of the Confederate Army who sought to resist Reconstruction. Their beliefs encompass white supremacy, anti-Semitism, racism, anti-Catholicism and nativism. Their typical intimidation methods have included terrorism, violence, lynching, hanging, cross burning and others. The KKK, or "Klan," entered a second period beginning in 1915. The silent film *The Birth of a Nation* controversially promoted their message. They also published a number of anti-Semitic newspaper articles. The group became a structured membership organization. Its membership did not begin to decline until the Great Depression.

Although the KKK began in the South, its membership at its peak extended into the Midwest, the Northern states, and even into Canada. Membership during the 1920s reached approximately 4 million, some 20% of the adult white male population in many regions and as high as 40% in some areas. The political influence of the group was significant, particularly in Tennessee, Indiana, Oklahoma, Oregon, and the Deep South.

Fearing radicalism, rampant racism and efforts to repress various ethnic and religious groups, several groups were formed to protect the civil rights and liberties guaranteed to all citizens by the U.S. Constitution. As a result, the *American Civil Liberties Union* (ACLU) was formed in 1920. The **ACLU** is a non-profit organization whose mission is "to defend and preserve the individual rights and liberties guaranteed to every person in this Country by the Constitution and laws of the United States (American Civil Liberties Union Web Site)." It accomplishes its goals through community education, litigation and legislation.

The ACLU was an outgrowth of the American Union Against Militarism, which had opposed America's involvement in WWI, and provided legal assistance to conscientious objectors. It also provided assistant to those who were being prosecuted under the Espionage Act of 1917 and the Sedition Act of 1918. With the name change came additional concerns and activities. The agency began to try to protect immigrants threatened with deportation and citizens threatened with prosecution for communist activities and agendas. They also opposed efforts to repress the Industrial Workers of the World and other labor unions.

The National Association for the Advancement of Colored People (NAACP) was founded in 1909 to assist African Americans. In the early years, the work of the organization focused on working through the courts to overturn "Jim Crow" statutes that legalized racial discrimination. The group organized a public protest oppose Woodrow Wilson's efforts to weave racial segregation into federal government policy. Between WWI and WWII, much energy was devoted to stopping the lynching of African Americans throughout the country.

In 1957, the formation of the **Southern Christian Leadership Conference** by civil rights leaders including Martin Luther King and, Rev. T. J. Jemison provided local training and assistance to fight segregation. Non-violence was its central doctrine and its major method of fighting segregation and **racism,** a belief that one's own race is superior and has the right to rule over others.

The Anti-Defamation League was created in 1913 to stop discrimination against the Jewish people. Its charter states, "Its ultimate purpose is to secure justice and fair treatment to all citizens alike and to put an end forever to unjust and unfair discrimination against ridicule of any sect or body of citizens." The organization has historically opposed all groups considered anti-Semitic and/or racist. This has included the Ku Klux Klan, the Nazis, and a variety of others.

The end of World War I and the decade of the 1920s saw tremendous changes in the United States. The shift from farm to city life continued at a quick pace. Social changes were occurring at such a fast pace that it was extremely difficult for many Americans to adjust to them. Politically, the eighteenth Amendment to the Constitution prohibited the distillation, transportation, and sale of alcoholic beverages throughout the United States. Prohibition resulted in problems affecting all aspects of society, including the rise of organized crime (i.e., "The Mafia," and "the Mob," etc). The passage of the nineteenth Amendment gave women **suffrage,** or the right to vote.

The "Roaring Twenties" were marked by rapid advancements in the economy, with a new middle class increasingly emerging along with a greater focus on consumerism. The rapid rise in popularity of the radio and its national programming along with the influence of motion pictures helped create a mass national culture. The Harlem Renaissance saw African American art, music, and literature flourish, and new art forms such as jazz swept the nation.

The impact of radio, mass production techniques, and the growth of cities on American society

Although the British patent for the **radio** was awarded in 1896, it was not until WWI that the radio's capabilities were recognized. One of the first developments in the twentieth century was the use of commercial AM radio stations for aircraft navigation. Thus, radio was used to issue orders and relay information between army and navy units on both sides of the war. Broadcasting subsequently became practical in the 1920s, as radio receivers were introduced on a wide scale. Thus, on August 31, 1920, the first radio program was broadcasted. The first entertainment broadcasts began in 1922 from England.

The relative economic boom of the 1920s made it possible for many households to own a radio. The beginning of broadcasting and the proliferation of receivers revolutionized communication. The news was transmitted into every home with a radio. With the beginning of entertainment broadcasting, people were able to remain in their homes for entertainment. Rather than obtaining filtered information, people were able to hear the actual speeches and information that became news. By the end of the decade, over half of all American households had purchased a radio.

Another innovation of the 1920s was the rise of **mass production**. This is the production of large amounts of standardized products on production lines. The method became very popular when Henry Ford used mass production to build the Model T Ford automobile. The process facilitates high production rates per worker. Thus, it created inexpensive products. The process is, however, capital intensive: it requires expensive machinery in high proportion to the number of workers needed to operate it.

Several factors promoted urbanization during the 1920s. The decline of agriculture, the drop in prices for grain and produce, and the end of financial support for farming after WWI caused many farmers to go under during the 1920s. Many sold or lost their farms and migrated to cities to find work.

Continuing industrialization drew increasing numbers of workers to the areas near or surrounding industrial or manufacturing centers. Cities were becoming the locus of political, cultural, financial and economic life. The cities, at once, became the workplace and the location of all of life's necessities.

The Great Depression and the New Deal

The 1929 Stock Market Crash generally marks the beginning of the Great Depression in the United States. Although the crash was not entirely unexpected, it was not without identifiable causes. The 1920s had been a decade of social and economic growth. But the attitudes and actions of the 1920s regarding wealth, production, and investment created several trends that quietly set the stage for the 1929 disaster.

One factor contributing to the Great Depression was the economic condition of Europe. During and after WWI, the United States and its banks lent a great deal of money to European nations to support the way effort and, later, to rebuild. Many of these countries used this money to purchase food and manufactured goods from the United States. But they were not able to pay off their debts, and in many cases the process of rebuilding the war-damaged countryside was slow and expensive. While the U.S. was providing money, food, and goods to Europe, however, it was not willing to buy European goods. Protective trade barriers were enacted to maintain a trade balance favorable to U.S. manufacturers.

Several other factors are cited by some scholars as contributing to the Great Depression. Primary among these were **stock speculation** and **buying on margin.** The stock market had soared through much of the 1920s as investors purchased large volumes of stock that they resold as prices rose. This speculative practice contributed to the overvaluing of many company's stocks. Further, many investors purchased those stocks with loans from stockbrokers that they planned to repay upon selling the stock. Lenders could issue **margin calls** at any time to demand the immediate repayment of the cash used to buy the stock.

In September 1929, stock prices began to slip somewhat, yet people remained optimistic. On Monday, October 21, prices began to fall quickly. The volume traded was so high that the tickers were unable to keep up. Investors were frightened, and they started selling very quickly. This caused further collapse. For the next two days prices stabilized somewhat. On October 24, **Black Thurs-day**, prices plummeted again. By this time investors had lost confidence. On Friday and Saturday an attempt to stop the crash was made by some leading bankers. But on Monday the 28th, prices began to fall again, declining by 13% in one day. The next day, **October 29, Black Tuesday,** saw 16.4 million shares traded. Stock prices fell so far that, at many times, no one was willing to buy at any price. Lenders began issuing margin calls that now-strapped investors could not repay with their valueless stock. Overnight, numerous investors went bankrupt.

When the stock market crashed, businesses collapsed. Without demand for products other businesses and industries collapsed. This set in motion a domino effect, bringing down the businesses and industries that provided raw materials or components to these industries. Hundreds of thousands became jobless. Often, the jobless then became homeless. Desperation prevailed. Little had been done to assess the toll that hunger, inadequate nutrition, or starvation took on the health of children during this time. Indeed, food was cheap, relatively speaking, but there was little money to buy it.

Unemployment eventually reached 25% nationwide. Unable to afford their rents or mortgages, homeless people created makeshift towns of cardboard, scraps of wood and tents that they called "**Hoovervilles**" after the increasingly unpopular President Herbert Hoover, whose hands-off approach to the economy had failed to bolster it during the downturn. Families stood in bread lines, rural workers left the Dust Bowl of the plains to search for work in California, and banks failed. More than 100,000 businesses failed between 1929 and 1932. The despair that swept the nation left an indelible scar on all who endured the Depression.

Hoover's bid for re-election in 1932 failed. The new president, Franklin Delano Roosevelt, won the White House on his promise to the American people of a "new deal." Upon assuming office, Roosevelt and his advisers immediately launched a massive program of federal spending to try to bring the Depression to an end and get the nation back on track. Congress gave the President unprecedented power to act in order to save the nation. During the next eight years, the most extensive and broadly based legislation in the nation's history was enacted. The legislation was intended to accomplish three goals: relief, recovery, and reform.

The first step in the "**New Deal**" was to relieve the day-to-day problems caused by massive unemployment, homelessness, and hunger. This was accomplished through a number of job-creation projects. The second step, the recovery aspect, was to stimulate the economy. The third step was to create social and economic change through innovative legislation.

To provide economic stability and prevent another crash, Congress passed the **Glass-Steagall Act**, which separated banking and investing. The Securities and Exchange Commission (SEC) was created to regulate dangerous speculative practices on Wall Street. The Wagner Act guaranteed a number of rights to workers and unions in an effort to improve worker-employer relations. The **Social Security Act of 1935** established pensions for the aged and infirm as well as a system of unemployment insurance. Some of the best-known jobs and public works programs included the **Works Progress Administration (WPA), Civilian Conservation Corps (CCC),** and **Tennessee Valley Authority (TVA).** These agencies provided jobs through numerous public works programs.

Many of the steps taken by FDR have had far-reaching effects. They eventually alleviated some of the effects the economic disaster of the Great Depression; they enacted controls that would mitigate the risk of another stock market crash; and they provided greater economic security for workers. The nation's economy, however, suffered a second decline in the late 1930s as spending decreased and interest rates increased, and did not fully recover until the United States entered World War II.

By far the worst natural disaster of the decade came to be known as the **Dust Bowl.** Due to severe and prolonged drought in the Great Plains and previous reliance on farming techniques that left the land barren, a series of devastating dust storms occurred in the 1930s. Ultimately, the dust storms resulted in destruction, economic ruin for many, and dramatic ecological change in the Great Plains. Crops were ruined, the land was destroyed, and people either lost or abandoned homes and farms. Fifteen percent of Oklahoma's population left, as did numerous other residents of the affected states, mostly to seek agricultural work in California. Because so many of the migrants were from Oklahoma, the migrants came to be called "**Okies**" no matter where they came from. Estimates of the number of people displaced by this disaster range from 300,000 or 400,000 to 2.5 million.

The gains and losses or organized labor in the 1930s

There were several major events or actions that are particularly important to the history of organized labor during the 1930s:

- The Supreme Court upheld the 1926 Railway Labor Act, including its prohibition of employer interference or coercion in the choice of bargaining representatives (1930).
- The Davis-Bacon Act provided that employers of contractors and subcontractors on public construction should be paid the minimum wage (1931).
- The Norris-LaGuardia Act prohibited Federal injunctions in most labor disputes (1932).
- Wisconsin created the first unemployment insurance act in the country (1932).
- The Wagner-Peyser Act created the United States Employment Service within the Department of Labor (1933).
- Half a million Southern mill workers walked off the job in the Great Uprising of 1934.
- The Secretary of Labor called the first National Labor Legislation Conference to get better cooperation between the Federal Government and the States in defining a national labor legislation program (1934).
- The United States joined the International Labor Organization (1934).
- The Wagner Act (The National Labor Relations Act) established a legal basis for unions, set collective bargaining as a matter of national policy required by the law, provided for secret ballot elections for choosing unions, and protected union members from employer intimidation and coercion. It also established the National Labor Relations Board (NRLBB). This law was later amended by the Taft-Hartley Act (1947) and by the Landrum Griffin Act (1959).
- The Guffey Act stabilized the coal industry and improved labor conditions (1935). It was later declared unconstitutional (1936).
- The Social Security Act was approved (1935).
- The Committee for Industrial Organization (CIO) was formed within the AFL to carry unionism to the industrial sector. (1935).
- The United Rubber Workers staged the first sit-down strike (1936).
- The United Auto Workers (UAW) used the sit-down strike against General Motors (1936).
- The Anti-Strikebreaker Act (the Byrnes Act) made it illegal to transport or aid strikebreakers in interstate or foreign trade (1936).
- The Public Contracts Act (the Walsh-Healey Act) of 1936 established labor standards, including minimum wages, overtime pay, child and convict labor provisions and safety standards on federal contracts.
- General Motors recognized the United Auto Workers in 1937.

- US Steel recognized the Steel Workers Organizing Committee in 1937.
- The Wagner Act was upheld by the Supreme Court (1937).
- During a strike of the Steel Workers Organizing Committee against Republic Steel, police attacked a crowd gathered in support of the strike, killing ten and injuring eighty. This came to be called **The Memorial Day Massacre** (1937).
- The CIO was expelled from the AFL over charges of dual unionism or competition (1937).
- The National Apprenticeship Act established the Bureau of Apprenticeship within the Department of Labor (1937).
- The Merchant Marine Act created a Federal Maritime Labor Board (1938).
- The Fair Labor Standards Act created a $0.25 minimum wage, stipulated time-and-a-half pay for hours over 40 per week. (1938)
- The CIO becomes the Congress of Industrial Organizations.

Major technological developments between 1945 and 1960

- Discovery of penicillin (1945)
- United States detonates world's first atomic bombs (1945)
- Xerography process invented (1946)
- Exploration of the South Pole
- Continuing studies of X-ray radiation
- U.S. airplane first flies at supersonic speed (1947)
- Invention of the transistor (1947)
- Long-playing record invented (1948)
- Studies begin in the science of chemo genetics (1948)
- Mount Palomar reflecting telescope (1948)
- Idlewild Airport (now JFK International Airport) opens in New York City (1948)
- Cortisone discovered (1949)
- USSR detonates their first atomic bomb (1949)
- U.S. guided missile launched and traveled 250 miles (1949)
- Plutonium separated (1950)
- Tranquilizer meprobamate comes to wide use (1950)
- Antihistamines become popular in treating colds and allergies (1950)
- Electric power produced from atomic energy (1951)
- First heart-lung machine devised (1951)
- First solo flight over the North Pole (1951)
- Yellow fever vaccine developed (1951)
- Isotopes used in medicine and industry (1952)
- Contraceptive pill produced (1952)
- U.S. detonates world's first hydrogen bomb (1952)
- Nobel Prize in medicine for discovery of streptomycin (1952)
- USSR detonates their first hydrogen bomb (1953)
- Lung cancer connected to cigarette smoking (1953)

- First U.S. submarine converted to nuclear power (1954)
- Polio vaccine invented (1954)
- Discovery of Vitamin B12 (1955)
- Discovery of the molecular structure of insulin (1955)
- Beginning of development of "visual telephone" (1956)
- Beginning of Transatlantic cable telephone service (1956)
- USSR launches first earth satellites (Sputnik I and II) (1957)
- Mackinac Straits Bridge in Michigan opens as the longest suspension bridge (1957)
- Stereo recordings introduced (1958)
- NASA created (1958)
- USSR launches rocket with two monkeys aboard (1959)
- Nobel Prize for Medicine for synthesis of RNA and DNA (1959)

Major domestic policies of presidential administrations from Harry S. Truman to the present

Notable Presidential Administrations

Harry S. Truman. Truman became president near the end of WWII upon the death of FDR. He is credited with some of the most important decisions in the war. When Japan refused to surrender, Truman authorized the use of atomic bombs on Japanese cities dedicated to war support: Hiroshima and Nagasaki. He took to the Congress a 21-point plan that came to be known as the **Fair Deal**. It included: expansion of Social Security, a full-employment program, public housing and slum clearance, and a permanent Fair Employment Practices Act. He also ordered the complete desegregation of the military in 1948.

The Truman Doctrine provided support for Greece and Turkey when they were threatened by the Soviet Union. The Marshall Plan (named for his Secretary of State) stimulated great economic recovery for Western Europe. Truman participated in the negotiations that resulted in the formation of the North Atlantic Treaty Organization (NATO). He and his administration believed it necessary to support South Korea when it was threatened by the communist government of North Korea. Though he contained American involvement in Korea so as not to risk conflict with China or the Soviet Union, the Chinese People's Liberation Army (PLA) eventually entered the war in support of North Korea.

The Truman Doctrine offered military aid to those countries that were in danger of communist upheaval. This led to the era known as the **Cold War** in which the United States took the lead along with the Western European nations against the Soviet Union and the Eastern Soviet Bloc countries. It was also at this time that the United States finally gave up on George Washington's' advice against "European entanglements" and joined the **North Atlantic Treaty Organization**, or **NATO**. This was formed in 1949 and comprised the United State, Canada and several Western European nations for the purpose of opposing communist aggression and supporting one another militarily.

At the close of World War II, Soviet troops had taken over the northern part of Korea from the surrendering Japanese, and American troops had occupied the southern part of the peninsula. Soon, a Communist government was established in the north and a democratic one in the south. The United Nations stepped in in1947, but failed to secure the existence of an independent South Korea amidst partisan fighting.

The first "hot war" in the post-World War II era was the Korean War, which began on June 25, 1950 and ended on July 27, 1953. Troops from Communist North Korea invaded democratic South Korea in an effort to unite both sections under Communist control. The UN asked its member-nations to furnish troops to help restore peace. Many nations responded, including the United States, which sent troops to help the South Koreans. The war dragged on for three years and ended with a truce, not a peace treaty. Korea remains divided to this day.

Causes: Korea was under control of Japan from 1895 to the end of the Second World War in 1945. At war's end, Soviet and U.S. troops both moved into Korea: U.S. troops were in the southern half, while Soviet troops were in the northern half, and were separated by the 38 degree North Latitude, or the 38th Parallel.

Participants were: North and South Korea, the U.S., Australia, New Zealand, the People's Republic of China (PRC), Canada. France, Great Britain, Turkey, Belgium, Ethiopia, Colombia, Greece, South Africa, Luxembourg, Thailand, the Netherlands, and the Philippines. It was the first war in which a world organization, the UN, played a major military role. As such, it presented quite a challenge to the UN, which had been in existence for only five years.

The war began on June 25, 1950 and ended on July 27, 1953. A truce was established and an armistice agreement was signed, which basically ended the fighting. It was a very costly and bloody war, which destroyed villages and homes, and displaced and killed millions of people. However, a permanent peace treaty has never been signed. Thus, technically, the country remains at war—divided between the Communist North and the Democratic South.

Dwight David Eisenhower, popularly known as "Ike," succeeded Truman as president. Eisenhower obtained a truce in Korea and development a policy of **containment** that aimed to control Soviet influence and expansion, contributing to the tensions of the Cold War. When Stalin died, he was able to negotiate a peace treaty with Russia that neutralized Austria. His domestic policy was a middle road. He continued most of the programs introduced under both the New Deal and the Fair Deal. When desegregation of schools began, he sent troops to Little Rock, Arkansas to enforce this controversial initiative. During his administration, the

Departments of Health, Education and Welfare were established, and the National Aeronautics and Space Administration (NASA) was formed.

John F. Kennedy is widely remembered for his Inaugural Address in which he famously proclaimed, "Ask not what your country can do for you—ask what you can do for your country." His campaign pledge was to get America moving again. During his relatively brief presidency, his economic programs created the longest period of continuous expansion in the country since WWII. He wanted the United States to again take up the mission as the first country committed to the revolution of human rights. Through the Alliance for Progress and the Peace Corps, the hopes and idealism of the nation reached out to assist developing nations. He supported equal rights for all Americans and drafted new civil rights legislation, although this program did not pass during his time in office. He also drafted plans for a broad attack on the systemic problems of privation and poverty. He believed the arts were critical to a society and instituted programs to support the arts.

In 1962, during Kennedy's presidency, Soviet Premier Nikita Khrushchev and his advisors decided, as a protective measure for Cuba against an American invasion, to install nuclear missiles on the island. In October, American U-2 spy planes photographed what were identified as missile bases under construction in Cuba. Because these missiles would be within ready striking distance of the eastern United States, Kennedy announced that the nation had set up a "quarantine"— effectively, a blockade—of Soviet ships heading to Cuba to prevent the arrival of Soviet arms. The **Cuban Missile Crisis** brought the two superpowers to the brink of war, but was eventually resolved. The Soviet removed existing missiles from Cuba and agreed not establish missile installations on the island; in return, Kennedy quietly agreed to remove U.S. missiles from Turkey.

Lyndon B. Johnson assumed the presidency after the assassination of John F. Kennedy. His vision for the nation was called the "Great Society" and built on the plans of Kennedy's "New Frontier." He won support in Congress for the largest group of legislative programs in the history of the nation. These included programs that Kennedy had been working on at the time of his death, including a new civil rights bill and a tax cut. He defined the "Great Society" as "a place where the meaning of man's life matches the marvels of man's labor." The legislation enacted during his administration included efforts to fight disease, urban renewal, Medicare, aid to education, conservation and beautification, development of economically depressed areas, a massive War on Poverty, voting rights for all, and control of crime and delinquency. Johnson managed an unpopular war in Vietnam and encouraged the exploration of space. During his administration, a number of new federal agencies, including the Department of Transportation, were formed and the first black Chief Justice, Thurgood Marshall, was nominated and confirmed to the Supreme Court.

Richard Nixon inherited social unrest and the unpopular Vietnam War, from which he eventually withdrew the U.S. military. His administration would have been best known for improved relations with both China and the USSR under a policy known as **détente** if not for the **Watergate scandal.** The investigation into this matter revealed wide-scale abuse of power and corruption that eventually led to Nixon's resignation in the face of certain impeachment. Nixon's major domestic achievements were: the appointment of conservative justices to the Supreme Court, passed new anti-crime legislation, introduced a broad environ-mental program, sponsored revenue sharing legislation, and ended the Vietnam War draft.

Probably the highlight of the foreign policy of President Richard Nixon, after the end of the Vietnam War and withdrawal of troops, was his 1972 trip to China. When the Communists gained control of China in 1949, the U.S. government refused to recognize the Communist government. Instead, it recognized the Republic of China (ROC) on the island of Taiwan under Chiang Kai-shek as the legitimate Chinese government. The Nixon administration changed this policy and altered the nation's relations with Soviet states from that of containment to one of discussion and diplomacy.

Republican representative **Gerald Ford** was the first Vice President, and, upon Nixon's resignation, President selected under the 25th Amendment. The challenges that faced his administration were a depressed economy scarred by **stagflation**, energy shortages, and the need to champion world peace. Ford, like Nixon before him, attempted several and mostly unsuccessful measure to curb inflation and jump start the economy. He tried to reduce the role of the federal government. He reduced business taxes and lessened controls on business. His international focus was on preventing a major war in the Middle East. He negotiated with the Soviet Union on limitations on nuclear weapons.

Jimmy Carter strove to make the government "competent and compassionate" in response to the American people and their expectations. The economy remained in recession when he took office. Although his administration made significant progress by creating jobs and decreasing the budget deficit, inflation and interest rates were nearly at record highs. There were several notable achievements: establishment of a national energy policy to deal with the energy shortage, decontrolling petroleum prices to stimulate production, civil service reform that improved government efficiency, deregulation of the trucking and airline industries, the creation of the Department of Education, negotiation of a framework for peace in Israel, furthering diplomatic relations with China, and establishing a Strategic Arms Limitation Agreement with the Soviet Union. He expanded the national park system, supported the Social Security system, and appointed a record number of women and minorities to government jobs.

Iran's Ayatollah Khomeini's extreme hatred for the United States was the result of the 1953 overthrow of Iran's Mossadegh government, sponsored by the CIA. The CIA had trained the Shah's ruthless secret police force, the SAVAK. The tensions within the country led to revolution, and the ruling Shah was overthrown and replaced with the Islamic leader, the Ayatollah Khomeini. The mood of Iran turned to traditional, conservative Muslim values, and a great deal of anti-Western sentiment emerged. In November of 1979, 66 Americans hostages were taken at the U.S. Embassy in Tehran, beginning an international incident.

President Carter later froze all Iranian assets in the United States, set up trade restrictions, and approved a risky rescue attempt, which failed. He had appealed to the UN for aid in gaining release for the hostages and to European allies to join the trade embargo on Iran. Khomeini ignored UN requests for releasing the Americans while European nations refused to support the embargo so as not to risk losing access to Iran's oil. American prestige was damaged and Carter's chances for reelection were doomed. The hostages were released on the day of Ronald Reagan's inauguration as President.

In 1983, 241 American Marines were killed in Beirut, Lebanon when an Islamic suicide bomber drove an explosive-laden truck into where the United States Marines headquarters was located. This tragic event came as part of the unrest and violence between the Israelis and the Palestinian Liberation Organization (PLO) forces in southern Lebanon.

A staunch conservative, **Ronald Reagan** introduced a reform program that came to be known as the Reagan Revolution. Its goal was to reduce the reliance of the American people upon government. For many, the Reagan administration restored hope in and enthusiasm for the nation. His legislative accomplishments include economic growth stimulation, curbing inflation, increasing employment, and strengthening the national defense. He won Congressional support for a complete overhaul of the income tax code in 1986. By the time he left office, the nation had enjoyed a sustained period of economic growth with no major wars. His foreign policy relied on "peace through strength." Reagan set the stage for the fall of the Berlin Wall and the end of the Cold War by spending billions of dollars on national defense—a figure that could not be matched by the Soviet Union, setting the stage of its economic collapse. He also nominated Sandra Day O'Connor as the first female justice on the Supreme Court.

George H. W. Bush was committed to "traditional American values" and to making America a "kinder and gentler nation." During the Reagan administration, Bush held responsibility for anti-drug programs and federal deregulation. When the Cold War ended and the Soviet Union broke apart, he supported the rise of democracy, but took a position of restraint toward the new nations. Bush ordered the invasion of Panama, codenamed Operation Just Cause, to remove drug-lord General Manuel Noriega from power. Following Iraq's August 2, 1990 invasion of

Kuwait, President Bush also ordered U.S. troops to Saudi Arabia to protect its vast oil fields, which became known as Operation Desert Shield. After Iraqi President Saddam Hussein refused to withdraw his military forces from Kuwait, President Bush, under UN authority, launched Operation Desert Storm —the largest military campaign since the Vietnam War. Thus, on January 16, 1991, the first Gulf War began, and ended with a relative quick allied victory on February 29, 1991. Although President Bush's international affairs record was strong, and despite an overwhelming military victory in the Middle East, he was not able to turn around increased violence in the inner cities and a struggling economy. During the 1992 presidential election, voters split their support among Bush, anti-deficit crusader and independent candidate Ross Perot, and Democratic nominee Bill Clinton, who ultimately carried the race.

William (Bill) Clinton led the nation in a time of greater peace and economic prosperity than has been experienced at any other time in history. His domestic accomplishments include maintaining the lowest inflation rate in 30 years, the lowest unemployment rate in modern days, the highest home ownership rate in history, lower crime rates in many places, and smaller welfare rolls. He proposed and achieved a balanced budget and even generated a budget surplus. However, due to widely publicized scandals involving political and personal matters, Clinton became the second President in American history to be impeached by the House of Representatives. He was later acquitted on all accounts following a Senate trial.

Modern Changes:
At the turn of the twentieth century, the world witnessed unprecedented strides in **communications**, a major expansion of international trade, and significant international diplomatic and military activity. The Internet connected people all over the world, opening new routes of communication and providing commercial opportunities. The expansion of **cell phone** usage and Internet access led to a **globalized** worldwide society that is interconnected like never before. In Asia, new economies matured, such as in India and China. As the technology sector expanded, so did India's economy, where high-tech companies found a highly educated work force. The formerly tightly controlled Chinese market became more open to foreign investment, which increased China's influence as a major economic power. The European Union made a bold move to a common currency, the Euro, in an effort to consolidate the region's economic strength. African nations, many struggling under international debt, appealed to the international community to assist them in building their economies. In South America, countries such as Brazil and Venezuela showed growth despite political unrest, even as Argentina suffered a near complete collapse of its economy.

Conflict between the Muslim world and the United States increased during the last decade of the twentieth century, culminating in a **terrorist attack** on New York and Washington, D.C. on September 11, 2001. These attacks, sponsored by the radical group Al-Qaeda, prompted a military invasion by the United States of Afghanistan, where the group is primarily based.   Shortly afterwards, the United States, United Kingdom, Spain, Australia, and several smaller countries became further involved in the region by ousting Iraqi dictator Saddam Hussein in a military campaign after a fruitless UN campaign to find **weapons of mass destruction (WMDs)**. In the eastern Mediterranean, tension between Israelis and Palestinians continued to build, regularly erupting into violence.

The threat of the spread of nuclear weapons, largely diminished after the fall of the Soviet Union and the end of the Cold War, reared its head again. North Korea claimed that it possessed nuclear weapons, while Iran was suspected of developing weapons-grade nuclear material. As international conflict and tension increased, the role of international alliances such as NATO and the United Nations grew in importance.

Skill 1.3   Analyze the influence of various factors on the development of societies

Spatial organization is a description of how things are grouped in a given space. In geographical terms, this can describe people, places, and environments anywhere and everywhere on Earth.

The most basic form of spatial organization for people is where they live. The vast majority of people live near other people, in villages and towns and cities and settlements. These people live near others in order to take advantage of the goods and services that naturally arise from cooperation. These villages' settlements are often near bodies of water, since water is a staple of survival for everyone, although towns formed in more recent years may be located farther from natural water sources. Water is also a powerful source of energy for factories and other industries, as well as a form of transportation for people and goods.

Another way to describe where people live is by the geography and topography around them. The majority of people on the planet live in areas that are hospitable to human settlement; consider the differences in the number of people living in the Himalayas and in the Sahara to the populations of such as the plains of China, India, Europe, and the United States. People naturally want to live where they will not have to struggle just to survive, and world population patterns reflect this.

Most places in the world are in some manner close to agricultural land, as well, for access to a ready supply of food. Rare is the city, however, that grows absolutely no crops. The kind of food grown is almost entirely dependent on the kind of land available and the climate surrounding that land. For instance, rice does not grow well in the desert, nor do bananas grow well in snowy lands. Certain crops are also easier to transport than others, and the ones that are not are usually grown near ports or land routes.

Science and technology have also had a significant impact on the emergence of various societies. Increased technological development improves agricultural, military, transportation, and communication systems, allowing a society to become more powerful within its sphere. Historically speaking, more technologically advanced societies have typically conquered less advanced ones; for example, European countries with superior military technologies fielded small armies that easily conquered Native Americans societies despite the higher populations of the latter.

See also Skill 1.1

Skill 1.4   Know common characteristics of communities, past and present

Human communities subsisted initially as **gatherers** who gathered edible berries, leaves, plants, and so on. With the invention of tools it became possible to dig for roots, hunt small animals, and catch fish from rivers and oceans. Humans observed their environments and in time learned to plant seeds and harvest crops, developing early agricultural techniques. As people migrated to areas in which game and fertile soil were abundant, communities began to develop. When people had the knowledge to grow crops and the skills to hunt game, they began to understand division of labor. Some of the people in the community tended to agricultural needs while others hunted game.

As habitats attracted larger numbers of people, environments became crowded and there was competition. The concept of division of labor and sharing of food soon came, in more heavily populated areas, to be managed. Groups of people focused on growing crops while others concentrated on hunting. Experience led to the development of skills and of knowledge that make the work easier. Farmers began to develop new plant species and hunters began to protect animal species from other predators for their own use. This ability to manage the environment led people to settle down, to guard their resources, and to manage them.

Camps soon became villages, which became year-round settlements. Animals were domesticated and gathered into herds that met the needs of the village. With the settled life it was possible to have more personal possessions. Pottery was developed for storing and cooking food.

By 8000 BCE, culture was beginning to evolve in these villages. Agriculture was developed for the production of grain crops, which led to a decreased reliance on wild plants. Domesticating animals for various purposes decreased the need to hunt wild game. Life became more settled. It was then possible to turn attention to such matters as managing water supplies, producing tools, and making cloth.

Social interaction and hierarchies grew, as did opportunity to reflect upon existence. Mythologies arose and various kinds of belief systems. Rituals reenacted the mythologies that gave meaning to life also developed.

The growth of settled agriculture enabled people to have a more reliable food supply and build stores for lean times. This improved availability of food and allowed for greater populations to be supported.

Two things seem to have come together to produce **cultures** and **civilizations**: a society and culture based on agriculture and the development of centers of the community with literate social and religious structures. The members of these hierarchies then managed water supply and irrigation, ritual and religious life, and exerted their own right to use a portion of the goods produced by the community for their own subsistence in return for their management.

Sharpened skills, development of more sophisticated tools, commerce with other communities, and increasing knowledge of their environment, the resources available to them, and responses to the needs to share goods, order community life, and protect their possessions from outsiders led to further division of labor and community development.

As trade routes developed and travel between cities became easier, trade led to labor specialization. Trade enables a people to obtain the goods they desire in exchange for the goods they are able to produce. This, in turn, leads to increased attention to refinements of technique and the sharing of ideas. The knowledge of a new discovery or invention provides knowledge and technology that increases the ability to produce goods for trade. As each community learns the value of the goods it produces and improves its ability to produce the goods in greater quantity, industry is born.

Skill 1.5   Apply knowledge of the concept of chronology and its use in understanding history and historical events

Chronology is the ordering of events through time. Chronologies are often listed along a timeline or in a list by date. It is closely related to the skill of **sequencing.** Chronology also helps show cause and effect and connections between events.

Chronologies allow for easy visualization of a wide expanse of history in one place. This allows a student to quickly get an overview of major events and changes over time. By including important related events, the causes and effects of major developments can be emphasized. By placing chronologies for different societies parallel to one another, comparisons in relative development can be quickly interpreted, providing material for further historical exploration.

Skill 1.6 **Apply different methods of interpreting the past to understand, evaluate, and support multiple points of view, frames of reference, and the historical context of events and issues**

Research into local history usually requires local sources, such as newspapers, family histories, memoirs, and oral interviews with local residents. Local records of births, deaths, land holdings, and other information can often be found at local courthouses and city halls. Local libraries and archives may also maintain extensive local records.

Historical events can affect local communities in more significant ways than when a larger viewpoint is taken. A factory closing may not have a large impact on a state's economy, for instance, but might be devastating for the town in which it was located. Interpreting historical events, issues, and developments of a specific locality requires a sharp focus on how relatively small groups of people are affected by larger historical forces.

Skill 1.7 **Understand similarities and differences among Native American groups in Texas, the United States, and the Western Hemisphere before European colonization**

Native Americans have made major contributions to the development of the nation and have been contributors, either directly or indirectly in every area of political and cultural life. In the early years of European settlement, Native Americans were both teachers and neighbors. Even during periods of extermination and relocation, their influence was profound.

Native American tribes lived throughout present-day North America in varying degrees of togetherness. They adopted different customs; different farming, hunting and gathering methods; and made slightly different weapons. They fought among themselves and with other peoples. Perhaps most importantly, they established cultures long before Columbus or any other European explorer arrived on the continent.

Archaeologists have discovered evidence of Native American civilization in Texas dating to at least 9,200 BCE. For the most part, these ancient peoples lived in temporary camps along river banks. Their subsistence was based on hunting and gathering. As the resources of an area were exhausted, they moved to another area. Although some of those Native American groups soon moved onto other areas, others stayed, in some cases for many years. Among the major settled tribes were the Caddo, Cherokee, Chickasaw, Choctaw, Comanche, Karankawa, Kickapoo, and Tonkawa.

The first known inhabitants of Texas were connected with the Clovis Complex. The Folsom Complex dates from around 8800–8200 BCE. The Archaic Period of

Texas history extended from about 6000 BCE to about 700 CE. The Late Archaic period (1000–300 BCE) continued to be a time of hunting societies. There is abundant evidence that bison became a vital source of food. The "Transitional Archaic" period (300 BCE–700 CE) was a time of some development in tool making, and the time of the first appearance of settled villages. The settlement of villages marks the emergence of agriculture and the beginning of social and political systems.

The Late Prehistoric period extends from about 700 CE to historic times. It was during this period that the bow and arrow first appeared along with new types of stone tools, pottery, and the creation and trade of ornamental items. Also during this period, the early Caddo culture began to emerge and mound building began. Agriculture spread and became more complex, and in some areas pit house dwellings appear. In particular, the presence of obsidian artifacts demonstrates the participation of these peoples in a north-south system of trade that extended to the Great Plains, and to Wyoming and Idaho, in particular.

The Caddo, in the east, were good at farming, trading, and making pottery. The Cherokee and Choctaw had advanced political structures, with an elected chief. The Chickasaw did not stay in Texas long but were known as good hunters and farmers. The Choctaw were also good farmers, hunters, toolmakers, and house-builders. The Comanche were famous horsemen and hunters. The Karankawa were good jewelers and shell-makers. The Tonkawa were famous for hunting bison and for gathering fruits and nuts.

An important northeastern Native American tribe was the **Algonquian**. We know a great deal about this tribe because they were one of the first to interact with the English settlers who had landed in Plymouth, Massachusetts. The Algonquians lived in longhouses or wigwams, wore clothing made from animal skins, and are known for introducing wampum (Native American bead work, which was traded as currency), and dream catchers to Native American culture. They were proficient hunters, gatherers, and trappers who also knew quite a bit about farming. Beginning with a man named Squanto, they shared this agricultural knowledge with the English settlers, including how to plant and cultivate corn, pumpkins, and squash. The Algonquian language group included several other related Native American groups. Other well-known speakers of Algonquin languages include Pocahontas and her father, Powhatan, who are immortalized in English literature, and Tecumseh and Black Hawk, who are known for their fierce fighting ability.

Another group of tribes who lived in the Northeast were the **Iroquois**, who were fierce fighters and progressive thinkers. They lived in longhouses and wore clothes made of buckskin. They, too, were expert farmers, growing the "Three Sisters" (corn, squash, and beans). Five of the Iroquois tribes formed a Confederacy, which was a shared form of government; they were later joined by a sixth group. The Iroquois also formed the False Face Society, a group of medicine men who shared their medical knowledge with others but hid their faces behind decorative masks. These masks are one of the enduring symbols of the Native American era.

Living in the Southeast were the **Seminoles** and **Creeks**, two related tribes who lived in log cabins or chickees (open, bark-covered houses) and wore clothes made from plant fibers. The Seminoles began in Florida as an offshoot of the Creek and included many African Americans who had fled from slavery. Both groups were expert farmers and hunters, and were proficient at making and paddling dugout canoes. The bead necklaces they created were some of the most beautiful on the continent. However, the Seminoles and Creeks are best known for their struggle against Spanish and English settlers, and the great Seminole leader, Osceola.

The **Cherokee** also lived in the Southeast. They were one of the more advanced Native American tribes, as they lived in domed houses and wore deerskin and rabbit fur. Accomplished hunters, farmers, and fishermen, the Cherokee were known throughout North America for their intricate and beautiful basketry and clay pottery. They also played an early form of the game lacrosse.

In the middle of the continent lived the Plains tribes, such as the **Sioux, Cheyenne, Blackfeet, Comanche**, and **Pawnee**. They lived in teepees and wore buffalo skins and feather headdresses. They hunted wild animals on the Plains, especially the buffalo. They were well known for their many ceremonies, including the Sun Dance, and for the ritual smoking of peace pipes. Famous Plains people include Crazy Horse and Sitting Bull, who defeated General George Custer and his Seventh Cavalry; Sacagawea, a Shoshone woman who led the Lewis & Clark Expedition; and Chief Joseph, who led the Nez Perce tribe.

Dotting the deserts of the Southwest was a handful of tribes, including the **Pueblo**, who lived in houses made of mud bricks known as adobe. They also wore clothes made of wool and woven cotton, and farmed crops in the middle of desert, sometimes aided by extensive irrigation system. Additionally, the Pueblo created exquisite pottery and Kachina dolls, and had one of the most complex religions of all the tribes. The Pueblo and other Southwestern tribes are perhaps best known for establishing villages upon cliffs and mountainsides (vistas.) Pueblos are also known to have chosen their own chiefs. This was perhaps one of the oldest representative governments in the world.

Another well-known southwestern tribe was the **Apache**, led for a time by **Geronimo**. The Apache lived in homes called wickiups, which were made of bark, grass, and branches. They wore cotton clothing, were excellent hunters and gatherers, and were adept at basketry. The Apache believed that everything in nature had special powers and that they were honored to be part of it.

The **Navajo**, also residents of the Southwest, lived in hogans (round homes built with forked sticks) and wore clothes of rabbit skins. Their major contribution to North American history was sand painting, weapon-making, silversmithing, and weaving. Some of the most beautiful woven rugs were created by the Navajo.

Living in the Northwest and frigid north were the **Inuit**, who lived either in tents made from animal skins or in igloos. They were excellent fishermen and hunters. They crafted kayaks and umiaks to take them through waterways, and harpoons with which to hunt animals. As a result, they wore clothes made of animal skins, usually seals or caribou. The Inuit are perhaps best known for their great carvings, notably ivory figures and tall totem poles.

See also Skill 1.1 and 1.2

Skill 1.8   Understand the causes and effects of European exploration and colonization of Texas, the United States, and the Western Hemisphere

Historic causation is the concept that events in history are linked to one another by an interwoven chain of cause and effect. The root causes of major historical events cannot always be seen immediately, and are only apparent when looking back from many years later. The advances made during the Renaissance in the areas of astronomy, cartography and shipbuilding opened the possibility of distant travel by sea. As cities grew and trade increased, Europe's monarchs began looking toward new lands to fuel growth. As Islam spread from the east, Christian nations also wished to find routes that bypassed areas of Islamic control. Thus, the Age of Exploration was underway.

Portugal led the first wave of exploration by sea in the early fifteenth century, under **Prince Henry the Navigator**. Using ships that borrowed technology from Arab sailing vessels, the Portuguese discovered new islands in the Atlantic and opened sea routes to the west coast of Africa. Over the next several decades, Portuguese explorers pushed farther south along the African coast. In 1498, Vasco De Gama became the first to navigate the Cape of Good Hope at the southern tip of Africa and opened a new sea route to India. Portugal's control over the African coast troubled the Spanish, who devised a plan to bypass the route entirely by sailing west, around the globe, to the profitable trade lands of Asia.

When Columbus landed in the New World in 1492, the full effect of his discovery could not have been measured at that time. By opening the Western Hemisphere to European economic and political development, Columbus changed the face of the world.

The native populations that had existed before Columbus arrived were quickly decimated by disease and warfare. Over the next century, the Spanish conquered most of South and Central America, while the English and French settlers that arrived in North America eventually displacing the natives there. This gradual displacement took place over many years and could not have been foreseen by those early explorers. Looking back it can be said that Columbus caused a series of events that greatly impacted world history.

Interaction among cultures, either by exploration and migration or war, often contributes directly to major historical events, but other forces can also influence the course of history. Religious movements, such as the rise of Catholicism in the Middle Ages, created social changes throughout Europe and culminated in the Crusades and the expulsion of the ruling Muslims from Spain.

The **Colonial Period** resulted in settlements being established by France, Spain and England; these grew and thrived. Settlers came to North America for various reasons, but mostly because it was a chance to own land and to experience freedom of one form or another. The first permanent settlement in North America was by the Spanish in **St. Augustine, Florida,** in 1565. Afterwards there was an influx of immigrants.

The **English** settlements spanned the Eastern seaboard from Maine to Georgia. The French settled between the Appalachian and Rocky Mountains, from New Orleans to Montreal, giving them control of most of the Great Lakes and the St. Lawrence and Mississippi Rivers. The Spanish settlements included Florida and the West Indies and the land west of the Mississippi. The fact that all three nations claimed the land west of the Mississippi set the stage for later conflicts.

Each of these regions had its own culture, as the settlers had brought with them many of the animals and agriculture from the regions from which they had immigrated, as well as their own customs. The New England colonies valued personal and religious freedoms and democratic governments. Their governments were based on the town hall where the adult males met to enact the laws. These British colonists brought British common law heritage with them.

The Middle Atlantic colonies were the considered melting pots of the colonies, since they included the Dutch settlements in New York and the region attracted settlers from all over Europe. They farmed the rich fertile land and produced a surplus of food that they traded with other regions. They also established commercial and manufacturing activities such as shipbuilding, mining, and textile, paper and glass manufacturing. Governmental units based on democracy, with unicameral or bicameral legislative bodies, were also established throughout the region.

Further south, the rich fertile land gave rise to large plantations. They also had mines in the South. There, the labor force was not large enough to staff the mines and plantations on the mainland, or even in the West Indies. Thus, mine and plantation owners began to import slaves from Africa. Virginia and the South also established democratic forms of governments. As the plantations grew, they required more and more slave labor. The South also had small family run and operated farms that did not use slaves. Other areas of the South were settled by different groups: Georgia became a haven for debtors from British prisons; North Carolina became settled by Virginia's expansion; and South Carolina was settled by different groups of European nationalities. Agriculture remained the primary form of economic activity for the region even though there was economic activity in lumber and the fur trade.

The common thread throughout all of the regions was a government based on democracy *for the settlers—not for the slaves*. The settlers came to North America in search of land ownership and various kinds of freedoms and this is evident in the forms of government they established.

Spain's influence was in Florida, the Gulf Coast from Texas all the way west to California, and south to the tip of South America and some of the islands of the West Indies. French control centered from New Orleans north to what is now northern Canada including the entire Mississippi Valley, the St. Lawrence Valley, the Great Lakes, and the land that was part of the Louisiana Territory. A few West Indian islands were also part of France's empire. England settled the eastern seaboard of North America, including parts of Canada and from Maine to Georgia. Some West Indies islands also came under British control. The Dutch had New Amsterdam for a period but later ceded it into British hands. One interesting aspect was in each of these three nations, especially in England, the land claims extended partly or all the way across the continent, regardless of the fact that the others claimed the same land. The wars for dominance and control of power and influence in Europe would undoubtedly and eventually extend to the Americas, especially North America.

The part of North America claimed by **France** was called New France and consisted of the land west of the Appalachian Mountains. This area included the St. Lawrence Valley, the Great Lakes, the Mississippi Valley, and all of the land westward to the Rockies. They established the permanent settlements of Montreal and New Orleans, thus giving them control of the two major gateways into the vast, rich interior of North America. The St. Lawrence River, the Great Lakes, and the Mississippi River along with its tributaries made it possible for French explorers and traders to roam at will, virtually unhindered in exploring, trapping, trading, and furthering the interests of France.

French and Spanish explorers reached **Texas** in the sixteenth century, and settlers soon followed. The first important Frenchman to arrive was La Salle, as part of his overall exploration of what became the Mississippi Territory. Other French explorers and settlers came to North America, but a combination of meager resources and a surge in Spanish explorers eliminated the French from further influence in the majority of Texas. The Spanish were far more successful in colonizing Texas. Spain had a whole colony called the Kingdom of Tejas, which was administered by forces of varying sizes. Conflict erupted over Louisiana, but the Spanish missions provided a strong base for settlement and defense, and French influence ended for good with the Louisiana Purchase.

Spanish exploration began with the search for the cities of gold. The failure of the French colony in Texas became internationally known, while Spain was quick to destroy the ruins of the French colony and establish itself in the area. Spain's interests included the Texan resources, the Catholic missionary zeal to convert native peoples, and expansion of its empire.

Colonization of Texas by Europeans affected the Native peoples in many ways, some of which were undesirable. The Spanish approach to occupation of a new region was to plant Catholic missions that would convert the natives, bring them into conformity with Spanish beliefs and ideas, and teach them subsistence agriculture. One of the negative effects of the Spanish arrival was the introduction of a number of diseases to which the native people had not been exposed and to which they had no natural immunities. This deadly combination of factors resulted in the deaths of thousands of Native American.

The Spanish colonists and missionaries introduced, however, a number of European crops, as well as irrigation methods that greatly improved the agricultural output of the native people. They also introduced animal husbandry methods. But throughout the early years of European occupation, Texas was primarily a buffer zone between the French, Spanish, English, and Americans, as each sought to expand its empire and exploit the native land and people. The greatest influence during this period, however, was that of the Spanish missions and presidios. These colonial institutions had been very successful in Hispanicize the native people.

Mexican independence from Spain resulted in Mexican control over much of Texas. This control was harsh and dictatorial. In the 1820s, Mexico reached an agreement with **Stephen Austin** to allow several hundred U.S. settlers, called Texians, to move to the area, as the Mexican government wanted to populate and develop the region. In a short period of time, thousands of settlers arrived to populate Texas. However, the Mexican government abolished slavery, a move with which many settlers refused to comply, and the Mexican government tried to tighten its control over the settlers' political and economic lives. Furthermore, the government expected "good citizens" to be members of the Catholic Church. However, most of the American settlers were Protestant. Emotions were aroused among the settlers and the local Tejanos that led to the Texas Revolution.

Spanish influence continued into the nineteenth century but ended with Mexico's independence in 1821. Texas was thus under Mexican control until the end of the

Mexican-American War, when it became part of the United States. One major result of the European occupation of Texas was the passage of Spanish culture into Texas culture, especially in the names of towns and foods. This legacy is still reflected in the state's culture, while French influence has largely disappeared.

See also Skill 1.1

Skill 1.9   **Understand the foundations of representative government in the United States, significant issues of the revolutionary era, and challenges confronting the U.S. Government in the early years of the republic**

The American nation was founded with the explicit idea that the people would have a large degree of autonomy and liberty. The famous maxim "no taxation without representation" was a rallying cry for the Revolution as colonists rejected not only the specific taxes placed upon them by the British Parliament but also their own lack of influence over the placement of those taxes. No American colonist had a seat in Parliament and no American colonist could vote for members of Parliament.

Representation, the idea that a people can vote—or even replace—their law-makers was not a new idea, except in the American colonies. Settlers in other British colonies did not have these rights, and according to the conventional wisdom of the British Government, America was just another colony. What the Sons of Liberty and other revolutionaries were asking for was to stand on an equal footing with Great Britain. Along with the idea of representation comes the notion that key ideas and concepts can be deliberated and discussed, with theoretically everyone having a chance to voice his views. This applied to both lawmakers and to the people who elected them.

Lawmakers would not just pass bills that became laws; rather, they would debate their strengths and weaknesses before voting on them. Members of both houses of Congress had the opportunity to speak out on the issues, as did the people at large, who could contact their lawmakers and express their views. This idea ran very much counter to the experience that the Founding Fathers had before the Revolution—that of taxation without representation. The different branches of government were designed to serve as a mechanism of checks and balances on each other so that no one branch could become too powerful. Each have its own specific powers.

Another key American ideal is **equality**, the notion that every person has the same rights and responsibilities under the law. The Great Britain that the American colonists knew was one of a stratified society, with social classes firmly in place. Not everyone was equal under the law or in the coffers; and it was clear for all to see that the more money and power a person had, the easier it was for that person to avoid things like serving in the army and being charged with a crime. The goal of the Declaration of Independence and the Constitution was to provide equality for all – not merely a few privileged.

Due process under law was also a big concern of the founders. Various amendments to the U.S. Constitution protect the rights of people, particularly those grouped under the **Bill of Rights**. This notion feeds into the idea of basic opportunity. The "American Dream" is that every individual has an equal chance to make his or her fortune in a new land and that the United States welcomes— even encourages —that initiative. The country's history is filled with stories of people who ventured to America and made their fortunes in the Land of Opportunity.

Causes of the War for Independence

With the end of the French and Indian War (the American arm of the Seven Years' War), Great Britain reasserted control over the American colonies. In particular, Britain needed revenues to pay for the war and to defend the new territory obtained as a result of the war.

British leaders imposed a tax that would pay for the defense of the colonies. The colonists rejected this for two reasons: (1) they were undergoing an economic recession, and (2) they believed it was unjust to be taxed unless they had representation in the Parliament. British leaders, however, believed that the tax was fair because of the high expenses that the nation had incurred as a result of defending its American holdings.

Opposition melded in Massachusetts. Leaders denounced "taxation without representation" and a boycott was organized against imported English goods. The movement rapidly spread to other colonies. Relations between the colonists and British troops became increasingly strained. Skirmishes between the two eventually led to the "Boston Massacre" in 1770. Angered at the heavy British military presence and other measures enacted by Great Britain, Bostonian colonists taunted a group of British troops. In response, British troops fired their muskets on unarmed Bostonians, resulting in five civilian deaths and increased hostility towards the British.

The Tea Act of 1773 gave the British East India Company a monopoly on sales of tea. In Boston, a group of the colonists responded by disguising themselves as Native Americans, boarding British merchant ships and tossing the crates of tea into Boston Harbor. In a tongue-in-cheek reference to the event, it became known as the "Boston Tea Party". England responded with the "Coercive Acts (called the "Intolerable Acts" by the colonists) in 1774. This closed the port of Boston, changed the charter of the Massachusetts colony, and suppressed town meetings. Eleven colonies sent delegates to the first Continental Congress in 1774. The group issued the "Declaration of Rights and Grievances," which vowed allegiance to the king but protested the right of Parliament to tax the colonies. Colonists also resumed their boycott of English goods.

Massachusetts mobilized its colonial militia, or Minutemen, in anticipation of difficulties with England. For the most part, the Minutemen were not formally trained soldiers. Rather, they were a loose confederation of colonists who, supposedly, could be called to duty within a minute's notice. The British troops attempted to seize their weapons and ammunition, which resulted in two clashes at Lexington and Concord. A month later, the Second Continental Congress met.

There, many of the delegates recommended a **Declaration of Independence** from Britain. The group also established the Continental Army and commissioned George Washington, the seasoned army officer who had fought the French and Indians under the British, as its commander.

When the war began, the colonies began to establish individual colonial—later state—governments. To a significant extent, the government that was defined for the new nation was intentionally weak; the colonies/states feared a strong, central government. But the lack of continuity between the individual governments was confusing and economically damaging.

The **Declaration of Independence** was the founding document of the United States of America. It sought to justify the colonies' separation from Great Britain. Conceived and written (mostly) by Thomas Jefferson, it is not only important for what it says, but also for how it was written. The Declaration is in many respects a poetic document. Instead of simply reciting the colonists' grievances, it clearly defined the reasons why the colonists sought their freedom from Great Britain. They had exhausted all peaceful means to resolve the dispute. Thus, it was their right to separate themselves from the government that was denying them their right to "life, liberty, and the pursuit of happiness".

By 1776, the colonists and their representatives in the Second Continental Congress realized that, in order to fulfill their wishes for self-determination, they had no choice but to break from Great Britain. The Declaration of Independence was drafted and issued July 4, 1776.

George Washington defied tremendous odds to wage a victorious campaign against the British. The turning point for Washington and the Continentals occurred in 1777 with the victory at Saratoga. The victory caused the French to join the colonies in their fight against the British. With the aid of Admiral De Grasse and French warships blocking the entrance to Chesapeake Bay, British General Cornwallis was trapped at Yorktown, Virginia. In 1781, General Cornwallis surrendered and the war was over. In 1783, the Treaty of Paris was signed and officially ended the war.

The Articles of Confederation, collectively, was the first political system under which the newly independent colonies tried to organize themselves. It was drafted after the Declaration of Independence in 1776, passed by the Continental Congress on November 15, 1777, ratified by the thirteen states, and took effect on March 1, 1781.

The newly independent states were unwilling to give too much power to a nation-al government. They were already fighting Great Britain, and did not want to replace one harsh, imperial ruler with another. After many debates, the form of the Articles was accepted. Each state agreed to send delegates to the Congress, where it would have one vote. The Articles gave Congress the power to declare war, appoint military officers, and coin money. It was also responsible for foreign affairs. The Articles of Confederation limited the powers of Congress by giving the states final authority. Although Congress could pass laws, at least nine of the thirteen states had to approve a law before it went into effect. Congress could not pass any laws regarding taxes. To get money, Congress had to ask each state for it; no state could be forcibly taxed.

Thus, the Articles created a loose alliance among the thirteen states. The nation-al government was weak, in part, because it did not have a strong chief executive to carry out laws passed by the legislature. This weak national government might have worked if the states were able to cooperate. However, many different disputes arose and there was no way of settling them. Thus, the delegates went to meet again to try to fix the Articles; instead they ended up scrapping them and creating a new Constitution that built on the lesson of these earlier mistakes.

The Constitutional Convention in 1787 devised an entirely new form of government and outlined it in the **Constitution of the United States**. It was ratified and took effect in 1789. Concerns that had been raised in or by the states regarding civil liberties and states' rights led to the immediate adoption of 12 amendments to the constitution, the first ten known as the **Bill of Rights**. Ratification of the U.S. Constitution was by no means a foregone conclusion. The representative government had powerful opponents, especially those who had seen firsthand the failure of the Articles of Confederation. The strong central government had its critics, as well, including some of the American Revolutionaries.

Those who wanted to see a strong central government, such as Alexander Hamilton and John Jay, were called **Federalists**, because they wanted to see a strong federal government in control. Hamilton and Jay, along with James Madison, wrote a series of letters to the New York newspapers, urging that that state ratify the Constitution. These became known as the *Federalist Papers*.

In the Anti-Federalist camp were Thomas Jefferson and Patrick Henry. These men and many like them were worried that a strong national government would descend into the kind of tyranny that they had just abolished. They, too, wrote a series of arguments to the New York newspapers; however, they argued *against* the Constitution, and were thusly called the **Anti-Federalist Papers.**

In the end, both sides got most of what they wanted. The Federalists got their strong national government, which was held in place by the famous "checks and balances." The Anti-Federalists got the Bill of Rights, the first ten Amendments to the Constitution and a series of laws that protect some of the most basic of human rights. The states that were in doubt for ratification of the Constitution signed on when the Bill of Rights was promised.

The three concepts of democracy—representation, civil rights, and a benign government—were basic reasons why people came to the New World. These concepts were embraced throughout the colonial and revolutionary periods, and were extremely influential in shaping the new central government under the U.S. Constitution.

Skill 1.10   Understand westward expansion and analyzes its effects on the political, economic, and social development of the United States

In the United States, westward territorial expansion occurred under the banner of **"Manifest Destiny."** This was the belief in the divinely given right of the nation to expand westward to the Pacific Ocean and incorporate more of the continent into the nation. Although the term was not coined until the mid-nineteenth century, the spirit of this doctrine had been expressed at the end of the Revolutionary War in the demand that Britain cede all lands east of the Mississippi River to America. Its goal was further confirmed with the Northwest Ordinance (1787) and the Louisiana Purchase (1803). Manifest Destiny was the justification of the **Mexican-American War** (1846-48) that resulted in the annexation of Texas and California, as well as much of the southwest. Due to U.S. involvement in that War, as well as the Spanish-American War and U.S. support of Latin America's fight for independence, the Spanish colonies eventually won their independence and their right to self-government.

After the United States purchased the Louisiana Territory, President Thomas Jefferson appointed Captains Meriwether Lewis and William Clark to explore the Territory to find out exactly what had been bought. The Corps of Discovery went all the way to the Pacific Ocean, returning two years later with maps, journals, and artifacts. This led the way for future explorers to reveal more about the territory, which in turn resulted in the Westward Movement and ultimately in the doctrine of Manifest Destiny.

Regarding the Oregon country, however, the United States and Britain had shared the land. By the 1840s, with increases in both free and slave populations and settlers' growing demand for U.S. control of the territory, the conflict had to be resolved. Thus, in a treaty signed in 1846 by both nations, a peaceful resolution occurred with Britain giving up its claims south of the 49th parallel.

In the American southwest, the results were exactly the opposite. Spain had claimed this area since the 1540s, had spread northward from Mexico City, and, in the 1700s, had established missions, forts, villages, towns, and very large ranches. After the purchase of the Louisiana Territory in 1803, Americans began moving into Spanish territory. A few hundred American families in what is now Texas were allowed to live there but had to agree to become loyal subjects of Spain. In 1821, Mexico successfully revolted against Spanish rule, won independence, and chose to be more tolerant towards the American settlers and traders.

The Mexican government encouraged and allowed extensive trade and settlement, especially in Texas. Many of the new settlers were Southerners and brought with them their slaves. Slavery was outlawed in Mexico and technically illegal in Texas, although the Mexican government looked the other way.

Friction increased between land-hungry Americans swarming into western lands and the Mexican government that controlled these lands. The clash was not only political but also cultural and economic. Spanish influence permeated all parts of southwestern life: law, language, architecture, and customs. By this time, Manifest Destiny was in the hearts and on the lips of those seeking new homes and new lives. Unlike the peaceful negotiations that ceded Oregon to the growing United States, it took two years of war to gain control of the Southwest.

In addition, the Mexican government owed debts to U.S. citizens whose property was damaged or destroyed during its struggle for independence from Spain. By the time war between Mexico and the United States broke out in 1845, Mexico had not paid its war debts. The government was weak, corrupt, irresponsible, torn by revolutions, and in dire financial straits. Mexico was also bitter over American expansion into Texas and the 1836 revolution, which resulted in Texas's independence. In the 1844 Presidential election, the Democrats pushed for annexation of Texas and Oregon and after winning, they began the process of admitting Texas to the Union.

When statehood occurred, diplomatic relations between the United States and Mexico ended. President Polk wanted U.S. control of the entire southwest, from Texas to the Pacific Ocean. He sent a diplomatic mission with an offer to purchase New Mexico and upper California but the Mexican government refused to even receive the diplomat. Consequently, in 1846, each nation claimed aggression on the part of the other and war was declared. The Treaty of Guadalupe-Hidalgo signed in 1848, followed by the Gadsden Purchase in 1853, completed the southwestern boundary of the United States, reaching to the Pacific Ocean, as President Polk wished.

Skill 1.11   Analyze ways in which political, economic, and social factors led to the growth of sectionalism and the Civil War

The character of the North and the South was quite distinct in the years leading up to the Civil War. From the earliest settlement of the colonies, the South had been more dependent on the cultivation of cash crops such as tobacco for its economic success. During the early nineteenth century, this division between North and South was furthered by the rise of "King Cotton" in the South and the beginnings of industrialization in the North. The Southern economy became even more dependent on the free labor provided by enslaved people to meet high demand for cotton exports, while Northern economies instead began to transform into ones based on manufacturing.

The growth of the United States also increased sectional tensions. As new states entered the Union, Southerners worried that the delicate balance of slave and free states maintained in the Senate would tip in favor of Northern interests, possibly endangering the continuation of the institution of slavery. Political solutions such as the Missouri Compromise and Compromise of 1850 attempted to correct the problem, but succeeded only in delaying the conflagration. Anti-slavery feeling rose in the North even as Southerners fought to maintain their way of life. When Abraham Lincoln won the presidency in the election of 1860, Southern leaders believed that division was inevitable and began seceding from the Union.

See also Skill 1.2 and 1.12

Skill 1.12   Know individuals, issues, and events of the Civil War and analyze the effects of Reconstruction on the political, economic, and social life of the nation

Civil War and Reconstruction

At the Constitutional Convention, one of the compromises reached on the issue of slavery concerned counting slaves for Congressional representation and taxation. Southerners pushed for counting slaves for representation but not for taxation, while Northerners pushed for the opposite. The resulting compromise, sometimes referred to as the "Three-Fifths Compromise," was that both groups agreed that three-fifths of the slaves would be counted for both taxes and representation.

The other compromise reached over slavery involved how much regulation the central government would have over commerce, such as international trade and the slave trade. It was agreed that Congress would regulate commerce with other nations including taxing imports. Southerners were worried about taxing slaves coming into the country and the possibility of Congress prohibiting the slave trade altogether. The agreement reached allowed the states to continue importation of slaves for the next 20 years until 1808, at which time Congress would make the decision as to the future of the slave trade. During the 20-year period, no more than $10 per person could be levied on slaves coming into the country.

An additional provision of this compromise was that with the admission of the state of Missouri, slavery would not be allowed in the rest of the Louisiana Purchase territory north of latitude 36 degrees 30'. This was acceptable to Southern Congressmen since it was not profitable to grow cotton on land north of this latitude anyway. The crisis had apparently been resolved but in the next year, it was discovered that Missouri's constitution discriminated against free blacks. Anti-slavery supporters in Congress went into an uproar, determined to exclude Missouri from the Union.

The Missouri Territory allowed slavery and, if admitted, Missouri would cause an imbalance in the number of U.S. Senators. Alabama had already been admitted as a slave state and that had balanced the Senate with the North and South each having 22 senators. The first Missouri Compromise resolved the conflict by admitting Maine as a free state along with Missouri as a slave state, thus continuing to keep a balance of power in the Senate with the same number of free and slave states.

Henry Clay, known as the Great Compromiser, then proposed a second Missouri Compromise that was acceptable to everyone. It stated that the U.S. Constitution guaranteed protections and privileges to citizens of states, and that Missouri's proposed constitution could not deny these to any of its citizens. The acceptance in 1820 of this second compromise opened the way for Missouri's statehood—a temporary reprieve, only.

These two "slavery' compromises were a necessary concession in order to have Southern support for the new Constitution and government. Many Americans felt that slavery would eventually die out in the United States, but by 1808, cotton was becoming increasingly important in the South. Thus, slavery became firmly entrenched in Southern culture. Conversely, as early as the Constitutional Convention, active anti-slavery sentiments were also very strong, which led to extremely active groups and societies.

The doctrine of **nullification** states that the states have the right to "nullify"— declare invalid—any act of Congress they believed to be unjust or unconstitutional. The nullification crisis of the mid nineteenth century climaxed over a new tariff on imported manufactured goods that was enacted by Congress in 1828. While this tariff protected the industrial interests of the North, it placed an additional economic burden on the South, which was only affected by the tariff as consumers of manufactured goods. The North had become increasingly industrial, while the South had become increasingly agricultural. Despite the fact that the tariff was primarily intended to protect Northern manufacturing interests in the face of imports from other countries, it merely raised the prices of vital goods in the South.

This disagreement peaked when John C. Calhoun, Jackson's vice president, led South Carolina to adopt the Ordinance of Nullification, which declared the tariff null and void within state borders. Although the crisis nearly escalated to a military conflict, it was resolved by the enactment of a new tariff in 1832.

The slavery issue was at the root of every problem, crisis, event, decision, and struggle from then on. The next crisis involved the issue concerning Texas. By 1836, Texas was an independent republic with its own constitution. During its fight for independence, Americans were sympathetic to and supportive of the Texans and some recruited volunteers who crossed into Texas to help the struggle. Problems arose when it petitioned Congress for statehood. Texas wanted to allow slavery but Northerners in Congress opposed admission to the Union because it would disrupt the balance between free and slave states and give Southerners in Congress increased influence.

The slavery issue soon flared again, but would not be fully addressed until the end of the Civil War. As the nation expanded, the newly acquired territory would be divided up into territories and later become states. In addition to the two factions of Northerners who advocated prohibition of slavery and of Southerners who favored slavery existing there, a third faction arose. This faction supported the doctrine of "**popular sovereignty,**" which stated that people living in territories and states should be allowed to decide whether or not slavery should be permitted. In 1849, California applied for admittance to the Union and the furor began.

The result was the **Compromise of 1850**, a series of laws designed as a final solution to the issue. Concessions made to the North included the admission of California as a free state and the abolition of slave trading in Washington, D.C. The laws also provided for the creation of the New Mexico and Utah territories. As a concession to Southerners, the residents there would decide whether to permit slavery when these two territories became states. In addition, Congress authorized stricter measures to capture runaway slaves.

A few years later, Congress considered new territories between Missouri and present-day Idaho. Again, heated debate over permitting slavery in these areas flared up. Those opposed to slavery used the Missouri Compromise to prove their point, showing that the land being considered for territories was part of the area the Compromise had designated as banned to slavery. But on May 25, 1854, Congress passed the **Kansas-Nebraska Act,** which nullified this provision, created the territories of Kansas and Nebraska, and allowed the people of these two territories to decide for themselves whether or not to permit slavery to exist there. Feelings were so deep and divided that any further attempts to compromise would meet with little, if any, success. As a result of the pro- and anti-slavery governments there, political and social turmoil were everywhere. Extreme violence and bloodshed ensued, and Kansas became known as "Bleeding Kansas."

In 1858, Abraham Lincoln and Stephen A. Douglas were running for the office of Illinois Senator and participated in a series of debates, which directly affected the outcome of the 1860 Presidential election. Douglas, a Democrat, was up for re-election and knew that if he won this race, he had a good chance of becoming President in 1860. Lincoln, a Republican, was not an abolitionist; however, he believed that slavery was wrong morally and supported the Republican Party principle that the practice must not be allowed to continue.

Douglas, on the other hand, instituted the doctrine of **popular sovereignty** and was responsible for supporting and getting through Congress the inflammatory Kansas-Nebraska Act. In the course of the debates, Lincoln challenged Douglas to show that popular sovereignty reconciled with the **Dred Scott** decision. Either way he answered Lincoln, Douglas would lose crucial support from one group or the other. If he supported the Dred Scott decision, Southerners would support him but he would lose Northern support. If he stayed with popular sovereignty, he would win Northern support but lose Southern support. His reply to Lincoln, stating that territorial legislatures could exclude slavery by refusing to pass laws supporting it, gave him enough support and approval to be re-elected to the Senate but it cost him support for the Democratic nomination for President in 1860.

Southerners realized that Douglas supported and was devoted to popular sovereignty but not necessarily to slavery's expansion. Conversely, two years later, Lincoln received the nomination of the Republican Party for President. The final straw came with the election of Lincoln to the Presidency the next year. Due to a split in the Democratic Party, there were four candidates from four political parties. With Lincoln receiving a minority of the popular vote and a majority of electoral votes, the Southern states, one by one, voted to secede from the Union as they had promised they would do if Lincoln and the Republicans were victorious. The die was cast.

South Carolina was the first state to secede from the Union and the first shots of the war were fired on Fort Sumter in Charleston Harbor. Both sides quickly prepared for war. The North had more in its favor, including a larger population, superior economic and transportation systems, and vast industrial, agricultural, and natural resources. The North possessed most of the nation's gold, had about 92% of all industries, and almost all known supplies of copper, coal, iron, and various other minerals.

Since most of the nation's railroads were in the North and Midwest, men and supplies could be moved wherever needed. Food could be transported from the farms of the Midwest to workers in the East and to soldiers on the battlefields. International trade could continue unabated due to the North's control of the navy and the merchant fleet. The Union states numbered 24 and included western

(California and Oregon) and border (Maryland, Delaware, Kentucky, Missouri, and West Virginia) states.

The Southern states numbered 11 and included South Carolina, Georgia, Florida, Alabama, Mississippi, Louisiana, Texas, Virginia, North Carolina, Tennessee, and Arkansas, making up the Confederacy. Although outnumbered in population, the South was completely confident of victory. Military leaders knew that all they had to do was fight a defensive war, protecting their own territory until the North, who had to invade and defeat an area almost the size of Western Europe, exhausted itself and gave up. Another Southern advantage was that a number of its best officers had graduated from the U.S. Military Academy at West Point and had had long years of army experience, some even exercising varying degrees of command in the Indian wars and the war with Mexico.

Southern soldiers were conditioned to living outdoors and were more familiar with horses and firearms than many men from northeastern cities. Since cotton was such an important crop, Southerners felt that British and French textile mills were so dependent on raw cotton that they would be forced to help the Confederacy in the war.

The South had specific reasons and goals for fighting the war, more so than the North. The major aim of the Confederacy never wavered: independence, the right to govern itself as they wished, and to preserve slavery. The North's goals were not as clearly defined. At the beginning, most believed, along with Lincoln, that preservation of the Union was paramount. Only a few extremely fanatical abolitionists viewed the war as a way to end slavery. However, by war's end, more and more Northerners had come to believe that freeing the slaves was just as important as restoring the Union.

The major military and political turning points of the war

The war strategies for both sides were relatively clear and simple. The South planned a defensive war, wearing down the North until it agreed to peace on Southern terms. The only exception to this defensive strategy was an aggressive plain to gain control of Washington, D.C., go north through the Shenandoah Valley into Maryland and Pennsylvania in order to drive a wedge between the Northeast and Midwest, interrupt the lines of communication, and end the war quickly.

The North had three basic strategies:

1. Blockade the Confederate coastline in order to cripple the South;
2. Seize control of the Mississippi River and interior railroad lines to split the Confederacy in two;
3. Seize the Confederate capital of Richmond, Virginia, driving southward and rendezvousing with Union forces coming east from the Mississippi Valley.

Until the Battle of Gettysburg (July 1–3, 1863), the South had winning clear victories in battle against the North. Until then, Lincoln's commanders—McDowell, McClellan, Burnside, and Hooker—had failed to demonstrate any great military prowess. Lee, on the other hand, had many able officers; he especially depended on "Stonewall" Jackson and Stuart. However, Jackson died at Chancellorsville and was replaced by Longstreet. Lee decided to invade the North; he depended on J.E.B. Stuart and his cavalry to inform him of the Union's troop locations and strengths. Four things worked against Lee at Gettysburg:

1. The Union troops gained the best positions and the best ground first, making it easier to make a stand there.

2. Lee's move into Northern territory put him and his army a long way from food and supply lines. They were more or less on their own.

3. Lee thought that his Army of Northern Virginia was invincible and could fight and win under any conditions or circumstances.

4. Stuart and his men did not arrive at Gettysburg until the end of the second day of fighting and by then, it was too little, too late. He and his men had had to detour around Union soldiers and were delayed in getting to Lee the information he needed.

Consequently, he made the mistake of failing to listen to Longstreet and following the strategy of regrouping back into Southern territory to the supply lines. Lee felt that regrouping was retreating and almost an admission of defeat. He was convinced the army would be victorious. Longstreet was concerned about the Union troops occupying the best positions and felt that regrouping to a better position would be advantageous. He was also very concerned about the distance from supply lines. The resulting Union victory helped turn the tide of the war.

The Civil War took more American lives than any other war in history. The South lost one-third of its soldiers in battle, while the North lost about one-sixth of theirs. More than half of the total deaths were caused by disease and the rudimentary conditions of field hospitals. Both sides paid a tremendous economic price but the South suffered more severely from direct damages, particularly in those areas affected by Sherman's devastating March to the Sea. Destruction was pervasive, with towns, farms, trade, industry, lives, and the homes of men, women, and children all destroyed. For the South, their entire way of life was lost. Deep resentment emerged, and it took the South decades to rebuild its infrastructure and economy.

The effects of the Civil War were tremendous. It changed the methods of waging war and has been called the first modern war. It introduced weapons and tactics that, when improved later, were used extensively in wars of the late 1800s and

1900s. Civil War soldiers were the first to fight in trenches, first to fight under a unified command, first to wage a defense called "major cordon defense," a strategy of advance on all fronts. They were also the first to use repeating and breech loading weapons. Observation balloons were first used during the war along with submarines, ironclad ships, and mines. Telegraphy and railroads were put to use first in the Civil War. It was considered a "total war," because it garnered all of the resources of the opposing sides.

By executive proclamation and constitutional amendment, slavery was officially ended, although deep prejudice and racism remained. The Union was preserved and the states were finally and truly united. Sectionalism, especially political, remained strong, but not to the degree and with as much violence as existed before the Civil War. It has been noted that the Civil War may have been American democracy's greatest failure; after all, from 1861 to 1865, calm reason, which is fundamental for democracy, gave way to human passion. Yet, democracy survived.

The Northern victory established that no state has the right to end or leave the Union. Because of unity, the United States became a major global power. Lincoln never proposed to punish the South; rather, he was most concerned with restoring it to the Union in a program that was flexible and practical rather than rigid and unrealistic. In fact, he never really felt that the states had seceded in leaving the Union; they had simply left the circle for a short time. His Presidential Reconstruction plans consisted of two major steps:

1. All Southerners taking an oath of allegiance to the Union promising to accept all federal laws and proclamations dealing with slavery would receive a full pardon. The only ones excluded from this were men who had resigned from civil and military positions in the federal government to serve in the Confederacy, those who were part of the Confederate government, those in the Confederate army above the rank of lieutenant, and Confederates who were guilty of mistreating prisoners of war and blacks.

2. A state would be able to write a new constitution, elect new officials, and return to the Union fully equal to all other states on certain conditions: a minimum number of persons (at least 10% of those who were qualified voters in their states before secession from the Union who had voted in the 1860 election) must take an oath of allegiance.

The economic and social chaos in the post-war South was unbelievable, with starvation and disease rampant, especially in the cities. The U.S. Army provided some relief, giving food and clothing to both white and blacks, but the major responsibility fell to the Freedmen's Bureau. Though, to a certain extent, the bureau agents helped southern whites, their main responsibility was to the freed slaves. They tried to assist the freedmen to become self-supporting and protect them from being taken advantage of by others. Northerners looked on it as a real, honest effort to help the South out of the chaos it was in. Most white Southerners charged the bureau with causing racial friction, deliberately encouraging the freedmen to consider former owners as enemies.

Lincoln and Johnson had considered the Civil War as a "rebellion of individuals." But Radical Republicans in Congress, such as Charles Sumner in the Senate, considered the Southern states as complete political organizations and were now in the same position as any unorganized territory and should be treated as such. Radical House leader Thaddeus Stevens considered the Confederate States not as territories, but as conquered provinces, and felt they should be treated as such. President Johnson refused to work with Congressional moderates, insisting on having his own way. As a result, the Radicals gained control of both Congressional houses; and when Johnson opposed their harsh measures, they came within one vote of impeaching him.

Plans for Reconstruction with its actual implementation

Following the Civil War, the nation was faced with repairing the torn Union and readmitting the Confederate states. **Reconstruction** refers to this period between 1865 and 1877 when the federal and state governments debated and implemented plans to provide civil rights to freed slaves and to set the terms under which the former Confederate states might rejoin the Union.

Planning for Reconstruction began early in the war, in 1861. Abraham Lincoln's Republican Party favored the extension of voting rights to black men, and Radical Republicans eventually sent the Fifteenth Amendment guaranteeing African American male suffrage to the states for ratification. In the case of former Confederate soldiers, moderates wanted to allow all but former leaders to vote, while the radicals wanted to require an oath from all eligible voters that they had never borne arms against the Union, which would have excluded all former rebels. Regarding readmission into the Union, moderates favored a much lower standard, with the Radicals demanding nearly impossible conditions for rebel states to return.

Lincoln's moderate plan for Reconstruction was actually part of his effort to win the war. He and the moderates felt that if it remained easy for states to return to the Union, Confederate States involved in the hostilities might be swayed to rejoin the Union rather than continue fighting. The radical plan was to ensure that Reconstruction did not actually start until after the war was over.

In 1865, Abraham Lincoln was assassinated leaving his Vice President Andrew Johnson to oversee the beginning of Reconstruction. A Southern Democrat who became Lincoln's vice-president in 1864, Johnson struck a moderate pose, and was willing to allow former confederates to keep control of their state governments. These governments quickly enacted Black Codes that denied the vote to blacks and granted them only limited civil rights.

The radical Republicans in Congress responded to the Black Codes by continuing their hard line on allowing former rebel states back into the Union. They also sought to override the Black Codes by granting U.S. citizenship to blacks by passing a civil rights bill. Johnson, supported by Democrats, vetoed the bill, but Congress had the necessary votes to override it, and the bill became law.

In 1866, the Radical Republicans won control of Congress and passed the Reconstruction Acts, which placed the governments of the southern states under the control of the federal military. With this backing, the Republicans began to implement their radical policies, such as granting all black men suffrage while denying it to former confederate soldiers. Congress had passed the 13th, 14th and 15th amendments granting citizenship and civil rights to blacks, and made ratification of these amendments a condition of readmission into the Union by the rebel states.

The Republicans found support in the south among Freedmen, as former slaves were called, white southerners who had not supported the Confederacy, called **Scalawags**, and northerners who had moved to the south, known as **Carpet-baggers**.

Federal troops were stationed throughout the South and protected Republicans who took control of Southern governments. Bitterly resentful, white Southerners fought the new political system by joining a secret society called the Ku Klux Klan (KKK, or "the Klan"), using violence to keep black Americans from voting and exercising other forms of equality. However, before being allowed to rejoin the Union, the Confederate states were required to agree to all federal laws. Between 1866 and 1870, all of them had returned to the Union, but Northern interest in Reconstruction was fading. Reconstruction officially ended when the last Federal troops left the South in 1877.

Under President Rutherford B. Hayes, the federal troops were removed from the South. Without this support, the Republican governments were replaced by so-called Redeemer governments, who promised the restoration of suffrage to those whites who had been denied it and limitations on civil rights for blacks.

The rise of the Redeemer governments marked the beginning of the **Jim Crow** laws and de facto segregation. Blacks were still allowed to vote, but ways were found to make it difficult for them to do so, such as literacy tests and poll taxes. Reconstruction, the goals of which had been reunification and the granting of civil rights to freed slaves, was a limited success, at best; in the eyes of blacks, it was a failure.

Skill 1.13   Demonstrate knowledge of major U.S. reform movements of the nineteenth century

Many **social reform movements** began during this period, including efforts to improve or establish public education, women's rights, labor, working conditions, and temperance, as well as reform prisons and insane asylums. But the most intense and controversial was the abolitionists' efforts to end slavery, an effort alienating and splitting the country, hardening Southern defense of slavery, and leading to four years of bloody civil war. The abolitionist movement had political fallout, affecting admittance of states into the Union and the government's continued efforts to keep a balance between total numbers of free and slave states. Congressional legislation after 1820 reflected this.

Religion has always been a factor in American life. Many early settlers came to North America in search of religious freedom, and the U.S. Constitution provided strong protections of religious freedom.

The **First Great Awakening** was a religious movement within American Protestantism in the 1730s and 1740s. This was primarily a movement among Puritans seeking a return to strict interpretation of morality and values, and an emphasis on the importance and power of personal religious or spiritual experience. Many historians believe the First Great Awakening unified the people of the original colonies and supported the colonists' independence.

The **Second Great Awakening** (the Great Revival) was a broad movement within American Protestantism that led to several kinds of activities that were distinguished by region and denominational tradition. Generally, the Second Great Awakening, which began in the 1820s, was a time of recognition that "awakened religion" must weed out sin on both a personal and a social level. It inspired a wave of social activism. In New England, the Congregationalists established missionary societies to evangelize the West. Publication and education societies arose, most notably the American Bible Society. This social activism gave rise to the temperance movement, prison reform efforts, and help for the handicapped and mentally ill. This period was particularly notable for the abolition movement. In the Appalachian region, the camp meeting was used to revive religion; it became a primary method of evangelizing new territory.

Closely allied to the Second Great Awakening was the **temperance movement**. This movement to end the sale and consumption of alcohol arose from religious beliefs, the violence many women and children experienced from heavy drinkers, and from the effect of alcohol consumption on the work force. The Society for the Promotion of Temperance was organized in Boston in 1826.

The **Third Great Awakening** (the Missionary Awakening) gave rise to the Social Gospel Movement. This period (1858 to 1908) resulted in a massive growth in membership of all major Protestant denominations through their missionary activities. This movement was partly a response to claims that the Bible was fallible. Many churches attempted to reconcile or change biblical teaching to fit scientific theories and discoveries. Colleges associated with Protestant churches began to appear rapidly throughout the nation. In terms of social and political movements, the Third Great Awakening was the most expansive and profound. Coinciding with many changes in production and labor, it won battles against child labor and stopped the exploitation of women in factories. Compulsory elementary education for children came from this movement, and reformers pushed to limit the working hours of women and children. Much was also done to protect and rescue children from abandonment and abuse, to improve the care of the sick, to prohibit the use of alcohol and tobacco, as well as numerous other social ills.

Skilled laborers were organized into a labor union called the **American Federation of Labor (AFL)**, in an effort to gain better working conditions and wages for its members. Farmers joined organizations such as the National Grange and Farmers Alliances. Farmers were producing more food than people could afford to buy. This was the result of (1) new farmlands rapidly opening on the plains and prairies, and (2) development and availability of new farm machinery, and newer and better methods of farming.

American **women** began actively campaigning for increased equality, including the right to vote. In 1869, Elizabeth Cady Stanton and Susan B. Anthony founded the National Women Suffrage Association the same year the Wyoming Territory gave women the right to vote. Soon after, a few states followed by giving women the right to vote, limited to local elections only.

Populism concerns itself with the common sense needs of average people. It often finds expression as a reaction against perceived oppression of the average people by the wealthy elite in society. Populism is often connected with religious fundamentalism, racism, or nationalism. Populist movements claim to represent the majority of the people and call them to stand up to institutions or practices that seem detrimental to their well being.

Governmental reform began in post-Reconstruction era. The secret ballot was adopted, and the passage of the Civil Service Act, also known as the Pendleton Act, provided for the Civil Service Commission, a federal agency responsible for giving jobs based on merit rather than as political rewards or favors. The **Progressive Era** was also a time of great political reform, with such measures as the direct primary, referendum, recall, and direct election of U.S. Senators by the people rather than by their state legislatures being enacted. Following the success of reforms made at the national level, the progressives were successful in gaining reforms in government at state and local levels.

The reforms initiated by these leaders and in the spirit of **Progressivism** were far-reaching. Politically, many states enacted the initiative and the referendum. The adoption of the recall occurred in many states. Several states enacted legislation that would undermine the power of political machines. On a national level, the two most significant political changes were (1) the ratification of the Seventeenth Amendment, which required that all U.S. Senators be chosen by popular election, and (2) the ratification of the Nineteenth Amendment, which granted women suffrage.

Responding to concern over the environmental effects of the timber, ranching, and mining industries, President Theodore Roosevelt set aside 238 million acres of federal lands to protect them from development. Wildlife preserves were established, the nation-al park system was expanded, and the National Conservation Commission was created. The Newlands Reclamation Act also provided federal funding for the construction of irrigation projects and dams in semi-arid areas of the country.

The Wilson Administration carried out additional reforms. The Federal Reserve Act created a national banking system, which provided a stable money supply. The Clayton Antitrust Act built upon the 1890 Sherman Act to define unfair competition, make corporate officers liable for the illegal actions of employees, and exempt labor unions from antitrust lawsuits. The Federal Trade Commission (FTC) was established to enforce these measures. Finally, the Sixteenth Amendment was ratified, which established an income tax. This measure was designed to relieve the poor of a disproportionate burden in funding the federal government and make the wealthy pay a greater share of the nation's tax burden.

Skill 1.14   Understand important issues, events, and individuals of the Twentieth Century in Texas, the United States, and the world

In 1900, a category 4 hurricane devastated Galveston, killing at least 6,000 people and destroying the city and its economy.

In 1901 the first major oil well was drilled at Spindletop. This event marked the discovery of the East Texas Oil Field—the largest in the United States—and the beginning of global oil boom. This led to great economic expansion and changed the state's economy.

The Stock Market Crash of 1929 and the ensuing Great Depression hit Texas hard. Thousands of city workers lost their jobs and became dependent upon federal relief programs. As cotton and livestock prices fell, farmers and ranchers were devastated. The Dust Bowl phenomenon destroyed agriculture in much of the state, leading to widespread hunger, joblessness, and homelessness. Many left Texas to seek new opportunities in the West, particularly in the agricultural state of California.

Before and during WWII, Texas military bases were expanded and new bases were built to train soldiers and aviators. Like the rest of the United States, wartime conditions in Texas fostered economic recovery and boom.

Since WWII, Texas has modernized, expanded its higher education system, developed new approaches to the distribution of its natural resources, and attracted numerous businesses, particularly in the electronic media sector. There has been a generalized migration from rural areas to the cities, and a general transition from an agricultural economy to a business and industrial economy. The economy would later be characterized by the high-tech and service industries.

Texas experienced the same struggles with racism and desegregation as the rest of the South. A growing rift between the conservatives and the liberals marked the political climate of the 1950s. Texas politics was essentially dominated by Lyndon Johnson during the 1950s and 1960s, both in terms of congressional politics, and of his term as John Kennedy's vice president, and then as President of the United States. The assassination of President Kennedy in 1963 in Dallas scarred the people of Texas in many ways.

The United States underwent significant social and economic changes during the twentieth century, and became a **dominant world power**. Economically, the nation saw periods of great prosperity as well as severe depression, nevertheless emerging as a global economic force. In the United States, the **industrialization** that began intensely after the Civil War continued into the early decades of the twentieth century. A wave of immigration in the late nineteenth and early twentieth centuries provided industry with a large labor pool and established millions of immigrants and their families in the working class.

The nation's inward focus was interrupted by U.S. entry into **World War I** in 1917. While reluctant to enter the hostilities, the nation played a decisive role in ending the war and creating, if not joining, the League of Nations. In establishing the League, President Wilson attempted to centralize the United States within international affairs, and increase its importance through the century.

The nation resumed its prosperous industrial growth in the years after WWI, but even as industrial profits and stock market investments skyrocketed, farm prices and wages fell. This created an unbalanced situation that contributed to an economic collapse in 1929, when the stock market crashed. The nation plummeted into an economic depression marked by extremely high unemployment known as the **Great Depression**.

President Franklin Delano Roosevelt proposed that the federal government assist in rebuilding the economy, something his predecessor, President Herbert Hoover, thought the government should not do. Roosevelt's **New Deal** policies were adopted with mostly successful results, and marked an important shift in the role that the federal government plays in economic matters and social welfare. Despite a brief step backward economically toward the end of the 1930s, the nation's recovery was generally underway when, in December 1941, it entered the Second World War against Japan, Germany and Italy (the Axis Powers) following the Japanese attack on Pearl Harbor. The domestic war effort fueled another period of economic prosperity that lasted through the post war years. As a result, the 1950s saw the emergence of a large consumer culture in the United States, which has since bolstered not only the American economy, but for the economies of other countries that produce goods for the United States.

The United States had first established itself as an important world military leader at the turn of the twentieth century during the **Spanish-American War**, and cemented this position during the two World Wars. Following WWII, with Europe struggling to recover from the fighting, the United States and the Soviet Union emerged as the two dominant competing world powers which, for forty-five years, engaged in a **Cold War** between the economic and political ideals of free enterprise democracy and communism.

Despite rising prosperity in the suburbs, poverty remained a serious problem in the central sections of large cities. This resulted in soaring crime rates and riots in the inner cities. The escalation of the war in Vietnam and the divide between those who supported U.S. involvement in the war and those who opposed it led to both pro- and anti-war demonstrations. Escalation of drug abuse, weakening of the family unit, and urban homelessness, poverty and mental illness further divided the country. As Vietnam veterans returned with a host of social, mental, and physical problems, they often received a cool welcome from a nation increasingly opposed to the conflict.

The **Watergate** scandal further troubled the nation, and resulted in the first-ever resignation of a sitting American president. Some say it was the most crucial domestic crisis of the 1970s. Facing Congressional impeachment for abusing executive power, President Richard M. Nixon resigned his office to Vice-President Gerald R. Ford, who had himself risen to office after resignation of Spiro Agnew amidst a scandal over misuse of governmental power. Ford served the remainder of Nixon's term and even campaigned for the presidency in 1976, but lost to James ("Jimmy") Carter.

Meanwhile, the U.S. population had greatly increased, as had the nation's industries and the amount of pollution they released into the environment. Factory smoke, automobile exhaust, waste from factories and other sources all combined to create hazardous air, water, and ground pollution; if they were not controlled and significantly reduced, they would severely endanger all life on earth.

Industry also proved it could be disastrous. In March 1979, the nation narrowly escaped disaster with the partial meltdown at the Three Mile Island Nuclear Plant in Pennsylvania. The Soviet Union was not so lucky. In 1985, a reactor at the Chernobyl nuclear power plant in the Ukraine suffered a severe meltdown, which released plumes of poisonous radiation that sickened and killed many throughout Eastern and Western Europe. Another energy disaster, the Exxon Valdez oil spill in 1989, devastated the Alaskan coastline. The effects of both Exxon Valdez spill and the Chernobyl meltdown are still seen and felt today.

Inflation increased in the late 1960s, and the 1970s witnessed a period of high unemployment, the result of a severe recession. The decision of **OPEC** (the Organization of Petroleum Exporting Countries) to curtail the supply of oil to the United States in response to U.S. support for Israel and later efforts to raise worldwide oil prices created a fuel shortage and raised the price of oil and gasoline in the United States, created two energy crises during the 1970s. In 1973–74, and again in 1979, Americans experienced shortages of heating oil and gasoline for automobiles.

The 1980s saw a sustained period of economic growth after a long period of high inflation and unemployment. Yet not all shared in the decade's economic successes. Foreign industrial competition and imports, the use of robots and other advanced industrial technology, and the relocation of American companies and factories to other countries for lower labor costs all contributed to high unemployment during the early part of the decade. The nation's farmers also experienced economic hardships.

On January 28, 1986, the NASA space shuttle "**Challenger**" blew up during launch; all seven crewmembers perished.

October 1987 saw another one-day significant drop in the Dow Jones on the New York Stock Exchange. Meanwhile, the reliability and soundness of numerous savings and loans institutions were jeopardized. After customers defaulted on their loans and mismanagement had been uncovered, hundreds of them failed and others went bankrupt. A massive bailout eventually shored up the industry, but costs taxpayers billions.

In November 1989, the Berlin Wall fell, striking a significant blow to the Cold War. Countries throughout Eastern Europe experienced democratic revolutions. On December 31, 1991, Soviet leader Mikhail Gorbachev resigned. Its economy had collapsed under the strain of decades of arms spending, marking the official end of the Cold War.

Globalization and the global economy surged during the 1990s, as advances in communications, such as the Internet, blurred the lines between markets. The personal computer, or PC, became a regular household appliance, and social and cultural interaction began to transform as more and more people connected online.

Globalization and communication continue to make great strides in the twenty-first century.

During the twentieth century, the rest of the world also witnessed unprecedented strides in **communications**, a major expansion of international trade, and significant inter-national diplomatic and military activity, including two world wars.

The rise of **nationalism** in Europe at the end of the nineteenth century led to a series of alliances and agreements among European nations. This eventually led to World War One as nations called on their military allies to provide assistance and defense. A new model of international relations was proposed following the devastation of WWI, one based on the mission to preserve peace. The **League of Nations** was formed to promote this peace, but it ultimately failed, having no way to enforce its resolutions. When Germany, led by Adolph Hitler, rebelled against the restrictions placed on it following WWI and began a campaign of military expansion through Europe, World War II ensued. Great Britain, the United States and other allied nations combined forces to defeat Germany and the Axis powers.

Taking a lesson from the failure of the League of Nations, the world's nations organized the **United Nations (UN)**, an international assembly given the authority to arrange and enforce international resolutions.

World War II left Europe in ruins. As a result, the United States and the Soviet Union emerged as the only two world powers. Although allies in the war, tension arose between the two powers as the United States attempted to halt the spread of communism sponsored by the Soviets and Communist China. The United States and Soviet Union never engaged in direct military conflict during this **Cold War**, but were each involved in protracted conflicts in Korea and Vietnam. The threat of nuclear war increased as each power produced more and more weapons in an extended arms race. The threat of the spread of nuclear weapons largely diminished after the breakup of the Soviet Union in the early 1990s, which ended the Cold War.

In Asia, new economies matured and the formerly tightly controlled Chinese market became more open to foreign investment, which increased China's influence as a major economic power. In Europe, the **European Union** made a bold move to a common currency, the Euro-dollar (or simply, the "Euro"), in an effort to consolidate the region's economic strength. In South America, countries such as Brazil and Venezuela showed growth despite political unrest, while Argentina suffered a near complete economic collapse. As the technology sector expanded, so did India's economy, where hi-tech companies found a highly educated work force.

Conflict between the Muslim world and the United States increased during the last decade of the twentieth century. On February 26, 1993, Islamic terrorists detonated a truck bomb beneath the World Trade Center in New York City, killing six and injuring more than a thousand. On June 26, 1996, terrorists bombed a housing complex in Khobar, Saudi Arabia, killing 19 U.S. servicemen and wounding hundreds more. Finally, on August 7, 1998, terrorists bombed U.S. embassies in Kenya and Tanzania, killing hundreds of U.S. and foreign diplomats.

The attacks spilled over into the twenty-first century. On October 12, 2000, the destroyer *USS Cole* was attacked by the radical Islamic terrorist group, Al Qaeda, in the Yemeni port of Aden, killing seventeen sailors. Less than a year later, on September 11, 2001, Al Qaeda terrorists attacked targets in New York City and Washington, D.C., killing more than 3,000 Americans. The 9/11 attacks prompted a U.S. military invasion of Afghanistan, where Al Qaeda and its leader, Osama bin Laden, were based. Shortly afterwards, the United States, Great Britain, and many smaller countries alleged that Iraqi dictator Saddam Hussein had been involved in the 9/11 attacks, and that he had retained or reconstituted his illicit **weapons of mass destruction** (**WMD**) stockpiles and programs. After months of inconclusive UN weapons inspections and Russian, French and Chinese reluctance to approve military action, the United States, United Kingdom, and their allies invaded Iraq and ousted Saddam Hussein and his government.

Meanwhile, in the eastern Mediterranean, tension between Israelis and Palestinians continued to build, regularly erupting into violence. This culminated in the July–August 2006 war in Southern Lebanon between Israel and **Hezbollah**, the Iranian and Syrian-backed terrorist group based out of Lebanon.

Skill 1.15   Understand the contributions of people of various racial, ethnic, and religious groups in Texas, the United States, and the world

The story of Texas is one awash with people of varying nationalities competing for a slice of life in what one relatively recent ad campaign called "a whole other country." At various times, the residents of what is now Texas have included Native Americans, French, Spanish, British, Mexican, and Americans. The current incarnation is a melting pot just like the United States.

Among the Native American tribes who made their home in Texas were the Apache, Cherokee, and Comanche. These were by no means the only tribes; numerous tribes roamed the great plains of Texas for many, many years before European settlers arrived. The Native American peoples of Texas have come from diverse parts of the nation and co-existed with the Spanish, Mexican, American, African American and other immigrants. The early Spanish civilization in Texas was marked by an intentional effort to Hispanicize the native people. This was done by converting them to Roman Catholicism, forcing them to give up traditional practices and beliefs, and incorporating them into a new culture marked by a sharing of some beliefs, values, and institutions. The influence of Spain, and later Mexico, is apparent at every turn throughout the state.

French and Spanish explorers reached the area in the sixteenth century, and settlers soon followed. The Rio Grande and other rivers provided avenues for transportation of both goods and people. Americans came in during the late eighteenth and early nineteenth centuries and made their presence felt for good after the **Louisiana Purchase**.

African Americans were brought to Texas first as slaves of the early white settlers. They worked both on cattle ranches and in cotton fields. After the Civil War, many African American migrated from Southern states in search of greater opportunity. In the later twentieth century, Curtis Graves became the first African American elected as a state legislator since Reconstruction, and Barbara Jordan served as state's first female African American representative to the state legislature and later to the U.S. House of Representative. The Mansfield School Desegregation Incident was a notable turning point in school desegregation in Texas.

The nineteenth century saw tremendous change in Texas. At the urging of the Mexican government, which wanted to expand the population possibilities of the newly independent territory, **Stephen F. Austin** and other Americans settled in the area. Austin soon led a movement to colonize the area as American. Tensions eventually arose between American settlers and Mexican leaders, culminating in the **Texas Revolution** that made Texas, briefly, an independent nation. In 1845, the United States annexed Texas. This, in part, brought on the **Mexican-American War.** The American victory in that war brought with it a tremendous influx of American settlers into Texas.

The state's population continued to grow at a rapid rate throughout the rest of the nineteenth century and into the twentieth century. Not even the devastating Civil War could stem the tide of new Texas residents. They came for economic and settlement opportunities, working at oil fields and on farms and ranches. They came to start new businesses and new lives.

In Texas, the latter half of the twentieth century saw a boom in high-tech companies and jobs, with **Houston**, **San Antonio**, and **Dallas** leading the way. These cities—and the state in general—continue to be a driving force in high tech and modern technologies.

The number of Mexicans moving into Texas began to grow in the twentieth century, reaching a staggering rate in the latter half of the century and into the twenty-first century (with the exception of the 1930s, when the Dust Bowl drove Texans away in droves). The proximity of the American state and the promise of new opportunity drove immigration to an all-time high. Texas to this day is home to many Mexican-Americans.

Stretching back through the history of the Mexican Territory, the number of Mexican residents who have migrated to Texas to seek their fortunes is very large indeed. The forecast is that Latinos will outnumber Caucasians in Texas by 2030. These Mexican-Americans serve in a variety of capacities throughout the state—in agriculture, at oil fields, on ranches, and in hundreds of other white-collar capacities.

Major cultural regions of the United States

The nation's immigrants were an important reason for American industrial growth from 1865 to 1900. Immigrants came seeking work and better opportunities for themselves and their families than what life in their native country could give them. Although the United States offered great opportunity, immigrants also faced discrimination and distrust by **nativists** who believed that immigrants took jobs from native-born Americans and from labor leaders who believed they kept wages down. Their languages, customs, and ways of living were different, especially among the different national and ethnic groups. Until the early 1880s, most immigrants were from parts of northern and western Europe, such as Germany, Scandinavia, the Netherlands, Ireland, and Great Britain. After 1890, the new arrivals increasingly came from eastern and southern Europe. Chinese immigrants on the Pacific coast, so crucial to the construction of the western part of the first transcontinental railroad, experienced this increasing distrust that eventually erupted into violence and bloodshed. From about 1879 to the mid-1960s, the U.S. Congress made, repealed, and amended numerous pieces of legislation concerning quotas, restrictions, and other requirements pertaining to immigrants. Immigrant and native-born laborers, both skilled and unskilled, were the foundation of the modern labor union movement, and helped gain recognition, support, respect, rights, fair wages, and better working conditions for all laborers.

New England is located in the northeastern part of the United States and includes the states of Maine, New Hampshire, Vermont, Massachusetts, Rhode Island and Connecticut. It was, along with Virginia, the first region of the United States to be heavily settled by Europeans, beginning in the seventeenth century. The largest city in the region is Boston. New Englanders share a tradition of direct involvement in government through small town meetings at which local decisions are made. Over the past several decades, the Democratic Party has been the dominant political group in the region; however, the Republican Party has grown in popularity over the years, particularly in Maine and New Hampshire. Education is highly regarded, and several of the nation's top universities are located in New England.

The **Mid-Atlantic** region is located in the central part of the east coast of the United States, and includes the states of New York, New Jersey, Pennsylvania, Delaware and Maryland. Virginia and West Virginia are sometimes included in this region, but are sometimes considered southern states. Some of the country's most densely settled urban areas are in this region, including New York City, Philadelphia, and Washington, D.C. The Mid-Atlantic region has always been more ethnically diverse than other east coast regions, with settlers from a wider range of the world. Today, political inclinations are mainly liberal within the urban areas, but political opinions of all types come together in Washington, D.C., which is the capital of the nation. The Mid-Atlantic area has provided much of the heavy industry and manufacturing for the country, and has a large working class population. From colonial times through the nineteenth century, this region has served as a kind of buffer zone between the northern and southern states, and its one-time central location contributed to the selection of the site of the nation's capital.

The **South** is one of the country's most distinctive cultural regions, and includes the states of North Carolina, South Carolina, Tennessee, Georgia, Florida, Alabama, Mississippi, Louisiana, Texas and Arkansas. Also sometimes considered part of the South are the states of Oklahoma, Missouri, Kentucky, Virginia and West Virginia. Major urban centers in the South include Atlanta, Miami, New Orleans, Dallas, and Houston, which is presently the nation's fourth-largest city.

With the exception of some French and Latin-settled regions, such as in Louisiana and Florida, the South is predominantly Protestant Christian in religion. The region's association with strong religious feeling and tradition has led to it being sometimes referred to as the Bible Belt. Texas, which was one of the Confederate States, extends westward into the Southwest region. Oklahoma has a large population of Native Americans who were relocated to the area from other parts of the eastern United States. Florida's warm climate has made it a popular retirement and vacation area for people from all over the nation, and its proximity to Cuba and Latino-settled islands has contributed a large Hispanic population in the region.

The **Midwest** is located in the north-central part of the United States, and traditionally includes the states of Minnesota, Wisconsin, Iowa, Illinois, Indiana, Ohio and Michigan. North Dakota, South Dakota, Nebraska, Kansas and Missouri are also sometimes thought of as being Midwestern states. Major Midwestern cities include Chicago, Minneapolis, Cincinnati, St. Louis, and Detroit. Outside the urban areas, the region is characterized by many small towns that grew around agriculture. Early settlers found rich soil drained by the Ohio, Missouri, and Mississippi Rivers. The western portions of the region contain rolling, grassy range land suitable for ranching.

Beginning in the 1790s, the Midwest was settled mainly by pioneers of western European heritage. They found several Native American peoples in the area, who were gradually pushed westward and eventually forcibly relocated to reservations. European Americans make up most of the population of the central Midwestern states. In the twentieth century, African Americans from the South migrated northwards to industrial areas such as St. Louis, Chicago, Cleveland, and Detroit.

Traditionally, Midwesterners are thought of as hard working and stoic, embodying the values of the American pioneer. Religion plays a central role in the social relationships of many Midwesterners, who are mainly Christian. The region extends westward to the Western cultural areas, but extends east-ward to the Mid-Atlantic, where parts of Ohio have perhaps more in common with the industrial East than the more agricultural Midwest.

The **Southwest** cultural region of the United States is an area where Native and Latin American culture has had the most influence. Arizona and New Mexico are the two states that make up the main part of the Southwest, with some of the surrounding states of California, Nevada, Utah, Colorado, Oklahoma and Texas extending into the region. Major cities in the region include Phoenix and Albuquerque. Once a part of Spanish territory, then a part of Mexico, the South-west has retained its cultural connection to these countries. Native American cultures established settlements here thousands of years ago, and their influence is still seen. Arizona has the largest population of Native Americans in the United States.

The **West** region extends from the Pacific Coast of eastward to the Rocky Mountain States, and includes the states of California, Colorado, Idaho, Montana, Nevada, Oregon, Utah, Washington, and Wyoming. Major western cities include Los Angeles, San Francisco, Denver, Salt Lake City, Portland, and Seattle. The West has some of the least densely populated areas in the country, particularly in areas of Montana and Wyoming. Immigration from the eastern United States began in earnest in the 1840s, along trails including the Oregon Trail to the Pacific Northwest region, the Santa Fe Trail, and the Mormon Trail. Mormons settled in Utah after facing opposition in the Midwest around this time, and are still prevalent there. In 1849, the discovery of gold near San Francisco brought thousands of new people to the area.

Situated along the Pacific Rim, the West has a high concentration of Asian immigrants, particularly in the coastal cities. It is a very diverse region with wide influence on American culture, especially from California, where most American television programs and movies are produced.

Major cultural regions of the world

North America includes the countries of the United States, Canada, and Mexico. Mexico, while geographically part of North America, is often thought of as being closer to Central and South America culturally. English is the primary language of North America, with large sections of French speakers in Quebec, Canada, and Spanish speakers in the southwestern United States and Mexico. Because of its history of immigration from wide areas, North America contains people of many cultures, with people of western European descent in the majority. Christianity is the primary religion, with significant populations practicing other religions such as

Judaism, Hindu, and Islam.

Latin America includes the mainly Spanish and Portuguese speaking countries of Mexico, Central America and South America. Culturally, this area has been heavily influenced by Spain and Portugal, who explored and conquered much of the region in the sixteenth century. Catholicism, introduced by the conquistadors and through subsequent missions, is the primary religious observance. Native practices are still observed in many areas, and several groups of indigenous peoples still inhabit the interior of South America.

Europe is a diverse collection of independent countries who have banded together economically. Primarily Christian in observance, Europe contains several significant groups that observe other religions. Turkey, a secular Muslim nation, is often considered to be part of Europe culturally, owing to its long history of interaction with the western countries.

The Middle East and North Africa (MENA) include the countries of Morocco, Algeria, Tunisia, Libya, Egypt, Israel, Lebanon, Syria, Jordan, Saudi Arabia, Yemen, Oman, Iraq, and Iran. Other Middle Eastern countries include Bahrain, the United Arab Emirates (UAE), Qatar (pronounced "cutter"), and Kuwait. These countries are located in and around the oil-rich **Persian Gulf**. The region is largely Islamic in faith, and once had great influence in parts of Europe, notably Spain. Arabic is the primary language, though Farsi, or Persian, is the official language of Iran. Israel is officially a Jewish state, with Hebrew as its national language. However, it also holds a sizable Arabic-speaking Palestinian population.

Sub-Saharan Africa is that portion of Africa located south of the great Sahara desert and includes the countries of South Africa, Kenya, Rwanda, and Ghana as well as 38 other nations. This is a culturally diverse area, stemming from the widespread colonization of the region by European countries upon whom many African countries still rely for assistance.

The region of **Russia and Central Asia** is made up of many former Soviet Union Republics, which are still dominated by the Russian language and culture. Russia observes the Eastern Orthodox religion, and is world renowned for its contributions to the arts, especially ballet and music. Since the breakup of the Soviet Union, several of the smaller states in Central Asia have re-established cultural connections with the Muslim nations of the Middle East and South Asia.

East Asia includes China, Taiwan, North and South Korea, and Japan. Historically, China has dominated this region, with the Korean and Japanese cultures developing independent cultures from the Chinese. Presently, China and North Korea are communist countries. However, China has developed a hybrid system that allows some free enterprise. Japan and South Korea are democratic countries with thriving economies. Religion varies within the region, and includes

Christianity, Buddhism, Taoism, Shinto, and the philosophy of Confucianism.

South Asia includes the countries of India, Pakistan, Bangladesh, Nepal, and Sri Lanka. This area is the most densely populated region of the world, and contains around 1.6 billion people. The predominant religions are Hindu, especially in India, although there is a long and rich Muslim culture as well, particularly in Pakistan. India, the largest nation in the region, gained independence in 1947 after a long period of British rule. British culture has contributed to the region significantly. Movies are a popular form of entertainment, and India is the second largest producer of motion pictures after the United States.

Southeast Asia includes the countries of Thailand, Vietnam, Cambodia, and Laos on the mainland of Asia, and Indonesia, the Philippines, Malaysia and Singapore off the shore of Asia. The mainland countries have been heavily influenced by the proximity of China and are mainly Buddhist, with several other faiths in observance. Indonesia is the world's most populous Muslim country, while the Philippines is mainly Christian.

Australia and New Zealand are two former British colonies that have much in common with western European and American cultures. Aboriginal culture has influenced the region, but these people are now in the minority.

Skill 1.16   Analyze ways in which particular contemporary societies reflect historical events

From the nation's beginnings, immigration has played a crucial role in the growth and settlement of the United States. With a large interior territory to fill and ample opportunity, the United States encouraged immigration throughout most of the nineteenth century, maintaining an almost completely open policy. Famine in Ireland and political unrest in Germany in the 1840s resulted in over 3.5 million immigrants resettling in the United States between 1830 and 1860.

Following the Civil War, rapid expansion in rail transportation brought the interior states within easy reach of new immigrants, most of whom entered the United States on the East Coast. As immigration increased, several states adopted individual immigration laws, and in 1875 the U.S. Supreme Court declared immigration a federal matter. Following a surge in European immigration in 1880, the United States began to regulate immigration, first by passing a tax to new immigrants, then by instituting literacy requirements and barring those with mental or physical illness. A large influx of Chinese immigrants to the western states had resulted in the complete exclusion of immigrants from that country in 1882 with the Chinese Exclusion Act.

In 1891, the Federal Bureau of Immigration was established. Even with these new limits in place, immigration remained relatively open in the United States to those from European countries, and increased steadily until World War I. From the 1890s through the mid-1920s, the primary point of entry for European immigrants was Ellis Island outside of New York City. An estimated 20 million immigrants passed through this point.

With much of Europe left in ruins after WWI, immigration to the United States thusly expanded. In 1920 and 1921, some 800,000 new immigrants arrived. Immigrations from southern and eastern Europe grew from already high levels. The United States responded to this shift with a quota system, first enacted by Congress in 1921. It limited immigration in proportion to the ethnic groups that were already settled in the U.S., which had been determined by previous census records. This national-origins policy was extended and further defined by Congress in 1924.

This remained the official policy of the nation for the next 40 years. Occasional challenges to the law from non-white immigrants reaffirmed that the intention of the policy was to limit immigration primarily to white, western Europeans, who the government felt were most likely to assimilate into American culture. Strict limitations on Chinese immigration were extended throughout the period, and only relaxed in 1940. In 1965, Congress overhauled immigration policy, removing the quotas and replacing them with a preference based system. Now, immigrants reuniting with family members and those with special skills or education were given preference. As a result, immigration from Asian and African countries began to increase. The 40-year legacy of the 1920s immigration restrictions had a direct and dramatic impact on the makeup of modern American society.

See also Skill 1.1

COMPETENCY 2.0   GEOGRAPHY

Skill 2.1   Understand and apply the geographic concept of region

A basic unit of geographic study is the region, an area on Earth's surface that is defined by certain unifying characteristics. The unifying characteristics may be physical, human, or cultural. In addition to studying the unifying characteristics of a region, geographers study how a region changes over time. Using the theme of regions, geographers divide the world into manageable units for study.

Skill 2.2   Know the location and the human and physical characteristics of places and regions in Texas, the United States, and the world

The state of Texas has varied geographical features and uses, which have changed over time, depending on who was living where at the time. Among the known settlers have been Native Americans, French, Spanish, and Americans.

Texas is divided into seven main regions: **Big Bend Country** in far west Texas, the **Gulf Coast** in the southeastern part of the state, **Hill Country** in the center, the **Panhandle Plains** through the northern panhandle, **Pineywoods** in the northeast, **Prairies and Lakes** in the north center, and the **South Texas Plains** in the far south of the state.

The majority of Texas topography is flat farmland. This is true in parts of West Texas, where the dominant crops are cotton, wheat, and sorghum. The land is semiarid and, for the most part, flat, with the exception of some hills and a mountain range, the Davis Mountains. Oil can be found in West Texas as well, near the Midland-Odessa corridor.

The antebellum and Civil Wartime civilizations in eastern Texas depended almost entirely on King Cotton, with the various hills and swamps dominated by vast plantations. Cotton's influence can still be felt there, but the dominant crop now is rice. The vast majority of the state's rice comes from this region. Lumber can be found here as well. As in nearly every other part of the state, however, oil is the new king of East Texas.

Houston, the fourth largest city in the United States, dominates the Gulf Coast. Houston is a port city, capitalizing on an early twentieth century canal to the Gulf of Mexico as a way to ship goods to the world. Indeed, only New York ships more than Houston. The lower Rio Grande area has citrus fruits and winter vegetables in abundance. The rest of the Rio Grande Valley is dotted with cattle ranches, some of them quite large.

Further north can be found the Blackland Prairies, a large range of agriculture and ranch land. Cotton and grain grow here in great numbers, as do cattle. The large cities of Dallas and Fort Worth can be found here. Together, they form one of the most burgeoning metropolitan areas, with big business in oil refining, grain milling, and cotton processing. The high plains have a somewhat varied landscape, although the semiarid climate falls mostly on flat land. Often noted is a dry-farming area near Lubbock, one of the larger cities of the region. Oil, grain, wheat, and cotton are the major industries there.

All major cities in Texas play a role in the advancement of modern technology, although Houston, Dallas, and Fort Worth are industry leaders, just as they were during World War II in weapons production. The people who live and have lived in Texas have made the land their own, turning flat, sometimes water-starved lands into vast plantations, ranches, and fields. Large cities have not been con-fined to waterways (although the state's largest city, Houston, can be found on the Gulf Coast). Dirt roads, railroads, and then paved roads have connected the large state's many, many towns and cities. Today, the Information Superhighway connects them all.

The most drastic change to the environment wrought by people has been the sheer number of square miles devoted to living space. Texas still maintains vast areas of agricultural and ranch land, but that number is shrinking by the year, as more and more people claim land designed to be lived on exclusively. The farmers of the past lived on their land *but also lived off it*. Their houses were part of their farms, and their jobs were working the land. Today, skyscrapers dot the skylines of large cities along with high-rise apartment buildings, which serve no function other than to provide living areas for the people who work there.

The continental United States is bordered by the Pacific Ocean on the west and the Atlantic Ocean on the east. The country is divided into two main sections by the Rocky Mountains, which extend from New Mexico in the south through the Canadian border on the north. The western portion of the country contains forested, mountainous areas in the Pacific Northwest and Northern California, including Mt. St. Helens, an active volcano in the Cascade Range. Dryer, warmer regions in the south include the Mojave Desert in the Southwest. The Great Salt Lake in Utah is at the foot of the Wasatch Mountains.

The Rocky Mountains slope down in the east to the Great Plains, a large, grassy region drained by the Mississippi River, the nation's largest river, and one of the largest rivers in the world. The Great Plains give way in the east to hilly, forested regions. The Appalachian Mountain chain runs along the eastern coast of the United States. Along the border with Canada between Minnesota and New York are the Great Lakes, of which there are five: Lake Huron, Lake Ontario, Lake Michigan, Lake Erie and Lake Superior.

Alaska is located in northwestern North America and contains Mt. McKinley, also called Denali, which is the highest mountain on the continent. Hawaii is a series of volcanic islands in the South Pacific.

Skill 2.3   Analyze ways in which humans adapt to, use, and modify the physical environment

By nature, people are essentially **social creatures**. They generally live in communities or settlements of some kind and of some size. Settlements are the cradles of culture, political structure, education, and the management of resources. The relative placement of these settlements or communities is shaped by the proximity to natural resources, the movement of raw materials, the production of finished products, the availability of a work force, and the delivery of finished products. Shared values, language, culture, religion, and subsistence will, at least to some extent, determine the composition of communities.

The theme of human-environmental interaction has three main concepts: humans adapt to the environment (e.g., wearing warm clothing in a cold climate), humans modify the environment (e.g., planting trees to block a prevailing wind), and humans depend on the environment (for food, water and raw materials). Environmental and geographic factors have affected the pattern of urban development in Texas and the rest of the United States. In turn, urban infrastructure and development patterns are interrelated factors (i.e., they affect one another).

The growth of suburbs had the effect in many cities of creating a type of economic segregation. Working-class people who could not afford new suburban homes and an automobile to carry them to and from work were relegated to closer, more densely populated areas. Frequently, these areas had to be passed through by those on their way to the suburbs, and rail lines and freeways some-times bisected these urban communities. Acres of farmland and forest were cleared to make way for growing suburban areas.

The environment means different things to different people, depending on their cultural backgrounds and technological resources. In studying human/environment interaction, geographers look at all the effects—positive and negative—that occur when people interact with their surroundings. Sometimes a human act, such as damming a river to prevent flooding or to provide irrigation, requires consideration of the potential consequences. The construction of **Hoover Dam** on the Colorado River, for example, changed the natural landscape, but it also created a reservoir that helps provide water and electric power for the arid South-west. Studying the consequences of human/environment interaction helps people plan and manage the environment responsibly.

Students should be able to recognize where resources are located, who needs them, and how they are transported over the earth's surface. The theme of movement helps students understand how they themselves are connected with, and dependent upon, other regions, cultures, and people in the world.

Skill 2.4   **Know how regional physical characteristics and human modifications to the environment affect people's activities and settlement patterns**

Geography involves studying location and how living things and Earth's features are distributed throughout Earth. It includes where animals, people, and plants live and the effects of their relationship with Earth's physical features. Geographers also explore the locations of Earth's features, how they got there, and why it is so important.

Another way to describe where people live is by the **physical geography** and **topography** around them. The vast majority of people on the planet live in areas that are hospitable, such as the agriculturally rich plains of China, Europe, and the United States. The fertility of these areas attracts humans, and settlement patterns reflect this.

Geographers typically organize geography along five main themes:

1. **Location:** This theme describes the physical location of a particular place, grouping, or characteristic
2. **Place:** This theme refers to both physical and human characteristics of a given place, and how those characteristics shape that place to give it a unique character.
3. **Regions:** This theme relate to the physical, human, or cultural regions that share characteristics.
4. **Movement:** This theme describes the movement of people, beliefs, and idea from place to place, as in immigration and cultural diffusion.
5. **Human-Environment Interaction:** This theme refers to both the ways that people have changed their environment and to ways that they have been affected by it.

Skill 2.5   **Analyze ways in which location (absolute and relative) affects people, places, and environments**

Every point on Earth has a specific *location* that is determined by an imaginary grid of lines denoting latitude and longitude. Parallels of latitude measure distances north and south of the origin line called the Equator. Meridians of longitude measure distances east and west of the origin line called the Prime Meridian. Geographers use latitude and longitude to pinpoint a place's absolute, or exact, location.

To know the absolute location of a place is only part of the equation. It is also important to know how that place is related to other places—in other words, to know that place's relative location. Words such as *north, south, east,* and *west* typically describe physical relative location. Relative location may also deal with the interaction that occurs between and among places. It refers to the many ways—by land, by water, even by technology—that places are connected.

See also Skill 2.4

Skill 2.6   Demonstrate knowledge of physical processes and their effects on environmental patterns

World weather patterns are greatly influenced by ocean surface currents in the upper layer of the ocean. These currents continuously move along the ocean surface in specific directions. Ocean currents that flow deep below the surface are called sub-surface currents. These currents are influenced by such factors as the location of landmasses in the current's path and the earth's rotation.

Climate is the average weather or daily weather conditions for a specific region or location over a period of time. Studying the climate of an area includes examining information gathered on the area's monthly and yearly temperatures and its monthly and yearly amounts of precipitation. In addition, a characteristic of an area's climate is the length of its growing season.

Natural changes can occur that alter habitats—floods, volcanoes, storms, earthquakes, etc. These changes can affect the species that exist within the habitat, either by causing extinction or by changing the environment in a way that will no longer support the life systems. Climate changes can have similar effects. Inhabiting species can also alter habitats, particularly through migration.

Plate tectonics is a geological theory that explains **continental drift**, which is the large movement of the solid portions of Earth's crust floating on the molten mantle. There are about twelve major tectonic plates, with several smaller plates. There are three types of plate boundaries: convergent, divergent and conservative, also called transform. Divergent boundaries occur at locations where plates are moving away from each other. Convergent boundaries are where plates are moving toward one another. When this happens, the two plates collide and fold up against one another, called **continental collision**, or one plate slides under the other, called **subduction**. Conservatives boundaries are those at which plates simply slide by each other.

Erosion is the displacement of solid earth surfaces such as rock and soil. Erosion is often a result of wind, water, or ice acting on surfaces with loose particles, such as sand, loose soils, or decomposing rock. Gravity can also cause erosion on loose surfaces. Factors such as slope, soil and rock composition, plant cover, and human activity all affect erosion.

Weathering is the natural decomposition of the Earth's surface from contact with the atmosphere. It is not the same as erosion, but can be a factor in erosion. Heat, water, ice and pressure are all factors that can lead to weathering. Chemicals in the atmosphere can also contribute to weathering

Transportation is the movement of eroded material from one place to another by wind, water or ice. Examples of transportation include pebbles rolling down a streambed and boulders being carried by moving glaciers.

Deposition is the result of transportation, and occurs when the material being carried settles on the surface and is deposited. Sand dunes and moraines are formed by transportation and deposition of glacial material.

Skill 2.7 Understand the characteristics, distribution, and migration of populations in Texas, the United States, and the world

Texas's modern population is made of mostly of the descendents of European settlers, with sizable minorities of African Americans and Mexican Americans. Other ethnic groups add further diversity to the state. Much of the state's population is centered in large cities such as Houston, San Antonio, Dallas, and Fort Worth, although the state is also home to the nation's largest rural population. One of the largest states in the nation by population, Texas has experienced significant population growth over the past several years that outpaces that of much of the rest of the country.

The United States is a growing and diverse country. White Europeans, African Americans, Mexican Americans, and Asian Americans each make up sizable portions of the population. The vast majority of the nation's population lives in cities or suburbs that make up urbanized areas. By population, the largest cities in the United States are New York City, Los Angeles, Chicago, Houston, and Phoenix.

The population of the world is approaching seven billion. The most populous nations of Earth are China and India, each of which counts more than one billion residents. Increasingly, nations of Asia and South America are joining Europe, the United States, and Canada as industrial powers.

See Skill 1.15

Skill 2.8   Understand the physical environmental characteristics of Texas, the United States, and the world, past and present, and how humans have adapted to and modified the environment

Earth's surface is made up of 70% water and 30% land. Physical features of the land surface include mountains, hills, plateaus, valleys, and plains. Other minor landforms include deserts, deltas, canyons, mesas, basins, foothills, marshes and swamps. Earth's water features include oceans, seas, lakes, rivers, and canals.

Mountains are landforms with rather steep slopes at least 2,000 feet or more above sea level. Mountains are found in groups called mountain chains or mountain ranges. At least one range can be found on six of the earth's seven continents. North America has the Appalachian and Rocky Mountains; South America, the Andes; Asia, the Himalayas and the Urals; Australia, the Great Dividing Range; Europe, the Alps; and Africa, the Atlas, Ahaggar, and Drakensburg Mountains.

Hills are elevated landforms rising to an elevation of about 500 to 2000 feet. They are found everywhere on earth including Antarctica where they are covered by ice.

Plateaus are elevated landforms that are usually level on top. Depending on location, they range from being an area that is very cold to one that is cool and healthful. Some plateaus are dry because they are surrounded by mountains that keep out any moisture. Some examples include the Kenya Plateau in East Africa, which is very cool. The plateau extending north from the Himalayas is extremely dry while those in Antarctica and Greenland are covered with ice and snow.

Plains are described as areas of flat or slightly rolling land, usually lower than the landforms next to them. Sometimes called lowlands (and sometimes located along **seacoasts),** they support the majority of the world's people. Some are found inland and many have been formed by large rivers. This resulted in extremely fertile soil for successful cultivation of crops and numerous large settlements of people. In North America, the vast plains areas extend from the Gulf of Mexico north to the Arctic Ocean and between the Appalachian and Rocky Mountains. In Europe, rich plains extend east from Great Britain into central Europe on into the Siberian region of Russia. Plains in river valleys are found in China (the Yangtze River valley), India (the Ganges River valley), and Southeast Asia (the Mekong River valley).

Valleys are land areas found between hills and mountains. Some have gentle slopes containing trees and plants; others have steep walls and are referred to as canyons. One example is Arizona's Grand Canyon of the Colorado River.

Deserts are large dry areas of land receiving ten inches or less of rainfall each year. Among the better-known deserts are Africa's large Sahara Desert, the

Arabian Desert on the Arabian Peninsula, and the Outback covering roughly one third of Australia.

Deltas are areas of lowlands formed by soil and sediment deposited at the mouths of rivers. The soil is generally very fertile and most fertile river deltas are important crop-growing areas. One well-known example is the delta of Egypt's Nile River.

Mesas are the flat tops of hills or mountains usually with steep sides. Some-times plateaus are also called mesas. **Basins** are considered to be low areas drained by rivers or low spots in mountains. **Foothills** are generally considered a low series of hills found between a plain and a mountain range. **Marshes** and **swamps** are wet lowlands providing growth of such plants as rushes and reeds.

Oceans are the largest bodies of water on the planet. The four oceans of the earth are the **Atlantic Ocean**, one-half the size of the Pacific and separating North and South America from Africa and Europe; the **Pacific Ocean**, covering almost one-third of the earth's surface and separating North and South America from Asia and Australia; the **Indian Ocean**, touching Africa, Asia, and Australia; and the ice-filled **Arctic Ocean,** extending from North America and Europe to the North Pole. The waters of the Atlantic, Pacific, and Indian Oceans also touch the shores of Antarctica.

Seas are smaller than oceans and are surrounded by land. Some examples include the Mediterranean Sea found between Europe, Asia, and Africa; and the Caribbean Sea, touching the West Indies, South and Central America. A **lake** is a body of water surrounded by land. The Great Lakes in North America are a good example.

Rivers, considered a nation's lifeblood, usually begin as very small streams, formed by melting snow and rainfall, flowing from higher to lower land, emptying into a larger body of water, usually a sea or an ocean. Examples of important rivers for people and countries affected by and/or dependent on them include the Nile, Niger, and Zaire Rivers of Africa; the Rhine, Danube, and Thames Rivers of Europe; the Yangtze, Ganges, Mekong, Hwang He, and Irrawaddy Rivers of Asia; the Murray-Darling in Australia; and the Orinoco in South America. River systems are made up of large rivers and numerous smaller rivers or **tributaries** flowing into them. Examples include the vast Amazon Rivers system in South America and the Mississippi River in the United States.

Canals are man-made water passages constructed to connect two larger bodies of water. Famous examples include the **Panama Canal** across Panama's isthmus connecting the Atlantic and Pacific Oceans; and the **Suez Canal** in the Middle East between Africa and the Arabian Peninsula connecting the Red and Mediterranean Seas.

Refer to Skill 2.2 for Texas and United States geography

Skill 2.9   Analyze how geographic factors have influenced the settlement patterns, economic development, political relationships, and policies of societies and regions in Texas, the United States, and the world

The varied geography of Texas has produced some vastly different settlement patterns, economic developments, and political conflicts over the hundreds of years that people have been migrating to the area. Some of these differences are bigger than others, some are more modern than others, and some areas have changed very little indeed.

The vast plains of central and western Texas are perfect for agricultural and ranch land, and that is largely what they have become. Among the areas that are inhabited or controlled by humans, wheat, cotton, sorghum, and cattle are the top-producing industries. The farms are big and the ranches bigger. This also means, of course, that the potential for land disputes is high, even today.

East Texas is similar in a way, in that huge rice fields dot the landscape, with corresponding towns built up around them. The crop might not be the same, but the interests and concerns definitely are.

The Gulf Coast is most known for its oil and its ports; though, the state's myriad products flow through the Gulf Coast, as well. Oil can be found in many places in the state, not just on the Gulf Coast. Texas is known for its oil production and exports, particularly in West Texas.

The larger cities of Texas—**Houston**, **Austin, Dallas**, and **Fort Worth**, most noticeably—are known for their high tech industries. Many Internet and computer companies make their home in Texas, and the state is a leader in scientific development efforts, as well.

Throughout Texas' history, politics have been contentious. Early on, it was the Americans versus the Mexicans, as American settlers moved into then-Mexican-owned territories and settled in for the long haul. After Mexico gave up all claims to Texas, a reverse immigration took place. This movement of people is still taking place, some years more than ever. The vast agricultural lands of Texas invite cheap labor, and many Mexican residents cross the border both legally and illegally to supply it. The problem of illegal immigration continues to be a significant policy debate today not only in Texas but in other Southwestern and Western states.

Another source of contention is the struggle between the ranch politics of yester-year and the high-tech politics of today. Farmers and ranchers have different interests than nuclear scientists, and these different interests often clash in the halls of Austin policy-makers.

In a sense, geography is driving all of this, since farmers and ranchers have their concerns largely because of their location and urban parties gain their perspectives from their environments, which are much more metropolitan. Oil companies and their lobbyists also play major roles in Texan policy. Oil continues to be a significant industry in Texas, and oil interests often clash with those of other industries.

Skill 2.10   Analyze interactions between people and the physical environment and the effects of these interactions on the development of places and regions

Environmental and geographic factors have affected the pattern of urban development in Texas and the rest of the United States. Urban infrastructure and development patterns are interrelated factors.

The growth of urban areas is often linked to the advantages provided by its geo-graphic location. Before the advent of efficient overland commercial routes, such as railroads and highways, commercial goods were primarily transported over water. Thus, many large American cities are situated along bodies of water.

As **transportation** technology advanced, the supporting infrastructure was built to connect cities with one another and to connect remote areas to larger com-munities. The railroad, for example, allowed for the quick transport of agricultural products from rural areas to urban centers. This newfound efficiency not only further fueled the growth of urban areas and the West, but also changed the economy of the rural United States. Where once most farmers had practiced only subsistence farming—growing enough to support one's own family—the new infrastructure meant that one could more readily convert agricultural products into cash by selling them at market. Food crops arose alongside traditional cash crops such as cotton and tobacco as important market commodities.

For urban dwellers, improvements in building technology and advances in transportation allowed for larger cities. Growth brought with it a new set of problems unique to each location. The bodies of water that had made the development of cities possible in their early days also formed natural barriers to growth. Further infrastructure in the form of bridges, tunnels and ferry routes were needed to connect central urban areas with outlying communities.

Today, advancements in **telecommunications** infrastructure may have an impact on urban growth patterns. Because information can pass instantly and freely between almost any two points on the globe, it allows access to some aspects of urban life to those in remote areas.

Cities are the major hubs of human settlement. Almost half of the population of the world now lives in cities. These percentages are much higher in developed regions. Established cities continue to grow. The fastest growth, however, is occurring in developing areas. While European and North American cities are usually well linked both by transportation and communication connections, there are other places in the world where inter-city communication may be inferior to international communication.

Natural resources are naturally occurring substances that are considered valuable in their natural form. A commodity is generally considered a natural resource when the primary activities associated with it are extraction and purification, as opposed to creation. Thus, mining, petroleum extraction, fishing, and forestry are generally considered natural-resource industries, while agriculture is not.

Natural resources are often classified into **renewable** and **non-renewable resources**. Renewable resources are generally living resources (e.g., fish, crops, and forests), which can restock (renew) themselves if they are not over-harvested. Thus, renewable resources can be used indefinitely if they are sustained. Once renewable resources are consumed at a rate that exceeds their natural rate of replacement, the standing stock will diminish and eventually run out. The rate of sustainable use of a renewable resource is determined by the replacement rate and amount of standing stock of that particular resource. Non-living renewable natural resources include soil, as well as water, wind, tides and solar radiation. Natural resources include soil, timber, oil, minerals, and other goods taken more or less as they are from the Earth. Non-renewable resources, however, are those that are not able to be replaced once they are used up. Many energy resources, including coal and oil, are non-renewable.

Deforestation or clear cutting is of particular concern in rainforest regions, which hold most of Earth's natural biodiversity. Conservation of natural resources is the major focus of environmental movements. Some view this depletion as a major source of social unrest and conflicts in developing nations.

Environmental policy is concerned with the sustainability of Earth, the region under the administration of the governing group or individual, or a local habitat. The concern of environmental policy is the preservation of the region, habitat, or ecosystem. Because humans, both individually and in community, live upon Earth, draw upon its resources, and affect the environment in many ways, environmental and social policy must be mutually supportive.

COMPETENCY 3.0 ECONOMICS

Skill 3.1   Understand that basic human needs are met in many ways

Economists divide goods and services into **needs** and **wants.** Needs include those items necessary for basic human survival, such as food, clothing, and shelter. Wants include luxury items such as consumer electronics or cars.

Throughout history, humans have met their basic needs in many ways. Ancient peoples obtained foods through hunting, gathering, and basic agriculture. They often made clothing out of woven natural fibers or animals skins, and lived in simple protective structures. Modern humans have the same basic needs, but typically have more selection in the specific items they use to meet them due to increased production of goods and improved worldwide shipping and transportation.

Skill 3.2   Understand and apply knowledge of basic economic concepts

Economics is the study of how a society allocates its scarce resources to satisfy what are basically unlimited and competing wants. A fundamental fact of economics is that resources are scarce while wants are infinite. The fact that scarce resources have to satisfy unlimited wants means that choices have to be made. **Scarcity** is thus a driving force behind all economic systems.

Economic choice often involves **opportunity cost,** or the benefit lost by the selection of an alternative. For example, choosing to allocate scarce agricultural land resources to the production of wheat creates an opportunity cost of not being able to grow corn upon that same land.

Economic systems refer to the arrangements a society has devised to answer what are known as the three basic economic questions: What goods to produce? How to produce those goods? For whom are the goods being produced? Different economic systems answer these questions in different ways.

A **free enterprise system,** or market economy, answers these questions in terms of demand, supply and the use of markets. **Demand** is based on consumer preferences and satisfaction and refers to the quantities of a good or service that buyers are willing and able to buy at different prices during a given period of time. **Supply** is based on costs of production and refers to the quantities that sellers are willing and able to sell at different prices during a given period of time. The determination of market equilibrium price is where the buying decisions of buyers coincide with the selling decision of sellers.

Consumers vote for the products they want with their spending. Goods acquiring enough dollar votes are profitable, signaling to the producers that society wants their scarce resources used in this way. This is how the "What" question is answered under the free enterprise system. The producer then works in accordance with the goods consumers want, looking for the most efficient or lowest cost method of production. The lower the firm's costs for any given level of revenue, the higher the firm's profits. This is the way in which the "How" question is answered.   The "For Whom" question is answered in the marketplace by the determination of the equilibrium price. Price serves to ration the goods to those who can and will transact at the market price of better. Those who can't or won't are excluded from the market. This mechanism results in market efficiency or obtaining the most output from the available inputs that are consistent with the preferences of consumers. Society's scarce resources are being used the way society wants them to be used.

Skill 3.3   Demonstrate knowledge of the ways in which people organize economic systems, and similarities and differences among various economic systems around the world

The United States primarily uses the **free enterprise system**. Under this system, the market determines what goods are produced, the price of those goods, and for whom they are produced. This system relies on the innovation of **entrepreneurs** to bring new products to them market.

The opposite of the free enterprise system is the **command economy**. In a command economy, the government makes all of the economic decisions about what is produced, how it is produced, and for whom goods and services are produced. The Soviet Union and other communist countries primarily used a command economy; today, communist nations such as China now have some free enterprise combined with the command system.

In between the two extremes is the **mixed economy.** This system uses both markets and government-controlled planning. Planning is usually used to direct resources at the upper levels of the economy, with markets being used to determine prices of consumer goods and wages. Under a mixed economy, the government may control utility companies or other major industries. Nearly all contemporary nations, including the United States, have some elements of a mixed economy.

See also Skill 3.2

Skill 3.4   Understand the value and importance of work and purposes for spending and saving money

Under the free enterprise system, consumers must acquire money to purchase goods and services. By far, the most common way for this acquisition to take place is through **employment.** Workers receive pay for their efforts, thus allowing them to purchase both needed and wanted goods and services.

Consumer spending not only allows consumers to obtain goods and services, but also drives the U.S. economy. Spending creates demand for certain goods and services, and in turn individuals and companies supply those goods and services to meet demand. When consumer spending rises, increased economic activity drives growth; when it falls, the economy tends to falter.

Just as spending helps the economy, saving helps consumers in several ways. Saving money provides a financial cushion against unexpected costs or job loss, and allows consumers to plan for long-term goals such as home ownership or retirement. Savings also provides a source of capital for financial institutions to loan out or to use as investments.

Economies with low savings rates are economies that don't domestically supply enough funds for investment purposes. These are economies that have lower growth rates because they don't have the investment funds required for growth. The banking sector with its financial markets is very important for economies. Without a well-developed banking center there is no mechanism for savings and therefore investment funds that are required for economic growth.

Skill 3.5 Demonstrate knowledge of patterns of work and economic activities in Texas, the United States, and the world, past and present

With its wide-open spaces, cattle, livestock and agriculture were initially important factors in the development of Texas. But as the nation developed, so did Texas. Many of the cities began as trading posts but then developed into their own production centers. Railroads and other modes of transportation aided the growth of the cities. Dallas became a focal point for the grain and cotton trade and was a stop off point for western migration. Houston was a center for the sugar trade. Texas also became a major oil-producing state, which resulted in the creation of many jobs and the infrastructure to support such an industry. In the 1940s major companies began to relocate to Texas, providing even more jobs. Houston has its major port and is a center for the oil and aeronautics industry.

The United States and Texas both have a history based on immigration. Immigrants settled in various parts of the country, assimilated, and thus contributed greatly to both American and Texan development. Texas's history is rich with Spanish and Mexican settlements. It also has diverse commercial and resource bases, beginning with agriculture and its oil industries, and then its aerospace industries.

Each commercial and ethnic group has different issues that are important to them. Agricultural areas are more concerned with issues pertaining to immigration and farm policy. Industrial workers are concerned mostly with issues of wages and benefits. Understanding the history of Texas illustrates how all of these different cultures and industries came into being and how the state is diverse enough to accommodate all of them.

Worldwide, countries may be roughly divided into industrialized, or developed, countries, and developing countries. In industrialized countries such as the United States and those of Western Europe, the majority of people are not concerned with the production of food but rather work to create goods and services. Most of these types of nations have regulated labor, and workplaces such as factories and offices provide employment. Developing nations have more in common with the patterns of work that typified the past. Economic activities in these places focus heavily on subsistence agriculture, and often have less division of labor than do industrialized economies.

Skill 3.6 Understand the characteristics, benefits, and development of the free-enterprise system in Texas and the United States

The **free enterprise system** in Texas developed as it did in the rest of the United States. In a free enterprise system the markets function on the basis of supply and demand and, if markets are free, the result is efficient resource allocation. Along with supply and demand, the innovations of **entrepreneurs** are vital to the success of the free enterprise system.

European and American settlers brought the concepts of the free enterprise system with them when they arrived in Texas. Trappers and other early settlers produced goods that they sold for profit in order to purchase other needed goods and services. In time, this system became larger and more sophisticated. Today, giant corporations and small businesses alike participate in the free enterprise system.

Economic interests played an important role in the foundation of the United States. Some of the nation's earliest colonies, such as Jamestown, were founded as profit-seeking ventures by British companies. Colonists sold natural resources to Europeans, and early industries including shipbuilding made up parts of the early free enterprise system. The principles of the U.S. Constitution discouraged government involvement in the economy, and for much of the nation's history the market ruled almost exclusively. With the rise of massive companies and long-distance travel during the nineteenth century, government regulation and involvement increased. Although this trend continued through much of the twentieth century, a trend toward **deregulation** emerged from the 1970s onward.

The free enterprise system offers many benefits. Among them are the potential to achieve great profits, the ability to pursue economic opportunity, and the encouragement of technological innovation.

Free enterprise, individual entrepreneurship, competitive markets, and consumer sovereignty are all parts of a market economy. Individuals have the right to make their own decisions as to what they want to do for a career. The financial incentives are there for individuals who are willing to take the risk. A successful venture earns profit. It is these financial incentives that serve to motivate inventors and small businesses. The same is true for businesses. They are free to determine what production technique they want to use and what output they want to produce within the confines of the legal system. They can make investments based on their own decisions; nobody is telling them what to do.

See skills 3.2, 3.3, and 3.9

Skill 3.7　Analyze the roles of producers and consumers in the production of goods and services

Producers and **consumers** both play important roles in determining what goods and services are produced under the free enterprise system. The interaction of producer and consumer is largely based upon the laws of supply and demand.

Producers create a good or service that is offered for sale to potential consumers. Thus, producers control the supply of a given good or service. Through economic innovation, producers may also offer an entirely new good or service.

When consumers buy a product or use a service, they establish the demand for that particular good or service. If demand is very high, the potential profits for producers increased, encouraging more producers to make greater quantities of that good or service to meet demand. The interaction of these forces typically leads to the establishment of an equilibrium at which enough of a particular good or service is produced to meet demand, but not so much as to unduly devalue an otherwise scarce and thus valuable commodity so that producers continue to generate a profit.

Skill 3.8　Demonstrate knowledge of how businesses operate in the U.S. free-enterprise system

The fundamental characteristics of the U.S. free enterprise system are competition and markets. Here, profit and competition are interdependent. **Competition** is determined by market structure and refers to the efforts of producers to sell to consumers, and consumers to find the best deal from producers. The most competitive of all market structures is **perfect competition**, characterized by numerous buyers and sellers, none of which are large enough to directly influence market price. Products are homogenous—the same—so buyers are indifferent as to whom they buy from. The absence of barriers to entry makes it easy for firms to enter and leave the industry.

At the other end of the spectrum is a **monopoly**, in which only one seller offers a unique product. Barriers to entry are significant enough to keep firms from entering or leaving the industry. In **monopolistic competition,** a relatively small number of firms sell similar products. An **oligopoly** is a market structure in which a few large firms selling heterogeneous or homogeneous products.

The existence of economic profits, or an above normal rate of return, attracts capital to an industry and results in expansion. Profit functions as a financial incentive for individuals and firms. The possibility of earning profit is why individuals are willing to undertake entrepreneurial ventures and why firms are willing to spend money on research and development (R&D), and innovation. Without these kinds of financial incentives, there would be little new product development or technological advancement.

Skill 3.9   Apply knowledge of the effects of supply and demand on consumers and producers in a free-enterprise system

In the free enterprise system, consumers and producers are both affected by the laws of **supply** and **demand. Supply** describes the amount of a particular good or service that producers are willing to sell at a given price. **Demand** reflects how much of a good or service that consumers are willing to buy at a given price. **Scarcity**—the relative lack of a resource—may have a significant influence on supply and demand.

All of these economic forces interact within the free enterprise system to set **prices.** When supply of a good or service is higher than demand, the price drops. When demand is higher than supply, however, prices rise. Consider the relative value of a sports ticket. If a sports team is doing well and many fans wish to attend its games, the team's owners may raise prices for the tickets. If the team is doing poorly and few fans wish to attend its games, however, team owners may instead run promotions lowering the price of the tickets in an attempt to generate greater demand.

Skill 3.10   Demonstrate knowledge of categories of economic activities and methods used to measure a society's economic level

Economic activities can be organized into a few basic categories. **Agricultural activities** are those economic activities relating to the growing of food or other crops. **Manufacturing activities** include the making of goods. **Wholesale activities then** involve the sale of large quantities of goods for resale directly to consumers at the **retail** level. The category of intangible **service activities,** such as health care or hair styling, make up the final category of economic activities.

A nation's overall economic performance may be measured by its Gross Domestic Product (GDP). GDP is a monetary measure of the economy's output during a specified time period. Tabulating the economy's output can be measured in two ways, both of which give the same result: the expenditures approach and the incomes approach. Basically, what is spent on the national output by each category of the economy is equal to what is earned producing the national output by each of the factors of production. The two methods have to be equal.

Economists may also measure a society's economic level with other economic indicators. The **unemployment rate** measures the proportion of a society's labor force that cannot find work, despite efforts to do so. **Stock indexes** such as the Dow Jones Industrial Average describe the overall performance of the stock market. The rate of **inflation,** usually measured in the United States by the **Consumer Price Index (CPI),** also reflects a society's economic level.

Skill 3.11   Use economic indicators to describe and measure levels of economic activity

Economists describe and measure levels of economic activity using several different types of **economic indicators.** Some of these indicators measure only economic data. A nation's overall **Gross Domestic Product (GDP)** describes that country's total economic output. GDP can also be measured as a ratio of GDP to population using to find **GDP per capita. Individual purchasing power** describes how many goods and services individuals within a given society can afford to buy. Other indicators, such as **stock indexes,** the **unemployment rate,** and the **inflation rate** provide valuable information about economies.

Other indicators of economic activity measure social, rather than inherently economic, factor. The **literacy rate** may indicate the relative education levels of a society's citizens, allowing conclusions to be drawn about likely economic activities. **Life expectancy** stems from a country's overall levels of health and societal development, so higher life expectancies can logically be tied to higher levels of economic activity.

See also Skill 3.10

Skill 3.12   Understand major events and trends in economic history

The **Agricultural Revolution**, initiated by the invention of the plow, led to a transformation of human society by making large-scale agricultural production possible and facilitating the development of agrarian societies. During the period in which the plow was invented, the wheel, numbers, and writing were also invented. This period was thus one of dramatic social and economic change. Results of the Agricultural Revolutions included higher populations, the development of settlements and, later, the emergence of societies and trade.

The **Industrial Revolution** of the eighteenth and nineteenth centuries resulted in great changes in human civilization, and yielded even greater opportunities for trade, increased production, and the exchange of ideas and knowledge. The **First Industrial Revolution** (1750–1830) saw the mechanization of the textile industry and vast improvements in mining. Also, due to the invention of the steam engine, there were numerous advances in transportation: the development or improvement of turnpikes, canals, and the invention of the railroad.

The **Second Industrial Revolution** (1830—1910) resulted in vast improvements in a number of industries that had already been mechanized through such inventions as the Bessemer steel process and the invention of steam ships. As a result, new Industries arose, such as photography, electricity, and chemical processes. New sources of power were harnessed and applied, including petroleum and hydro-electric power. Precision instruments were developed and engineering was launched. It was during this second phase that the Industrial Revolution spread to other European countries, to Japan, and to the United States.

The direct results of the Industrial Revolution, particularly as they affected industry, commerce, and agriculture, included:
- Enormous increase in productivity
- Significant increase in world trade
- Specialization and division of labor
- Standardization of parts and mass production
- Growth of giant business conglomerates and monopolies
- A new revolution in agriculture facilitated by the steam engine, machinery, chemical fertilizers, processing, canning, and refrigeration

The social results of the Industrial Revolution include:
- Increase of population, especially in industrial centers
- Advances in science applied to agriculture, sanitation and medicine
- Growth of great cities
- Disappearance of the difference between city dwellers and farmers
- Faster lifestyles and greater stress from the monotony of the work routine

Increased mobility produced a rapid diffusion of knowledge and ideas. It also resulted in wide-scale immigration to industrialized countries. Cultures clashed and melded. As the economy developed and expanded to the north, south and west, the areas developed in different ways. As the nation expanded southward, the southern states developed slave labor-economies. The vast plantations required a cheap source of labor to make the South's exports low priced in world markets. Westward expansion was based on family occupation of farms that did not need slaves to operate them. The North and the South developed in different ways that brought them into conflict over the issue of slavery. This led to different patterns of economic activity in the different areas of the country.

Skill 3.13   Analyze the interdependence of the Texas economy with the United States and the world

Economic **interdependence** describes the relationships among various regional, national, and international economies. Interdependent economics rely upon one another for economic needs such as resources, finished goods, and labor. As transportation and communication have improved during the late twentieth and early twenty-first centuries, increased economic interdependence has contributed to the **globalization** of the economy.

Interdependence plays a significant role in the Texas and U.S. economy. For example, a Texas high-tech company may manufacture a computer microchip using component parts made in China and Germany. That microchip may then be sent to California, where it is added to an mp3 player that is later sold in Canada.

As interdependence grows, local and regional economies have closer relationships with national and international economies. Thus, an increase in a supply cost in Asia may raise manufacturing costs in Europe and consumer prices in Texas.

Skill 3.14   Apply knowledge of significant economic events and issues and their effects in Texas, the United States, and the world

Throughout its history, the United States relied on trade. Early North American colonists grew cash crops such as tobacco and extracted natural resources that were sold to Europeans. However, most U.S. economics interests were focused on protection of American manufacturing and other internal growth until the World War I era. The end of the war began a period of prosperity that lasted until 1929. The economy, freed from its wartime restraints, had to satisfy the pent up demand caused by the rationing of war. Thus, mass production satisfied mass demand, and supplied the wages for the people to buy the output.

Manufacturing output doubled during this period. The building sector experienced a boom that eventually faded. The financial sector provided loans for all the building. The stock market was booming with almost unlimited buying and selling on margin. When the stock prices fell, many speculators could not meet their margin calls. This, along with several other national and global economic factors, contributed to the onset of the **Great Depression**. However, FDR's **"New Deal"** policies of public spending and the onset of World War II eventually brought the economy out of the Great Depression.

The United States and the Soviet Union emerged as the new global superpowers after World War II. The European economies were shattered by the war, as was their infrastructure. America embarked on a program of massive aid called **the Marshall Plan** to help the war devastated economies rebuild.

The Bretton Woods System was established to provide stable exchange rates. The General Agreement on Tariffs and Trade (GATT), the International Bank for Reconstruction and Development (IBRD, or simply, the World Bank), and the International Monetary Fund (IMF) were established to help lower trade barriers and facilitate international development. This system worked well and the world economies recovered from the war. Under the Bretton Woods System, the U.S. dollar was expressed in terms of gold, at $35 per ounce, and all other world currencies were pegged to the dollar. Nations were required to keep their currency values within specified range and nations would settle their Balance of Payments imbalances at the end of the year.

The Bretton Woods System worked well until the 1960s when the world consistently experienced exchange rate crises that resulted in the exchange markets closing. The situation continued until 1973 when world exchange rates began to float. This eliminated the need for the settlement of payments imbalances because the exchange rate adjusts to eliminate any payments disequilibrium. A deficit results in currency depreciation, while a surplus results in currency appreciation. As firms and traders became more adept at hedging, currency problems were eliminated and international trade continued to grow. After this time, many industries began to relocate to Texas and the oil and aeronautics industries, as well as others developed. As a result, Houston remains a major international shipping center.

Today, all nations are members of a global economy: what happens in one nation affects other nations because they are practically all related through international trade and finance. For example, if one nation lowers its interest rates to stimulate its domestic economy, the lower interest rates cause an outflow of dollars to a foreign country with higher interest rates. This results in dollar depreciation and an appreciation of the foreign currency. The cheaper dollar makes U.S. exports more attractive to foreigners because they are cheaper due to the lower priced dollar. Thus, foreigners buy more U.S. exports. The higher value of the foreign currency makes foreign imports more expense to U.S. citizens so they buy fewer foreign imports and more domestic goods. This ultimately leads to higher employment in the U.S. but lower employment in the foreign country. A nation cannot act in isolation in today's world.

See also Skill 1.10, 1.11, 1.12, 1.16

COMPETENCY 4.0 GOVERNMENT AND CITIZENSHIP

Skill 4.1   Understand the purpose of rules and laws; the relationship between rules, rights, and responsibilities; and the individual's role in making and enforcing rules and ensuring the welfare of society

Rules and **laws** are essential for the organization of society. When people establish rules and laws, they agree upon social values and practices. Just as students follow classroom laws to ensure that the classroom is an orderly and well-functioning place with defined borders and behaviors, societies agree upon laws so that they will be safer.

Federal laws are passed by Congress, and can originate in either the House of Representatives or the Senate. The first step in the passing of a law is for it to be introduced in one of the houses of Congress. A proposed law is called a **bill** while it is under consideration by Congress. A bill can be introduced, or sponsored, by a member of Congress by giving a copy to the clerk or by placing a copy in a special box called a hopper.

Once a bill is introduced, it is assigned to one of several standing committees of the house in which it was introduced. The committee studies the bill and researches the issues it would cover. Committees may call experts to testify on the bill and gather public comments. The committee may revise the bill. Finally, the committee votes on whether to release the bill to be voted on by the full body. A committee may also lay aside a bill so that it cannot be voted on, often called "killing" a bill. Once a bill is released, it can be debated and amended by the full body before being voted on. If it passes by a simple majority vote, the bill is sent to the other house of Congress, where the process begins again.

Once a bill has passed both the House of Representatives and the Senate, it is assigned to a conference committee that is made up of members of both houses. This committee resolves differences between the House and Senate versions of a bill, if any, and then sends it back to both houses for final approval. Once a bill receives final approval, it is signed by the Speaker of the House and the Vice President, who is also the President of the Senate, and sent to the President for consideration. The President may either sign the bill or **veto** it. If he vetoes the bill, it may be overruled if two-thirds of both the Senate and the House vote to do so. Once the President signs it the bill becomes a law.

Federal laws are enforced by the executive branch and its departments. The Department of Justice, led by the U.S. Attorney General is the primary law enforcement department of the federal government. The Justice Department is aided by other investigative and enforcement departments such as the Federal Bureau of Investigation (FBI) and the U.S. Postal Inspectors.

The U.S. Constitution and Congressional laws provide many rights to U.S. citizens. These civil rights include freedom of religion, assembly, speech, voting, holding public office, and traveling through-out the country. American citizens have the right to live in the Unites States and cannot be forced to leave. Citizenship is guaranteed and will not be taken away for any reason, unless one commits certain serious actions. Civil rights have limitations such as minimum age for voting and limited free speech, forbidding the damage to someone's reputation by slander and lying.

Popular sovereignty grants citizens the ability to directly participate in their own government by voting and running for public office. This ideal is based on the notion that all citizens have an equal right to engage in their own governance, and is established in the U.S. Constitution. The Constitution also contains a list of specific rights that citizens have and that upon which the government cannot infringe. Popular sovereignty also allows for citizens to change their government if they feel it is necessary. The Declaration of Independence embodied this idea, and the Founders provided for this in the U.S. Constitution.

The **rule of law** is the ideal that the law applies not only to the governed, but also to the government. This core value gives authority to the justice system, which grants citizens protection from the government by requiring that any accusation of a crime be proved by the government before a person is punished. This is called due process and ensures that any accused person will have an opportunity to confront his accusers and provide a defense. Due process follows from the core value of the right to liberty. The government cannot take away a citizen's liberty without reason or without proof. The correlating ideal is also a core value— that someone who *does* harm another or break a law receives justice under the democratic system. The ideal of justice holds that a punishment will fit the crime, and that any citizen can appeal to the judicial system if he feels he has been wronged.

Citizens' duties also vary from nation to nation. Duties demanded by law— also considered civic responsibilities—include paying taxes, obeying laws, and compulsory military service through the U.S. Selective Service. Although some governments, including that of the United States, require jury duty a compulsory duty of citizenship, others consider it a voluntary duty, like voting, volunteer work, and public awareness.

Citizenship is granted one of two ways: either by birth or by naturalization. Some Americans, particularly those who have emigrated from another country, hold dual citizenship (that is, they are citizens of the United States and of their country-of-origin).

Skill 4.2   Know the basic structure and functions of the U.S. Government, the Texas government, and local governments (including the roles of public officials) and relationships among national, state, and local governments

The United States is a **republic.** In a republic, individual voters select representatives to their government. Those representatives then are charged with acting on the behalf of the interests of those who elected them.

The American governmental system is a **federal system** with fifty individual states federating, or uniting, as one nation. The federal and state governments share the powers of government. This federal system required decentralization, which makes it impossible to coexist with totalitarianism. Both federal and state governments exist and govern by the will of the people who are the source of their authority. Local governmental systems operate under the same guidelines.

The American political system is a **two-party system**, consisting of the Democratic and Republican parties. Political parties in America have approximately five major functions: (1) Choose candidates who will run for public office; (2) assist in organizing the government; (3) formulate political platforms and policies; (4) obtain the funds needed to conduct election campaigns; and (5) take the initiative to make sure voters are aware of issues, problems to be solved, and any other information about public affairs. The two-party system in the United States operates at the national, state, and local levels.

The Texas state government is organized along the same lines as the federal government. It has three branches of government: **executive, legislative,** and **judicial**. The governor leads the executive branch, vetoes or signs bills into law, commands the state militia, and can call special sessions of the legislature. That legislature has two houses—a House of Representatives with 150 members and a Senate with 31—and meets in regular session lasting two years. The judicial branch has many overlapping courts, of which the Supreme Court (civil cases) and the Texas Court of Criminal Appeals are the highest. Judges are elected, as are members of the legislative branch and many members of the executive branch.

At the United States Federal level:

Legislative – Article I of the Constitution established the legislative or law-making branch of the government, the Congress. It is made up of two houses, the House of Representatives and the Senate. Voters in all states elect the members who serve in each respective house of Congress. The legislative branch is responsible for making laws, raising and printing money, regulating trade, establishing the postal service and federal courts, approving the President's appointments, declaring war and supporting the armed forces. The Congress also has the power to change the Constitution itself, and to *impeach* (bring charges against) the President. Charges for impeachment are brought by the House of Representatives, and are then tried in the Senate.

Executive: Article II of the Constitution created the executive branch of the government, led by the President, who leads the country, recommends new laws, and can veto bills passed by the Legislative branch. As the Chief of State, the President is responsible for carrying out the country's laws and the treaties and declarations of war passed by the Legislative branch. The President also appoints federal judges and is Commander-in-Chief of the military when it is called into service. Other members of the executive branch include the Vice-President, also elected, and various cabinet members as he might appoint: ambassadors, presidential advisors, members of the armed forces, and other appointed and civil servants of government agencies, departments and bureaus. Though the President appoints them, the Legislative branch must approve them.

Judicial: Article III of the Constitution established the judicial branch of government, led by the Supreme Court. The Supreme Court has the power to rule that a law passed by the legislature, or an act of the Executive branch is illegal and unconstitutional. Citizens, businesses, and government officials can, as the highest possible appeal, ask the Supreme Court to review a decision made in a lower court if someone believes that the ruling by a judge is unconstitutional. The judicial branch also includes lower federal courts, known as federal district courts, which have been established by the Congress. These courts try lawbreakers and review cases referred from other courts.

Powers delegated to the federal government:	Powers reserved to the states:
1. To tax	1. To regulate intrastate trade
2. To borrow and coin money	2. To establish local governments
3. To establish postal service	3. To protect general welfare
4. To grant patents and copyrights	4. To protect life and property
5. To regulate interstate & foreign commerce	5. To ratify amendments
6. To establish courts	6. To conduct elections
7. To declare war	7. To make state and local laws
8. To raise and support the armed forces	
9. To govern territories	
10. To define and punish felonies and piracy on the high seas	
11. To fix standards of weights and measures	
12. To conduct foreign affairs	

Concurrent powers of the federal government and states.

1. Both Congress and the states may tax.
2. Both may borrow money.
3. Both may charter banks and corporations.
4. Both may establish courts.
5. Both may make and enforce laws.
6. Both may take property for public purposes.
7. Both may spend money to provide for the public welfare.

Implied powers of the federal government.

1. To establish banks or other corporations implied from delegated powers to tax, borrow, and to regulate commerce.
2. To spend money for roads, schools, health, insurance, etc. implied from powers; to establish post roads, to tax to provide for general welfare and defense, and to regulate commerce.
3. To create military academies, implied from powers to raise and support armed forces.
4. To locate and generate sources of power and sell surplus implied from powers to dispose of government property, commerce, and war powers.
5. To assist and regulate agriculture implied from power to tax and spend for the general welfare and to regulate commerce.

State governments are much like the federal government with a few important exceptions. Governors are not technically commanders in chief of armed forces; state supreme court decisions can be appealed to federal courts; terms of state representatives and senators vary; judges, even of the state supreme courts, are elected by popular vote; governors and legislators often have term limits that vary by state.

Local governments, including cities, counties, and **special districts** such as school and water districts, vary widely across the country. Some local governments consist of a city council, of which the mayor is a member and has limited powers. In other cities, the mayor is the head of the government and the city council are the chief lawmakers. Local governments also have more lenient requirements for people running for office than do the state and federal governments.

Skill 4.3   Demonstrate knowledge of key principles and ideas in major political documents of Texas and the United States and relationships among political documents

The Declaration of Independence was a condemnation of the British king's tyrannical government, and emphasized the American colonists' belief that a government received its authority to rule from the people, and its function should be to protect —not suppress—the rights of the governed. This included protection from the government itself. These two ideals, **popular sovereignty** and the **rule of law,** remain core values of the U.S. government.

Popular sovereignty grants citizens the ability to directly participate in their own government by voting and running for public office. This ideal is based on a belief of **equality** that holds that all citizens have an equal right to engage in their own governance. The ideal of equality has changed over the years, as women and non-white citizens were not always allowed to vote or bring suit in court. Now, all U.S citizens above the age of 18 (with few exceptions, such as felons) are allowed to vote. This expansion of rights since the adoption of the Constitution demonstrates an American value of **respect for minority rights.**

The republican system of election and representation is based on **majority rule**. In most public elections, the candidate receiving the most popular votes is awarded the office. Majority rule is also used to pass legislation in Congress. Majority rule is meant to ensure that authority cannot be concentrated in one small group of people.

The rule of law is the ideal that the law applies not only to the governed, but also to the government. This core value gives authority to the justice system, which grants citizens protection from the government by requiring that any accusation of a crime be proved by the government before a person is punished. This is called **due process** and ensures that any accused person will have an opportunity to confront his accusers and provide a defense. Due process follows from the core value of a right to liberty. The government cannot take away a citizen's liberty without reason or proof. The correlating ideal is also a core value - that someone who *does* harm another or break a law will receive **justice** under the democratic system. The ideal of justice holds that a punishment will fit the crime, and that any citizen can appeal to the judicial system if he feels he has been wronged.

Central to the ideal of justice is an expectation that citizens will act in a way that promotes the **common good**, that they will treat one another with **honesty** and respect and will exercise **self-discipline** in their interactions with others. These are among the basic responsibilities of a citizen of a democracy.

The U.S. Constitution created a federal government solidly based on four fundamental principles. The first principle is that of federalism, a system of government in which power is divided between the federal and state governments. This, in turn, set up four types of governmental powers: (1) delegated or expressed—those listed directly; (2) implied powers—not stated directly but suggested; (3) reserved powers—not given to the federal government but reserved for the people or for the states; and (4) concurrent powers—given to both federal and state governments at the same time.

The second constitutional principle is the separation of powers with the system of checks and balances. The writers of the Constitution were greatly concerned with protecting the new nation from any form of tyranny, seizure of power by a military dictator, or any one branch of government becoming stronger and more powerful than the others. Thus, it was determined to keep the three branches separate and equal in power.

Also, a system of checks and balances was written into the Constitution, which gives each of the three branches some powers that affect the other two. Some examples include:

- Congress checks the President by having the authority to appropriate funds for running the government.
- Congress checks the judicial branch due to its power to make laws.
- The President can check Congress with the power to veto bills it passes.
- The President checks the courts with the power to appoint judges and justices.
- The courts can check both Congress and the President by reviewing executive orders and legislative acts and declaring them unconstitutional.

A third principle provides for the protection of individual rights and liberties. These provisions include the following:

- The Constitution prohibits the passage of "ex post facto laws" (laws passed "after the deed" providing the penalty for an act that was not an illegal act at the time it was committed), and **bills of attainder** (laws that render punishment to someone through fines, imprisonment, and confiscation of property without a court trial first).
- Individual rights are also protected through the **writ of habeas corpus,** which requires release from jail or prison if an individual has not been formally charged with or convicted of a crime.
- Special protection is given to those accused of treason as well as their innocent relatives. The accused is entitled to a fair trial and due process of law and would be protected against being accused merely because of criticism against the government. Treason was defined by the Constitution as waging war against the U.S., or supporting enemies of the U.S. It would require at least two witnesses testifying for conviction. Only the guilty would be convicted and punished; no punishment is allowed against one's family or relatives.

The first ten amendments to the Constitution, known as the **Bill of Rights,** guarantee protection for individuals against any action by the federal government which would threaten the loss of their life, liberty, or property without due process. These laws guarantee freedoms such as speech, press, assembly, religion, petition, and protect against unreasonable searches, seizures, and arbitrary arrest and punishment.

The fourth constitutional principle is adaptation to changing times and circumstances. One important process is the ability to meet needed changes through amendments. The other is the inclusion of what is known as the "elastic clause." In addition to its specific powers, the writers granted to Congress the power to make any additional laws needed to implement other powers.

The U.S. Constitution is the oldest federal constitution used among national governments today, and one of the most enduring among all forms of government. It has stood the test of time for two reasons: (1) It has set out procedural rules that must be followed, even in extreme and critical circumstances; and (2) due to amending along with customs and practices, it is flexible and adaptable making it possible to meet the demands and changes of a growing nation.

Bill Of Rights - The first ten amendments to the United States Constitution dealing with civil liberties and civil rights. They were written mostly by James Madison. They are in brief:

1. Freedom of Speech, Religion, and the Press.
2. Right to Bear Arms
3. Security from the quartering of troops in homes
4. Right against unreasonable search and seizures.
5. Right against self-incrimination
6. Right to trial by jury, right to legal counsel
7. Right to jury trial for civil actions
8. No cruel or unusual punishment allowed.
9. These rights shall not deny other rights the people enjoy.
10. Powers not mentioned in the Constitution shall be retained by the states or the people.

The U.S. Constitution built on the ideas established in a number of earlier English and colonial governmental documents. These include the **Magna Carta (1215)**, the first significant document that limited the power of the monarchy; the Declaration of Rights, a forerunner of the Bill of Rights; and the Virginia Declaration of Rights and Statute of Religious Freedom.

The current Texas Constitution dates from 1876. Since then, it has been amending many times. It bears several important similarities to the U.S. Constitution. Like that document, the state constitution establishes a structure for government based on three branches. It also guarantees many individual rights under the Texas Bill of Rights. Unlike the U.S. Constitution, however, Texas's guiding document does not grant the government those powers considered **necessary and proper** to perform its duties. Partially as s a result of this, the Texas Constitution has been amended hundreds of times to grant powers to the state or to further refine those powers.

Skill 4.4 Know how people organized governments in colonial America and during the early development of Texas

Colonial government differed depending on the type of colony. Each colony had an elected lower legislative assembly, and a higher council and governor that were elected or appointed differently depending on the how the colony was initially organized. In most colonies, the councils and governors were appointed by the King of England, or by British property owners or agencies. In corporate colonies the council and governors were elected by colonial property owners who maintained a close connection to England.

Thus, while the colonies were allowed to tax themselves and regulate much of their daily lives through representation in the colonial assemblies, Britain maintained control of international affairs and international trade by controlling the upper levels of colonial government. In practice, Britain allowed the colonies to go about their business without interference, largely because the colonies were providing important raw materials to the home country.

One important innovation in colonial government was the **town meeting** common in New England. This event brought together colonists to discuss and vote on local issues in a direct democracy. Although this form of government did not spread out of New England, it is still used in some communities in the region today.

The early presidential administrations established much of the form and many of the procedures still present today. George Washington, the first U.S. President, established a cabinet form of government, with individual advisors overseeing the various functions of the executive branch and advising the President, the final decision-maker. Divisions within his cabinet and within Congress during his administration eventually led to the development of political parties, which Washington opposed. Washington was elected to two terms and served from 1789 to 1797.

From its earliest days, Texas was governed by a document of some sort. The Republic of Texas had a Constitution that closely resembled the U.S. Constitution, with a government that had three branches, checks and balances, a stipulation for democratic elections of officials, and a Bill of Rights. It also had certain Spanish and Mexican traditions, such as provisions for community property and debt relief, which remain today.

Texas's modern government dates from the Reconstruction Era, when the state was readmitted to the Union and set back up its state government under the strict rules placed upon former Confederate states by the U.S. Congress.

Skill 4.5   **Understand the political process in the United States and Texas and how the U.S. political system works**

The U.S. political process today takes place at the local, state, and national levels. At the federal (or national) level, political processes stem from the agenda-setting power of the President and executive branch, and the law-making power of the legislative branch. Members of these branches are chosen by voters through regular **elections** that typically follow lengthy political **campaigns.** Political agendas at both the state and national levels may also be influenced by **lobbyists** and **special interest groups.**

Texas has, primarily, two political parties, the Democratic and Republican Parties. The Democratic Party was the dominant party for years, but the Republican Party has enjoyed resurgence in the past few decades and now controls much of the state government. The state legislature, with its two houses, drafts, writes, and passes laws, which the governor either approves (signs into law) or rejects (vetoes). The state courts can weigh in on matters of dispute or constitutionality regarding laws that the Legislature passes and the governor signs. The legislature itself meets only every two years but for an extended period of time. Amendments to the Constitution are relatively easily passed. A proposed amendment needs only two-thirds of both houses of the legislature to approve and then a simple majority of the registered state voters.

See also Skills 4.2 and 4.3

Skill 4.6   **Demonstrate knowledge of types of government and their effectiveness in meeting citizens' needs**

Governments may be divided into a few broad categories. **Limited** governments exercised political authority that is limited in some way, often by a constitution of other founding document. Under a limited government, all people and the government must follow established laws. **Unlimited** governments, however, exercise total, unfettered political authority. These types of governments are more likely to experience abuse of power.

Types of governments may also be characterized by the number of people who have political authority. A government with just one leader uses the **rule of one** form. Under the **rule of few,** a select body of some type of elites oversees the government. Democratic forms of government rely on **rule of many.** Governments that are based on the will of many are more likely to serve the needs of both the majority and minority groups within that society.

Some major forms of government:

Communism: This political system, characterized by the ideology of class conflict and revolution, and government ownership of the means of production and distribution of goods and services. Historically, communism was practiced in the Soviet Union; the largest communist country today is China. The centralized control exercised by communist governments has typically resulted in economic and political hardships for its citizens.

Dictatorship: The rule by an individual or small group of individuals (Oligarchy) that centralizes all political control in itself and enforces its will with a strong police force. Dictatorships may exist with varying degrees of success, but often become repressive.

Monarchy: The rule of a nation by a monarch, a non-elected and usually hereditary leader, most often a king or queen. Most monarchies today are **constitutional monarchies,** under which an elected legislative body such as a parliament shares authority with the monarch.

Parliamentary System: A system of government with a legislature, usually involving a multiplicity of political parties and often coalition politics. There is a division between the head of state and head of government. Head of government is usually known as a Prime Minister. This person is typically the head of the largest political party. The head of government and cabinet usually both sit and vote in the parliament. Head of state is most often an elected president, (though in the case of a constitutional monarchy, such as Great Britain, the sovereign may take the place of a president as head of state). A government may fall when a majority in parliament votes "no confidence" in the government.

Presidential System: A system of government with a legislature; it can involve few or many political parties, no division between head of state and head of government. The president serves in both capacities. The president is elected either by direct or indirect election. A president and cabinet usually do not sit or vote in the legislature and the President may or may not be the head of the largest political party. A president can thus rule even without a majority in the legislature. He can only be removed from office before an election for major infractions of the law.

Skill 4.7   Know the formal and informal process of changing the U.S. and Texas constitutions and the impact of changes on society

Both the U.S. and Texas constitutions can be formally changed with **amendments.** At the federal level, amending the Constitution is often a long and difficult process. A proposed amendment must first be approved by Congress before going to the states for ratification. A majority of three-fourths of the states must then vote to ratify the amendment in order for it become enacted. Proposed amendments may have a time limit for ratification by the states. Amending the Texas Constitution is a simpler process. After being passed on to voters by the Texas legislature, a proposed amendment must win approval by only a simple majority of voters.

Constitutions may also be affected more informally by the judicial branch. The power of **judicial review** allows the U.S. Supreme Court to formally interpret the U.S. Constitution, including rulings on matters that are not directly addressed by the Constitution. These decisions directly impact how U.S. law is applied within society. These decisions may thus be quite controversial; for example, the Supreme Court found in the hotly debated *Roe* v *Wade* ruling that the U.S. Constitution's implied right to privacy guaranteed access to abortion services.

Skill 4.8   Understand the impact of landmark Supreme Court cases

The first landmark decision of the U.S. Supreme Court was, fittingly enough, the one that granted itself the power to make significant legal decisions. The case of **Marbury *v.* Madison** (1803), on the surface a case regarding the legality of a judicial appointment. More important, however, the case established the principle of **judicial review.** This principle states that the U.S. Constitution established the U.S. Supreme Court as the ultimate authority to interpret the nation's founding document.

The case of **McCulloch *v.* Maryland** (1819) supported the authority of the federal government over the states. Involving a dispute over the right of the state of Maryland to levy a tax on federal business conducted by the First Bank of the United States, the decision first found that the federal government had the right to create such a bank because the Constitution granted the federal government certain implied—that is, not directly stated—powers. It then determined that the states had no power to tax the federal government. **Gibbons *v* Ogden** (1824) found that the U.S. Constitution permits the federal government to regulate interstate commerce.

Several landmark Supreme Court cases have related to civil rights issues. One the first major civil rights case was **Dred Scott *v.* Sandford** (1857). In this case, an enslaved man named Dred Scott sued for his freedom, claiming that he had ceased to be a slave when his former master had moved with him from Missouri (a slave state) to Illinois (a free state). The Court, however, ruled not only that Scott was not free, but that he was not a citizen of the United States and thus had no right to sue. African Americans would not win formal citizen ship rights until after the Civil War.

Even after the conflict, however, segregation and discrimination remained common in the South. In **Plessy *v.* Ferguson** (1896), the Court affirmed the legality of segregation and created the "separate but equal" doctrine that characterized the South for the next several decades. However, legal segregation began to topple with the Court's decision in **Brown v. Board of Education of Topeka, Kansas** (1954), which ruled that separate but equal public schools were illegal under the Constitution's Equal Protection Clause. Later, the decision in **Regents of the University of California v. Bakke** (1978) established the legality of the practice of affirmative action.

The Warren Court of the mid-twentieth century also made several landmark decisions regarding the rights of suspected criminals. In **Mapp v. Ohio** (1961), the Court ruled that evidence obtained as part of a search conducted illegally—for example, without a proper search warrant—is not admissible in court. The decision is **Gideon v Florida** declared that the Sixth Amendment requires states to appoint a lawyer to act on the behalf of accused people who cannot afford to hire their own lawyers. Finally, the Court decision in **Miranda v. Arizona** (1966) found that police were required to read arrested persons their legal rights, such as their right against self-incrimination. The **Miranda Rights** reflect this ruling.

The Supreme Court reasserted the power of judicial review in **United States v. Richard Nixon**. The issue was whether the president had the ability to keep certain items secret under the doctrine of "executive privilege." In this case, the items were secret recordings that President Richard Nixon had made of conversations he had had with his advisers that were suspected of being related to the Watergate break-in. Nixon claimed that presidential "executive privilege," used to protect matters of national security, kept him from having to relinquish the recordings to Congress and its special prosecutor. Like John Marshall before him, Chief Justice Warren Burger declared that the judicial branch could trump both other branches in its pursuit of justice and that no one, not even the president, was above the law.

Skill 4.9   Understand components of the democratic process and their significance in a democratic society

The most important part of the democratic process is **voting.** By voting, citizens of a democratic society formally state their preferences for a certain candidate, law, or other matter. Voting may take place in a **legislative assembly,** which determines laws for a society, or be part of an **election** in which voters choose people to serve in certain offices.

In the United States, the democratic process is part of a **republican** form of government. This means that citizens vote democratically to choose representatives who then vote on laws and issues on their behalf.

See Skill 4.5

Skill 4.10   Demonstrate knowledge of important customs, symbols, and celebrations that represent American beliefs and principles and contribute to national unity

The United States recognizes several national **holidays** that reflect patriotic views. Presidents' Day honors two of the country's most beloved leaders, George Washington and Abraham Lincoln. Veterans Day honors the American ideal of military service as an honorable endeavor in defense of the country's ideals. Independence Day celebrates the founding of the country in 1776, when independence from England was declared. These celebrations contribute to the shared experience of all Americans and promote patriotic ideals and unity.

The U.S. flag is perhaps the most important symbol of the country. It displays 13 stripes representing the original colonies that gained independence from Great Britain, as well as 50 stars, one for each state in the union. The flag symbolizes both the independence and unity of the 50 states, an important ideal in the republican form of government.

The bald eagle is another widely-used symbol of the United States, and appears on the currency and the Presidential Seal. It was chosen by the founding fathers to represent the strength and independence of the new nation.

Skill 4.11   Analyze the relationship among individual rights, responsibilities, and freedoms in democratic societies

Citizenship in a democracy bestows on an individual certain rights, foremost being the right to participate in one's own government. Along with these rights come responsibilities, including the responsibility of a citizen to participate.

The most basic form of participation is the **vote**. Those who have reached the age of 18 in the United States are eligible to vote in public elections. With this right comes the responsibility to be informed before voting, and not to sell or otherwise give away one's vote. Citizens are also eligible to run for public office, which requires office-holders to represent their electors as fairly as possible and to perform the duties expected of a government representative.

In the United States, citizens are guaranteed the right to **free speech**, or to express an opinion on public issues. In turn, citizens have the responsibility to allow others to speak freely. At the community level, this might mean speaking at a city council hearing while allowing others with different or opposing view-points to have their say without interruption.

The U.S. Constitution also guarantees **freedom of religion.** This means that the government may not impose an official religion on its citizens, and that people are free to practice any religion they prefer. Citizens are also responsible for allowing those of other religions to practice freely without obstruction. Occasion-ally, religious issues will be put before the public at the state level in the form of ballot measures or initiatives. To what extent it should be acceptable for religious beliefs to be expressed in a public setting, such as a public school, is an issue that has been debated recently.

In making decisions on matters like these, the citizen is expected to become informed of the issues involved and to make his vote based on his own opinion. Being informed of how one's government works and what the effects of new legislation will be is an essential part of being a good citizen.

The U.S. Constitution also guarantees that all citizens are **equal under the law.** In addition, federal and state laws make it a crime to discriminate against citizens based on their sex, race, religion and other factors. To ensure that all people are treated equally, citizens have the responsibility to follow these laws.

These rights and responsibilities are essentially the same whether one is voting in a local school board race, for the passage of a new state law, or for the President of the United States. Being a good citizen means exercising one's own rights while allowing others to do the same.

Almost all representative democracies in the world guarantee similar rights to their citizens, and expect them to take similar responsibilities to respect the rights of others. As a citizen of the world one is expected to respect the rights of other nations, and the people of those nations, in the same way.

Skill 4.12 Apply knowledge of the rights and responsibilities of citizens in Texas and the United States, past and present

People who live in Texas have a host of rights and responsibilities as part of their contract with the state. The state constitution protects them from harm, from un-fair government and laws, and from violence. The state government also protects their right to a legal job at a fair wage.

Texas residents are expected to obey their state, local, and national laws, to pay their taxes and vote in elections at all three levels of government. They are expected to represent their state well when they travel outside its borders.

Respect is an attitude toward other people or groups that recognizes and values their feelings, interests and beliefs, without necessarily agreeing with them. The idea of the rights of individuals and groups is a socially normalized outgrowth of respect.

Dissent is a belief or opinion in opposition to an accepted ideology, or to those who hold particular beliefs, powers, or policies. It may be expressed in a number of ways, some of which are socially and politically acceptable while others are not.

Voting is an approach to decision-making that permits each entitled individual to express a view or opinion on a matter or a person seeking political leadership office. It is generally considered a hallmark of democratic government.

Skill 4.13 **Understand how the nature, rights, and responsibilities of citizenship vary among societies**

Citizenship is membership in a political unit such as a city, country, or state. With citizenship comes the right to participate politically in a society. Citizenship and nationality are closely related, but are not always the same thing. A person can hold citizenship in one country, for instance, but live and work in a different country.

According to the U.S. Constitution, anyone born in the United States is a citizen of the United States regardless of their parents' nationality or citizenship. Other countries have different rules about obtaining citizenship that may be based on parental heritage or ethnicity. Some countries, such as Switzerland, hold local elections on whether a person may become a citizen.

Historically, many countries required an oath of allegiance to become a citizen, and some still do. Some countries, such as Israel, require all citizens to serve at least one term in the military.

At times, countries that grant individual citizenship may join together and create a combined political group that has citizenship rights and responsibilities of its own. The British Commonwealth and the European Union are examples of this kind of group. Citizens of the member states hold additional rights and share additional responsibilities of the larger group. They may also have the right to move freely within the member states. In all cases, citizenship also implies a responsibility to participate in the general improvement of one's society.

See also Skill 4.6 and Skill 4.7

COMPETENCY 5.0 CULTURE, SCIENCE, TECHNOLOGY AND SOCIETY

Skill 5.1   Understand basic concepts of culture and the processes of cultural adaptation, diffusion, and exchange

Innovation is the introduction of new ways of performing work or organizing societies, and can spur drastic changes in a culture. Prior to the innovation of agriculture, for instance, human cultures were largely nomadic and survived by hunting and gathering their food. Agriculture led directly to the development of permanent settlements and a radical change in social organization. Likewise, technological innovations in the Industrial Revolution of the nineteenth century changed the way work was performed and transformed the economic institutions of western cultures. Recent innovations in communications are changing the way cultures interact today.

Adaptation is the process that individuals and societies go through in changing their behavior and organization to cope with social, economic and environmental pressures.

Cultural diffusion is the movement of cultural ideas or materials among populations independent of the movement of those populations. Cultural diffusion can take place when two or more populations are close to one another; through direct interaction; or across great distances through mass media and other routes. Historically, the spread of Buddhism from India to other parts of Asia is an example of cultural diffusion. A contemporary example of cultural diffusion is the spread of the popularity of American movies to other nations.

Acculturation is an exchange or adoption of cultural features when two cultures come into regular direct contact. An example of acculturation is the adoption of Christianity and western dress by many Native Americans in the United States.

Assimilation is the process by which a minority ethnic group largely adopts the culture of the larger group with which it coexists. These groups are typically immigrants moving to a new country, as with the European immigrants who traveled to the U.S. at the beginning of the twentieth century who assimilated to American culture.

Cultural exchange takes place when two or more people from different cultures interact, with each learning or adopting a small part of the other's culture. For example, cultural exchange takes place when a foreign exchange student resides in the home of a host family, and each prepare cultural foods for the other.

Extinction is the complete disappearance of a culture. Extinction can occur suddenly, from disease, famine or war when the people of a culture are completely destroyed. It can also happen over time, as a culture adapts, acculturates or assimilates to the point where its original features are lost.

Skill 5.2   Analyze similarities and differences in the ways various peoples at different times in history have lived and met basic human needs

Food, clothing, and shelter are the three basic needs of human beings. As early humans increased in number and moved into new parts of the world, they had to adapt to their new environments by adopting new ways to obtain these needs.

Early humans hunted animals and gathered food from wild sources. Taking their basic support from nature like this required them to move with their food sources. Game animals might migrate, and seasonal food sources might require groups to travel to the regions where the food could be had. To take full advantage of varying areas where food could be found, portable methods of shelter were developed, such as the Native American teepee or the Mongolian yurt. These shelters could be carried from place to place, allowing for a greater range.

Clothing allowed humans to adapt to the wider range of climates they discovered as they migrated, both in their annual circuit and as they moved into newer and colder climates. Clothing protects the body from cold, sun exposure, and the elements. In very hot climates, early humans wore little or no clothing. The advantages of having an extra layer of protection were soon realized, however, and basic coverings were fashioned from animal skin. Foot coverings were developed to protect their feet from rough ground and sharp rocks. In colder climates, clothing was crucial for survival. Animal pelts with the fur attached provided warmth. Foot coverings could also be fur-lined or stuffed with grass. Mittens or gloves kept vulnerable fingers warm and protected.

As humans drifted from hunting and gathering to agriculture, other materials for clothing became available. Wool-bearing animals were domesticated and plant fibers were woven into cloth. During the Industrial Revolution, cloth-weaving methods advanced rapidly, greatly expanding the use of woven cloth clothing.

Agriculture also expanded the types of food that were available. Grains and fruits could be grown in place and meat could be harvested from domesticated animals. Not all climates are suitable for all crops, however, and humans have had to adapt varieties and methods to successfully produce food.

Just as their environment shaped their needs, so did the environment provide the means to meet those needs. For thousands of years, food and shelter had to be obtained from local resources, or from resources that could be grown locally. However, human technology has reached the point where we are able to supply food to any location on the planet and adapt clothing and shelter to any environment, even outer space.

See also Skill 3.1

Skill 5.3   Apply knowledge of the role of families in meeting basic human needs and how families and cultures develop and use customs, traditions, and beliefs to define themselves

In most societies, the **family** is the primary social unit. It is through the family that children learn the most essential skills for functioning in their society, such as language and appropriate forms of interaction. The size of the family unit varies among cultures, with some including grandparents, aunts, uncles and cousins as part of the basic family, who may all live together. The family is also related to a society's economic institutions, as families often purchase and consume goods as a unit. A family that works to produce its own food and clothing, as was the case historically in many societies, is also a unit of economic production.

One important function of the family is to introduce children to their society's customs, traditions, and beliefs. This prepares young people to take part in their culture.

Customs are the typical practices of a culture or society. Customs vary from place to place and over time. Customs typically do have the force of law, but are generally recognized within a society. **Traditions** are customs that have become standardized over time and are an important part of a society's cultural heritage.

Beliefs and values are similar and interrelated systems. **Beliefs** are those things that are thought to be true. They are often associated with religion, but beliefs can also be based on political or ideological philosophies. "All men are created equal," is an example of an ideological belief. **Values** are what a society thinks are right and wrong, and are often based on and shaped by beliefs. The value that every member of the society has a right to participate in his government might be considered to be based on the belief that "All mean are created equal," for instance.

Skill 5.4   Demonstrate knowledge of institutions that exist in all societies and how characteristics of these institutions may vary among societies

Sociologists have identified five different types of institutions around which societies are structured: family, education, government, religion and economy. These institutions provide a framework for members of a society to learn about and participate in a society, and allow for a society to perpetuate its beliefs and values to succeeding generations.

The **family** is the primary social unit in most societies. It is through the family that children learn the most essential skills for functioning in their society, such as language and appropriate forms of interaction. The family is connected to ethnicity, which is partly defined by a person's heritage.

Education is an important institution in a society, as it allows for the formal passing on of a culture's collected knowledge. The institution of education is connected to the family, as that is where a child's earliest education takes place. The United States has a public school system administered by the states that ensures a basic education and provides a common experience for most children.

A society's **governmental** institutions often embody its beliefs and values. Laws, for instance, reflect a society's values by enforcing its ideas of right and wrong. The structure of a society's government can reflect a society's ideals about the role of an individual in his society. The American form of democracy emphasizes the rights of the individual, but in return expects individuals to respect the rights of others, including those of ethnic or political minorities.

Religion is frequently the institution from which springs a society's primary beliefs and values, and can be closely related to other social institutions. Many religions have definite teachings on the structure and importance of the family, for instance. The U.S. Constitution guarantees the free practice of religion, which has led to a large number of denominations practicing in the United States today.

A society's **economic** institutions define how an individual can contribute and receive economic reward from his society. The U.S. economy relies on the free enterprise system. While this system allows for the economic advancement of the individual, it can also produce areas of poverty and economic depression.

Skill 5.5   **Understand how people use oral tradition, stories, real and mythical heroes, music, paintings, and sculpture to create and represent culture in communities in Texas, the United States, and the world**

Societies use a number of means to create and transmit their cultures. One of the most ancient of these means is the **oral tradition.** In the oral tradition, people tell **stories** about **real or mythical heroes,** historical and fictional events, and other cultural topics. This tradition creates a series of set stories that may vary somewhat from teller to teller. Ancient Native Americans in Texas relied on the oral tradition to pass on historical and cultural ideas. Modern oral traditions range from historical stories such as those of Johnny Appleseed to urban legend.

Other artistic output also defines and expresses cultural ideals and values. **Music** has long been a way for people to express religious beliefs, enjoy beauty, or share stories. In the antebellum United States, for example, enslaved people created a distinctive culture partially characterized by **spirituals.**

Visual art such as **painting** and **sculpture** has also been an important part of various cultures. Paintings may depict important cultural or historical scenes and people, creating iconic images. During the Renaissance, for example, artists expressed their interest in the rebirth of classical Greek and Roman ideas by recreating classical sculptural techniques, as in Michelangelo's *David.*

Skill 5.6   **Understand the contributions of people of various racial, ethnic, and religious groups in Texas, the United States, and the world**

See Skill 1.1 and Skill 1.2

Skill 5.7   **Demonstrate knowledge of relationships among world cultures and relationships between and among people from various groups, including racial, ethnic, and religious groups, in the United States and throughout the world**

Biologically speaking, a **race** of people shares a common genetic lineage. An **ethnic group** is a group of people who identify themselves as having a common social background and set of behaviors, and who perpetuate their culture by traditions of marriage within their own group. Ethnic groups often share a common language and ancestral background, and frequently exist within larger populations with which they interact. Ethnicity and race are sometimes interlinked, but differ in that many ethnic groups can exist within a population of people thought to be of the same race. Ethnicity is based more on common cultural behaviors and institutions than common physical traits.

Race, ethnicity, and religion are three lines along which many people group themselves and view themselves as distinct from other groups. Tension among groups can arise for various reasons, leading to longstanding conflict among some groups. Groups that have minority status within a larger group are often disadvantaged, owing to the dominant group favoring its own members in social and political policies and in daily interactions. These kinds of majority/minority relationships can be based on race, ethnicity, and religion.

Ethnic and religious tension can also arise from traditional historical relationships among groups. Ethnicity and religion are two frameworks by which social views can be passed from generation to generation, perpetuating tension and conflict between groups. Religion can also play an important role in relationships between groups. Some religious beliefs directly conflict with others, giving rise to disagreement.

Some of the major racial groups within the United States are white Caucasians, African Americans, and Asian Americans. Within those groups exist smaller ethnic groups, such as Hispanic Americans (white Caucasians) and Chinese Americans (Asian Americans). Major religious groups around the world include Catholics, Protestant Christians, Jews, Hindus, and Muslims.

Skill 5.8 Analyze relationships among religion, philosophy, and culture, and the impact of religion on ways of life in the United States and world areas

Religion is a formalized set of spiritual beliefs. Religion may be based on a broader **philosophy,** or a set of ideas about the world, morality, and other ideas. Religion may also influence various philosophies.

Both religion and philosophy play important roles in influencing the values and beliefs of cultures. In the modern United States, religion is officially separated from government. However, religious beliefs—particularly Christian religious beliefs—influence much of American culture. Many Americans base their personal moral codes on the tenets of Christian behavior, and significant portions of the population attend church services or make faith otherwise a part of their daily lives.

Religious practice in culture around the world varies. Some nations, such as Israel, draw much of their shared culture from religious identity and practice. Other states, such as Iran, are governed by religious leaders. Many places have relatively secular cultures in which people choose to incorporate religious practice into their lives as much as they choose.

Skill 5.9 Understand the concept of diversity within unity

The United States prides itself on its cultural **diversity**. From its beginnings, colonists came to the nation from various European nations. They soon began developing distinct, unified regional cultures. Over the ensuing centuries, people have immigrated to the United States from all parts of the world. Today, European Americans, African Americans, Asian Americans, Hispanic Americans, and others have all made important cultural contributions to the shared American culture. Within this mass American culture, individuals also have diverse cultural practices, and various cultural groups have developed distinctive practices.

The Hispanic heritage of many Texas citizens is officially honored by the preservation of early settlements and artifacts, such as Ceremonial Cave, Espiritu Santo and Morhiss Mound and ethnic and cultural concentrations of people currently thrive.

Skill 5.10   Analyze the effects of race, gender, and socioeconomic class on ways of life in the United States and throughout the world

Throughout history, social divisions have often occurred along lines of race, gender, and **socioeconomic class.** Often, men have been dominant over women; Northern white Europeans dominant over those o f other races; and the wealthy, dominant over lower and middle classes.

Racial differences have been the source of considerable difficulty throughout the world. For centuries, racist ideas greatly influenced social practices such as slavery, segregation, and discrimination. In the United States, these practices have been outlawed.

In the modern United States, men and women are increasingly equal. Since the 1960s, women have held more and more importance in the work place, and in recent decades men have begun sharing more of the traditional home and family responsibilities assumed by women. However, some inequalities in areas such as pay continue to persist.

Throughout the world, differences in socioeconomic class have a considerable influence on daily life. In countries that use a market economy, those of the upper socioeconomic classes have more economic buying power and typically enjoy great social influence. The working and middle classes, however, may also have considerable social power, as exemplified through the achievements of labor unions. Social class—which can be fluid—may influence a person's relative education, earning potential and family life.

Skill 5.11   Understand the various roles of men, women, children, and families in cultures past and present

During colonial times, residents of the New England colonies were primarily small farmers from England. Each family had its own subsistence farm with supporting livestock. Women were expected to care for the children and take care of the household, while men tended to the farming and livestock. Families encouraged their sons to continue to farm, and provided them with land and livestock to establish them. Women were expected to marry.

The middle colonies had a more diverse population than New England, with immigrants from Holland, Scotland, Ireland and Germany making up the largest groups. These peoples were also largely farmers, each group bringing its own methods and techniques. Family structure was similar to that in New England, but unlike their Puritan counterparts, German and Dutch women were allowed to hold property and could often be found working in the fields.

Until the early twentieth century, working children were typically expected to contribute financially to their families. As child labor laws began limited children's work and public education increased, childhood and the teen years increasingly became a time of learning, exploration, and personal and development. Women made great strides in the workplace, largely shedding traditional practices that limited them to the home.

Skill 5.12   Understand how the self develops and the dynamic relationship between self and social context

Socialization is the process by which humans learn the expectations their society has for their behavior so that they might successfully function within that society. It takes place primarily in children as they learn and are taught the rules and norms of their culture. For example, children who attend school are introduced to the social patterns of group behavior and develop an understanding of the importance of following rules. By observing adults and older children, young children learn about gender roles, and appropriate ways to interact. The family is the primary influence in this kind of socialization, and contributes directly to a person's sense of self-importance and personal identity, or **self**.

Through socialization, a person gains a sense of belonging to a group of people with common ideals and behaviors. When a person encounters people affiliated with other groups, their own group affiliation can be reinforced in contrast, contributing to their own sense of personal identity.

Skill 5.13   Apply knowledge of the effects of scientific discoveries and technological innovations on political, economic, social, and environmental developments and on everyday life in Texas, the United States, and the world

The **microscope** first appeared around 1590 and was steadily improved upon in later years. It revealed an entire world of invisible activity by bacteria and fungus, and laid bare the cell structure of complex organisms. Advancements in microscopy directly led to important discoveries of germs, viruses and the cause of disease, greatly aiding the field of medicine.

Electrical power is a phenomenon that has been known about for centuries, but not until the late nineteenth century had understanding and technology advanced to the point at which it could be reliably produced and transmitted. The ability to transmit power by wire over distances changed the nature of industry, which previously had relied on other sources, such as steam plants or waterpower to move machinery.

Albert Einstein's **Theory of Relativity** revolutionized physics. He proposed that the measurement of time and space changed relative to the position of the observer, implying that time and space were not fixed but could warp and change. This had radical implications for Newtonian physics, particularly as it related to gravity, and opened new fields of scientific study.

Penicillin was developed in the mid-twentieth century, and rapidly became an important drug, saving countless lives. Penicillin is derived from a mold, which, it was discovered, inhibited and even killed many kinds of germs. In drug form, it could be used to fight various kinds of human infections. Penicillin and similarly derived drugs are called antibiotics. Other important medical advances, such as the polio vaccine, also appeared during the twentieth century.

The **microchip** was developed in the 1950s as a way to reduce the size of transistor-based electronic equipment. By replacing individual transistors with a single chip of semiconductor material, more capability could be included in less space. This development led directly to the microprocessor, which is at the heart of every modern computer and most modern electronic products.

The religious beliefs and institutions of a culture can greatly influence scientific research and technological innovation. Political factors have also affected scientific advancement, especially in cultures that partially support scientific research with public money. Warfare has traditionally been a strong driver of technological advancement as cultures strive to outpace their neighbors with better weapons and defenses. Technologies developed for military purposes often find their way into the mainstream. Significant advances in flight technology, for example, were made during the two World Wars.

Socially, many cultures have come to value innovation and welcome new products and improvements to older products. This desire to always be advancing and obtaining the latest, newest technology creates economic incentive for innovation.

Skill 5.14 Analyze how science and technology relate to political, economic, social, and cultural issues and events

Science and technology have increasing effects on the daily lives of Americans. The scientific method and scientific experiments allow people to more fully understand many natural phenomena.

Technological developments have long been drivers of significant economic and social change. The development of the cotton gin in the early nineteenth century, for example, allowed cotton to be cleaned at a faster rate by fewer people, raising its profit margin and permitting more of it to be produced. This technological shift quickly encouraged Southern planters to grow and clean more cotton, an activity that required increasing amounts of slave labor. Thus, the invention cotton gin can be traced to the political tensions of sectionalism and, later, the Civil War.

As technological developments began to appear rapidly at the end of the nineteenth century, American life changed greatly. Industrial improvements contributed to the urbanization and industrialization of the United States as manufacturing began the primary economic activity in many parts of the country. The ability to construct railroads led not only to faster transit times and increased trade between distant areas but also to the creation of time zones due to the need for standardized train timetables.

Twentieth century technology has been no less impactful. The rise of radio, movies, and television created a shared, mass American culture. The emergence of the Internet in the late twentieth century contributed to greater globalization and improved communication and access to information. All of these technological improvements have greatly changed the ways that people live.

Skill 5.15   Demonstrate knowledge of the origins, diffusion, and effects of major scientific, mathematical, and technological discoveries throughout history

Historic causation is the concept that events in history are linked to one another by an endless chain of cause and effect. The root causes of major historical events cannot always be seen immediately, and are only apparent when looking back from many years later.

The **Agricultural Revolution**, initiated by the invention of the plow, led to a thoroughgoing transformation of human society by making large-scale agricultural production possible and facilitating the development of agrarian societies. During the period in which the plow was invented, the wheel, numbers, and writing were also invented. Coinciding with the shift from hunting wild game to the domestication of animals, this period was one of dramatic social and economic change.

The **Scientific Revolution** and the **Enlightenment** were two of the most important movements in the history of civilization, resulting in a new sense of self-examination and a wider view of the world than ever before. The Scientific Revolution was, above all, a shift in focus from belief to evidence. Scientists and philosophers wanted to see the proof, not just believe what other people told them. It was an exciting time, if you were a progressive thinker.

Refer to Skill 1.1 for further discussion of the Scientific Revolution and the Enlightenment

The **Industrial Revolution** of the eighteenth and nineteenth centuries resulted in great changes in human civilization and even greater opportunities for trade, increased production, and the exchange of ideas and knowledge. The First Industrial Revolution (1750–1830) saw the mechanization of the textile industry and vast improvements in mining.   Also, due to the invention of the steam engine, there were numerous advances in transportation: the development or improvement of turnpikes, canals, and the invention of the railroad.

Refer to Skill 3.12 for further discussion of the Industrial Revolution

The **Information Revolution** refers to the sweeping changes in information technology that occurred during the latter half of the twentieth century. It resulted from technological advances and a new respect for the information provided by a variety of trained, skilled, and experienced professionals. This approach arose from the ability to make computer technology both accessible and affordable. In particular, the development of the computer chip has led to such technological advances as the Internet, the cell phone, Cybernetics, wireless communication, and the ability to instantly access and disseminate a large amount of information.

In terms of economic theory and segmentation, it is now standard to think of three basic economic sectors: agriculture and mining, manufacturing, and services. Indeed, labor is now often divided between manual labor and informational labor. The fact that businesses are involved in the production, distribution, processing and transmission of information has, according to some, created a new business sector.

Skill 5.16   Know how developments in science and technology have affected the physical environment; the growth of economies and societies; and definitions of, access to, and use of physical and human resources

From the beginning of human history, technology has affected human-environment interaction. As early peoples developed basic agricultural technologies, for example, they began changing the soil by cultivating crops and eventually developed settlements, cities, and societies.

Technological innovations have generally contributed to the movement of people to cities and, by the nineteenth century, the development of advanced industrial manufacturing practices. This revolutionized economies as factory work began to overtake agriculture in economic importance. Technology also allows humans greater access to physical resources. The development of advanced mining techniques, for example, has permitted greater access to underground mineral resources.

Technological progress and innovation allow for the production of more goods and services at lower prices. This leads to increased consumption for consumers. Technology can also result in unemployment by displacing workers. This is referred to as structural unemployment. The displaced workers must be retrained and find jobs in other industries.

See also Skill 3.9

Skill 5.17   Know how changes in science and technology affect moral and ethical issues

Nuclear energy was once hailed as a cheap and relatively clean alternative to fossil fuels, but fell largely out of favor in the United States due to some high-profile accidents at nuclear plants (i.e., Three Mile Island, Chernobyl). Nuclear technology has continued to advance, and nuclear energy is gaining attention once again as a potential resource. One of the crucial considerations in the use of nuclear energy is safety. Nuclear fuels are highly radioactive and very dangerous should they enter the environment. The waste from creating nuclear energy is another important issue, as the dangerous byproduct must be carefully and safely stored. Internationally, there is concern that nuclear power plants may be used to produce fissile material for nuclear weapons, which has created another controversy over the spread of nuclear technology.

Biotechnology is another area that shows promise, but also brings controversy. Advances in biotechnology have opened the possibility of cloning and genetically altering organisms. Serious ethical issues have been raised about proceeding with this type of research, especially involving human beings and tissues. In recent years, political and public debate over the use of human **stem cells** in medical research has become a hot button issue

In the area of **ecology**, scientific research is focused primarily on finding efficient fuel alternatives. Advances in solar and wind power technology have made these options feasible in some geographic areas. Hybrid technology that uses electricity and fuel cells to supplement fossil fuels has found a market niche that expands yearly.

DOMAIN II	SOCIAL STUDIES FOUNDATIONS, SKILLS, AND INSTRUCTION

COMPETENCY 6.0   SOCIAL STUDIES FOUNDATIONS AND SKILLS

Skill 6.1   Understand the philosophical foundations of the social science disciplines and knows how knowledge generated by the social sciences affects society and people's lives

The social sciences are built upon the philosophy that human movements and interactions can be measured, studied, and ultimately predicted using a variety of methods and research techniques. By studying how humans act individually and within their societies, the social sciences seek to discover and explain common motivations and reactions among humans.

The body of knowledge generated by the social sciences has great influence on both the individual and societal levels. Methods of individual psychological treatment, for instance, are based on ongoing research in psychology. In the larger scheme, a country bases its foreign policy largely on the analysis of political scientists and other social research.

Skill 6.2   Understand how social science disciplines relate to each other

The major disciplines within the social sciences are intertwined and interrelated. Knowledge and expertise in one requires background that involves some or most of the others.

Anthropology is the study of human culture—how different groups of people live; how they have adapted to their physical environment; what they make or produce; and their relationship to other cultures, behavior, differences and similarities. To pursue the study of people, the anthropologist must know the history of the people being studied; their human geography and physical environment; their governmental structure, organization, and its impact on the people; their goods and produce and how they are used. Thus, a background in economics, geography, history, political science and sociology is helpful.

Archaeology studies past human cultures, typically by examining artifacts left behind to determine how certain people or groups lived their daily lives. Certainly, knowledge of history gives a background as a foundation of study. Geography makes its contribution by not only knowing where to look for remains but also how geographic conditions contributed to and affected the people or cultural groups being studied; how physical factors contributed to artifacts left behind.

Civics deals with what is required and expected of a region's citizens, along with their rights and responsibilities to government and to one another. Knowledge of history gives the background and foundation, while knowledge of government or political science explains not only the organization of the government but also its place with-in international affairs.

Economics is tied in mainly with history, geography, and political science. The different interrelationships include: history of economic theory and principles combined with historical background of areas; economic activities in the different countries and regions of the world, and how international trade and relations are affected; political science or government—how political organization and government affect an area's economic activities.

Geography is the study of Earth, its people, how they adapt to life on Earth, and how they use its resources. It is undeniably connected to history, economics, political science, sociology, anthropology, and archaeology. Geography not only deals with people and the physical environment today but also with: How did it all begin? What is the background of the people of an area? What kind of government or political system do they have? How does that affect their ways of producing and distributing goods? What kind of relationships do these people have with other groups? How is the way they live their lives affected by their physical environment? In what ways do they effect change in their way of living? All of this is tied in with physical and human geography.

History is an integral part of every other discipline in the social sciences. Knowing historical background on anything and anyone anywhere goes a long way towards explaining that what happened in the past leads up to and contributes to the events of the present.

Political Science is the study of government, international relations, political thought and activity, and comparison of governments. It is tied in with history (historical background), anthropology (how government affects a group's culture and relationship with other groups), economics (governmental influence and regulation of producing and distributing goods and products), and sociology (in-sight into how social developments affect political life). Other disciplines are also affected, as the study of political science is crucial to understanding political processes, the influence of government, and responsibilities of people.

Psychology is defined as scientifically studying mental processes and behavior. It is related to anthropology and sociology, two social sciences that also study people in society. All three closely consider relationships and attitudes of humans within their social settings. Anthropology considers humans within their cultures, how they live, what they make or produce, how different groups or cultures relate to each other. Sociology follows the angle of looking at behaviors, attitudes, conditions, and relationships in human society. Psychology focuses on individual behavior and how actions are influenced by feelings and beliefs.

Sociology studies human society, particularly the attitudes, behaviors, conditions, and relationships of people. It is closely related to anthropology, especially applied to groups outside of one's region, nation, or hemisphere. History puts it in perspective with an historical background. Political Science is tied to sociology with the impact of political and governmental regulation of activities. Awareness, influence, and use of the physical environment as studied in geography also contributes to understanding. Economic activities are a part of human society. The field of psychology is also related to sociology in its study of the actions of people.

Skill 6.3   Understand practical applications of social studies education

In measuring the social significance of an event or issue, one of the first questions to ask is how many people are affected. Wide sweeping events such as wars, natural disasters, revolutions, etc., are significant partly because they can change the way of life for many people in a short time.

Sometimes significant changes take place over long periods of time, however, so it is also important to look at long-term effects of an event or phenomenon, following the chain of causes and effects. In this way, sometimes events that seem insignificant at the time they occur, or which affect only a small number of people, can be linked directly to large societal changes.

Participation in self-government is one of the United States' core democratic values. By participating in democratic institutions, citizens become better informed of their rights and responsibilities in a democracy, and thus better citizens. While elementary students are too young to participate directly by voting, class-room activities that simulate elections can help develop a sense of the importance of participating. Encouraging structured discussion or debate on issues directly affecting the students can help establish respect for minority viewpoints and the importance of free expression, both of which are core democratic values.

Studying social studies allow young people to grow up into informed citizens. By understanding history, government, economics, geography, and other social studies topics, students can develop the skills they need to fulfill their duties as adult citizens.

Skill 6.4   Relate philosophical assumptions and ideas to issues and trends in the social sciences

Human societies can differ in an infinite number of ways, but all are faced with similar problems as they develop and change. Identifying how different peoples cope with and solve these challenges illustrates differences among cultures, as well as the common traits they share.

By identifying and analyzing these different approaches to social challenges, one can draw conclusions about the societal sources and causes of these differences that may be unique to each society. These conclusions can then be examined further by themselves, which may lead to the discovery of other social phenomena.

Skill 6.5 **Know characteristics and uses of various primary and secondary sources and use information from a variety of sources to acquire social science information and answer social science questions**

Primary sources are those historical documents and artifacts that were created directly by a person involved with a historical time or event. Examples of primary sources include:

- Letters
- Diaries
- Newspapers
- Photographs
- Advertisements
- Oral histories

Primary sources can be interpreted to learn not only about the events of the past but also about the thoughts and opinions of the people living during that time. However, researchers should keep in mind that primary sources should be interpreted within their historical context, and that they may reflect some misunderstandings or errors on the part of the person who created them.

Secondary sources are those sources created by scholars or historians writing about historical events, but who did not directly experience them. Examples of secondary sources include:

- Textbooks
- Nonfiction historical books and articles
- Encyclopedias
- Documentaries

Guidelines for the use of secondary sources:

- Do not rely upon only a single secondary source.
- Check facts and interpretations against primary sources whenever possible.
- Do not accept the conclusions of other historians uncritically.
- Place greatest reliance on secondary sources created by the best and most respected scholars.
- Do not use the inferences of other scholars as if they were facts.

- Ensure that you recognize any bias the writer brings to his or her interpretation of history.
- Understand the primary point of the book as a basis for evaluating the value of the material presented in it to your questions.

Students and researchers may obtain information from a variety of sources. Today, **electronic resources** offer rich, diverse sources of information. Reliable online encyclopedias and databases provide quick access to countless primary and secondary sources on nearly every aspect of history. Learning to use and evaluate electronic resources is an important skill for students to master.

Skill 6.6   Know how to formulate research questions and use appropriate procedures to reach supportable judgments and conclusions in the social sciences

There are many different ways to find ideas for **research problems**. One of the most common ways is through experiencing and assessing relevant problems in a specific field. Researchers are often involved in the fields in which they choose to study, and thus encounter practical problems related to their areas of expertise on a daily basis. The can use their knowledge, expertise and research ability to examine their selected research problem. For students, all that this entails is being curious about the world around them. Research ideas can come from one's background, culture, education, experiences, etc. Another way to get research ideas is by exploring literature in a specific field and coming up with a question that extends or refines previous research.

Once a **topic** is decided, a research question must be formulated. A research question is a relevant, researchable, feasible statement that identifies the information to be studied. Once this initial question is formulated, it is a good idea to think of specific issues related to the topic. This will help to create a hypothesis. A research **hypothesis** is a statement of the researcher's expectations for the outcome of the research problem. It is a summary statement of the problem to be addressed in any research document. A good hypothesis states, clearly and concisely, the researcher's expected relationship between the independent (causal) variable(s) and dependent (effect) variable that they are investigating. Once a hypothesis is decided, the rest of the research paper should focus on analyzing a set of information or arguing a specific point. Thus, there are two types of research papers: analytical and argumentative.

Analytical papers focus on examining and understanding the various parts of a research topic and reformulating them in a new way to support your initial statement. In this type of research paper, the research question is used as both a basis for investigation as well as a topic for the paper. Once a variety of information is collected on the given topic, it is coalesced into a clear discussion

Persuasive papers focus on supporting the question or claim with evidence or reasoning. Instead of presenting research to provide information, an argumentative paper presents research in order to prove a debatable statement and interpretation.

The scientific method is the process by which researchers over time endeavor to construct an accurate (that is, reliable, consistent and non-arbitrary) representation of the world. Recognizing that personal and cultural beliefs (i.e., biases) influence both our perceptions and our interpretations of natural phenomena, standard procedures and criteria minimize those influences when developing a theory.

The scientific method has four steps:

1. Observation and description of a phenomenon or group of phenomena.
2. Formulation of a hypothesis to explain the phenomena.
3. Use of the hypothesis to predict the existence of other phenomena or to predict quantitatively the results of new observations.
4. Performance of experimental tests of the predictions by several independent experimenters and properly performed experiments.

While the researcher may bring certain biases to the study, it's important that bias not be permitted to enter into the interpretation. It's also important that data that doesn't fit the hypothesis not be ruled out. This is unlikely to happen if the researcher is open to the possibility that the hypothesis might turn out to be null. Another important caution is to be certain that the methods for analyzing and interpreting are flawless. Abiding by these mandates is important if the discovery is to make a contribution to human understanding.

Skill 6.7   Understand social science research and knows how social scientists locate, gather, organize, analyze, and report information using standard research methodologies

Primary sources are works, records, memoirs or interviews that were created or conducted during or immediately after the period being studied. Secondary sources are works written significantly after the period being studied and are based upon primary sources.

Suppose you are preparing for a presentation on the Civil War and you intend to focus on causal factors, an issue that has often been debated. If you are examining slavery as a cause, a graph of the increase in the number of slaves by area of the country for the previous 100 years would be very useful in the discussion. If you are focusing on the economic conditions that were driving the politics of the age, graphs of GDP, distribution of wealth geographically and individually, and the relationship of wealth to ownership of slaves would be useful.

If you are discussing the war in Iraq, detailed maps with geopolitical elements would help clarify not only the day-to-day happenings but also the historical features that led up to it. Depending on the issue, a map showing the number of oil fields and their location relative to the various political factions, along with charts showing daily and yearly output of those fields might be useful. If you are teaching the history of space travel, photos of famous astronauts will make the discussion more interesting. If you are discussing the growth of the Texas oil industry, graphs illustrating this growth and charts showing oil discoveries and their relationship to the lives of everyday Americans would be helpful.

See Skill 6.5

Skill 6.8   Evaluate the validity of social science information from primary and secondary sources regarding bias issues, propaganda, point of view, and frame of reference

Making a decision based on given information requires a careful interpretation to decide the strength of the evidence supplied and what it means.

A chart showing that the number of foreign-born inhabitants of the United States has increased annually over the last ten years might allow one to make some preliminary conclusions. These might concern population growth and changes in the sizes of ethnic groups in the United States relative to one another and to white Caucasians as a whole. However, the chart would not give information about the *reasons* why this number increased, or appropriately and effectively address matters of immigration status. Drawing conclusions from this information would thus be premature.

Bias describes a personal slant upon an issue or event. For example, a political bias may draw on a conservative or liberal view of a particular issue. Historical bias may also reflect the historical context of a particular time period. Identifying bias within a piece can help a researcher determine whether information presented in the source is valid.

A person's **point of view** is related to, but not the same as, bias. Point of view describes an individual person's take on a situation or event and draws on his or her own personal experience, ideas, and opinions. **Frame of reference**—the context in which a writer created or a reader examines a document—can also influence interpretation.

A work of **propaganda** aims to convince a reader or viewer of a certain idea or to behave in a certain way. Recognizing propaganda can help a person determine the message of a source and think about it critically. Several common types of propaganda exist. These include:

- Glittering generalities
- Bandwagon
- Star appeal, or testimonial
- Stereotyping

Skill 6.9   Understand and evaluates multiple points of view and frames of reference relating to issues in the social sciences

Historical interpretation is typically influences by the interpreter's **point of view**—the lens through which one interprets events—and **frame of reference,** the personal and societal historical context through which one interprets events. Thus, two different people may have nearly opposing interpretations of the same event or idea depending on each person's point of view and frame of reference.

Analyzing an event or issue from multiple points of view involves seeking out sources that advocate or express those perspectives, and comparing them with one another. Listening to the speeches of Martin Luther King, Jr. provides insight on one group's perspective of civil rights in the United States in the 1950s and 1960s. Public statements of George Wallace, an American governor and segregationist, provide another perspective from the same time period. Looking at the proposed legislation at the time and how it was passed sheds light on public attitudes regarding race and segregation during the 1950 and 1960s.

Comparing these perspectives on the matter of civil rights provides information on the key issues that each group was concerned about, and gives a fuller picture of the societal changes that were occurring at that time. Analysis of any social event, issue, problem or phenomenon requires that various perspectives be taken into account in this way. One way to analyze historical events, patterns and relationships is to focus on historical themes. There are many themes that run throughout human history, and they can be used to make comparisons between different historical times, as well as between nations and peoples. While new themes are always being explored, a few of the widely recognized historical frames of reference are as follows:

Politics and political institutions can provide information on the prevailing opinions and beliefs of a group and how they change over time. Historically, Texas has produced several important political figures, and was a consistent supporter of the Democratic Party for nearly a century. This has changed in recent years, with the Republican Party gaining more influence and power in Texas politics. Looking at the political history of the state can reveal the popular social ideals that have developed there, and how they have changed over time.

Race and ethnicity are other historical themes that run through the history of Texas and the nation. Texas was formerly part of Spanish territory and then part of Mexico. Thus, Hispanic settlers have been present from the earliest days of settlement. American settlers began moving into the area in the early nineteenth century and soon made up most of the Texas population. Recently, this has changed, with ethnic minority groups in Texas now outnumbering white Caucasians. Researching the history of how peoples of different races treated one another reveals many other social aspects, and can be a fruitful method of historical interpretation.

The study of **gender issues** is a theme that focuses on the relative places men and women hold in a society; it is connected to many other social themes, such as politics and economics. For many years, American women were denied suffrage, or the right to vote. Economically, married middle class women were expected not to hold jobs, except perhaps in a family business; among working class women, employment opportunities were still limited, and women were paid less than men for the same work. Investigating gender legacies can reveal changes in public attitudes, economic changes and shifting political attitudes, among other things.

Economic factors drive many social activities, such as where people live and work and the relative wealth of nations. As a historical theme, economic history can connect events to their economic causes and explain the results. Mexican immigration is a national political issue currently. Economic imbalances between the U.S. and Mexico are driving many Mexicans to look for work in the United States. As a border state formerly belonging to Mexico, Texas absorbs many of these immigrants. Thus, it has the second largest Hispanic population in the country, which plays a crucial role in Texas' current economy. The subject of immigration in Texas is an example of how the historical themes of politics, economics and race can intersect, with each providing a line of historic interpretation into Texas' past.

Historical concepts are movements, belief systems, or other phenomena that can be identified and examined, either individually or as part of a trend. Capitalism, communism, democracy, totalitarianism, isolationism and globalization are all examples of historical concepts. Historical concepts can be interpreted as part of larger trends and provide insight into historical events by placing them in historical context.

Colonialism, for example, is a historical concept that is connected to Texas history. Colonialism is the concept that a nation should seek to control areas outside of its borders for economic and political gain by establishing settlements and controlling the native inhabitants. Beginning in the seventeenth century, the nations of France and Spain were both actively colonizing North America, with the French establishing a colony at the mouth of the Mississippi River. Spain moved into the area to contain the French and keep them away from their settlements in present-day Mexico. These colonial powers eventually clashed, with Spain maintaining its hold over the region. France finally sold its holdings to the United States in the Louisiana Purchase, which positioned the U.S. beside New Spain's frontier.

The eighteenth and early nineteenth centuries were a time of revolutionary movements in many parts of the world. The American and French Revolutions had altered the balance of world power in the 1770s and 1780s, and by the 1820s Mexicans living under Spanish colonial control won independence. Thus, Texas became part of Mexico, but would, itself, declare independence from Mexico and become an independent country. It would eventually be annexed by the United States and become a state.

Also refer to Skill 6.8

Skill 6.10   Know how to analyze social science information

Social studies provide an opportunity for students to broaden their general academic skills in many areas. By encouraging students to ask and investigate questions, they apply critical thinking skills to past, present, and future social issues. Providing them with a range of sources requires students to make judgments about the best sources for investigating a line of inquiry, and to assess authenticity among those sources. Collaboration develops students' ability to work as part of a team and to respect the viewpoints of others, which are crucial tenets in government, public service, and the social sciences.

Historic events and social issues cannot be considered apart from each other. People and their actions are connected in many ways, and events are linked through cause and effect over time. Identifying and analyzing these social and historic links is a primary goal of the social sciences. The methods used to analyze social phenomena borrow from several of the social sciences. Interviews, statistical evaluation, observation and experimentation are just some of the ways that people's opinions and motivations can be measured. From these opinions, larger social beliefs and movements can be interpreted, and events, issues and social problems can be placed in context to provide a fuller view of their importance.

Skill 6.11   Communicate and interpret social science information in written, oral, and visual forms and translates information from one medium to another

An **atlas** is a collection of maps usually bound into a book. Atlases and contain maps on geographic features, political boundaries, and perhaps social, religious and economic statistics. Atlases can be found at most libraries and they are widely available on the Internet. The United States Library of Congress holds more than 53,000 atlases, one of the largest and most comprehensive collections in the world.

Statistical **surveys** are used in social sciences to collect information on a sample of the population. With any kind of information, careful attention must be given to randomly selecting interviewees and accurately recording information so the results are not skewed or distorted.

Opinion polls are used to represent the opinions of a population by asking a number of people a series of questions about a product, place, person, or event and then applying the answers to a larger group or population. Polls, like surveys, are subject to errors in the process. Errors can occur based on whom is asked the question, how, when and where they are asked, or the biases one may hold in relevance to the poll being taken.

Also refer to Skill 6.5, 6.15

Skill 6.12 Know how to use problem-solving processes to identify problems, gather information, list and consider options, consider advantages and disadvantages, choose and implement solutions, and evaluate the effectiveness of solutions

The problem-solving process involves a series of six steps designed to help you to identify your problem, plan and choose a solution, implement that solution, and evaluate its success. The steps in the problem-solving process are described below.

1. Identify the problem. Defining the problem that needs to be solved will help you begin thinking about the problem-solving process.

2. Analyze the problem. Consider the various facets of the problem, and ask questions to help you get to the root of the problem. Many problems have many aspects, so analyzing the problem can help you determine what the most important part of the problem is.

3. Brainstorm solutions. Thinking up many possible solutions to the problem—even ones that seem unrealistic—will help you creatively and thoroughly consider various ways to solve the problem.

4. Choose and plan a solution. Consider the pros and cons of each of the options you have generated, and then choose the one you think it best. Make a plan to help you execute your solution. Your plan may include listing resources you need to gather or people you need to talk to, for example.

5. Implement your solution. Use the plan that you made to follow through with your solution.

6. Evaluate your solution. After you have implemented your solution, take a few minutes to consider its success. Did you solve your problem? Were there any unintended consequences, either positive or negative? Would you use the same solution again?

Refer to Skill 5.14 and Skill 6.6 for discussion on scientific method

Skill 6.13   Know how to use decision-making processes to identify situations that require decisions, gather information, identify options, predict consequences, and take action to implement decisions

Decision-making can be broken down into methodical steps that will result in sound decisions based on the relevant facts. Here, the first step is to identify situations that require decisions. These situations often present themselves in daily life. For example, students may need to choose what extracurricular activities to pursue, and adults choose between candidates in elections. The steps in the decision making process are described below.

Skill 6.14   Know how to create maps and other graphics to present geographic, political, historical, economic, and cultural features, distributions, and relationships

We use various **illustrations** because it is sometimes easier to demonstrate a given idea visually instead of orally. Among the more common illustrations and graphic aids used in the social sciences are various types of **diagrams, graphic organizers, maps, graphs,** and **charts**.

Photographs and globes are also useful, but as they are limited in the kind of information that they can show, they are rarely used. Unless, as with photographs, it is of a particular political figure or a time that one wishes to visualize.

Although maps have advantages over globes and photographs, they do have a major disadvantage: most maps are flat while Earth is spherical. It is impossible to reproduce exactly on a flat surface an object shaped like a sphere. In order to put the earth's features onto a map they must be stretched in some way. This stretching is called **distortion**.

Distortion does not mean that maps are wrong; it simply means that they are not perfect representations of Earth or its parts. **Cartographers,** or mapmakers, understand the problems of distortion, and try to design maps so that there is as little distortion as possible.

The process of putting the Earth's features onto a flat surface is called **projection**. All maps are really map projections, and there are many different types. Each one deals in a different way with the problem of distortion. Map projections are made in a number of ways. Some are done using complicated mathematics.

However, the basic ideas behind map projections can be understood by looking at the three most common types:

(1) **Cylindrical Projections**: These are done by taking a cylinder of paper and wrapping it around a globe. A light is used to project the globe's features onto the paper. Distortion is least where the paper touches the globe. For example, suppose that the paper was wrapped so that it touched the globe at the equator, the map from this projection would have just a little distortion near the equator. However, in moving north or south of the equator, the distortion would increase as you moved further away from the equator. The best-known and most widely used cylindrical projection is the **Mercator Projection.** Gerardus Mercator, a Flemish mapmaker, first developed it in 1569.

(2) **Conical Projections**: The name for these maps comes from the fact that the projection is made onto a cone of paper. The cone is made so that it touches a globe at the base of the cone only. It can also be made so that it cuts through part of the globe in two different places. Again, there is the least distortion where the paper touches the globe. If the cone touches at two different points, there is some distortion at both of them. Conical projections are most often used to map areas in the **middle latitudes**. Maps of the United States are most often conical projections. This is because most of the country lies within these latitudes.

(3) **Flat-Plane Projections**: These are made with a flat piece of paper, and touch the globe at one point only. Areas near this point show little distortion. Flat-plane projections are often used to show the areas of the north and south poles. One such flat projection is called a **Gnomonic Projection**. On this kind of map all meridians appear as straight lines. Thus, Gnomonic projections are useful because any straight line drawn between points on it forms a **Great-Circle Route**.

Great-Circle Routes are best demonstrated by simply stretching a string from one point to the other to find the shortest route between two points. However, if the string was extended in reality, so that it accounted for the globe's curvature, it would then make a great-circle. A Great-Circle is any circle that cuts a sphere, such as the globe, into two equal parts. Because of distortion, most maps do not show great-circle routes as straight lines. Gnomonic projections, however, do show the shortest distance between the two places as a straight line. Because of this, they are valuable for navigation and are called Great-Circle Sailing Maps.

To properly analyze a given map one must be familiar with the various parts and symbols that most modern maps use. For the most part, this is standardized, with different maps using similar parts and symbols, which can include:

Title All maps should have a title that tells you what information can be found on the map.

Legend: Most maps have a legend, which tells the reader about the various symbols that are used on that particular map and what they represent (also called a *map key*).

Grid: A grid is a series of lines that are used to find exact places and locations on the map. There are several different kinds of grid systems in use; however, most maps use the longitude and latitude system, known as the **Geographic Grid System**.

Directions: Most maps have some directional system to show which way the map is being presented. Often on a map, a small **compass rose** will be present, with arrows showing the four basic directions: north, south, east, and west. More complex compass roses also include indicators for northeast, southeast, southwest, and northwest.

Scale: This is used to show the relationship between the map's unit of measurement versus the real world measure on Earth. Maps are drawn to many different scales. Some maps show a lot of detail for a small area, while others show a greater span of distance. Though, whichever is used, one should always be aware of how it is scaled. For example, a map showing a small area might have a scale of 1 inch = 10 miles, whereas a map of the world might have a scale of 1 inch = 1,000 miles. The point is that one must know what units of measurements the map is using in order to determine relative distances and locations.

Maps have four main properties: (1) the size of the areas shown on the map, (2) the shapes of the areas, (3) consistent scales, and (4) straight-line directions. A map can be drawn so that it is correct in one or more of these properties, but no map can be correct in all of them.

Equal areas: One property of particular maps is that of equal areas. In an equal area map, the meridians and parallels are drawn so that the areas shown have the same proportions as they do on the Earth. For example, Greenland is about 1/18 the size of South America, thus it will be show proportionately on an equal area map. The Mercator projection is an example of a map that does not have equal areas. Here, Greenland would appear to be about the same size as South America. This is because the distortion is very bad at the poles and Greenland lies near the North Pole.

Conformal: A second map property is conformal, or correct shapes. There are no maps that can show very large areas of the earth in their exact shapes; only globes can really do that. However, conformal maps appear as closely to true shapes as possible. The United States is often shown by a Lambert Conformal Conic Projection Map.

Consistent Scales: Many maps attempt to use the same scale on all parts of the map. Sometimes, inset maps appear to show more detail of a specific area using a smaller scale.

Maps showing physical features often try to show information about the elevation or **relief** of the land. **Elevation** is the distance above or below the sea level, and is usually shown with colors. For instance, all areas on a map that are at a certain level will be shown in the same color.

Relief Maps: These indicate the terrain of the earth's surface, such as flat, rugged or steep. Relief maps usually give more detail than simply showing the overall elevation of the land's surface. Relief is also shown with colors, or with **contour lines**. These lines connect all points of a land surface which are the same height surrounding the particular area of land.

Thematic Maps: These show more specific information about a given area, often on a single **theme**, or topic. Population density, climate, economic information, cultural, political information, and other data may be represented on thematic maps.

Spatial organization is a description of how things are grouped in a given space. In geographic terms, this can describe people, places, and environments anywhere and everywhere on Earth.

We can examine the spatial organization of the places where people live. For example, in a city, where are the factories and heavy industry buildings? Are they near airports or train stations? Are they on the edge of town, near major roads? What about housing developments? Are they near these industries, or are they far away? Where are the other industry buildings? Where are the schools, hospitals and parks? What about the police and fire stations? How close are homes to each of these things? Towns and especially cities are routinely organized into neighborhoods, so that each house or home is near most things that its residents might need regularly. This means that large cities have multiple schools, hospitals, grocery stores, fire stations, and so on.

Related to this is the distance between cities, towns, villages, or settlements. In certain parts of the United States and certainly in many countries in Europe, the population settlement patterns achieve megalopolis standards, with no clear boundaries from one town to the next. Other, more sparsely populated areas have towns that are few and far between and have relatively few people in them. Some exceptions to this exist, of course, like oases in the deserts; for the most part, however, population centers tend to be relatively near one another or at least near smaller towns.

Skill 6.15   Analyze social science data by using basic mathematical and statistical concepts and analytical methods

Demography is the branch of statistics most concerned with the study of groups of people. **Demographic tables** may include information such as the following:

(1)   Analysis of the population on the basis of age, parentage, physical condition, race, occupation and civil position, giving the actual size and the density of each separate area;
(2)   Shifts in the population as a result of birth, marriage, and death;
(3)   Statistics on population movements and their effects on and relations to given economic, social and political conditions;
(4)   Statistics of crime; and
(5)   Levels of education and economic and social statistics.

Demography is indispensable in studying social trends and making important legislative, economic, and social decisions. Such demographic information is gathered from census data, registrar reports, and the like.

Social scientists analyze data in a variety of ways, ranging from the construction of simple charts to complex analysis requiring knowledge of advanced calculus and statistics. Social scientists use statistics to describe and explain a variety of observations that might include the characteristics of a population, the result of a survey, and the testing of a hypothesis. Based on this analysis, social scientists may then attempt to predict future events or trends. A viable theory or statistical model should do all three (describe, explain, and accurately predict phenomena).

Measures of central tendency include the common average or **mean** routinely calculated by summing the value of observations and dividing by the number of observations; the **median** or middle score of observations; or the **mode** that is the most repeated observation.

It is typically not possible to secure data on a full **population**. Social scientists routinely collect data on **samples** that are based on measurements or observations of a portion of a population. The samples are described using measures of central tendencies but also by its range from the low score to the high score. Samples ideally are collected **randomly,** meaning that each observation in a population had an equal chance of being selected.

Hypothesis testing involves analyzing the results of a sample to show support for a particular position.   A social scientist will establish a hypothesis regarding some pattern in the world. This may be that a particular counseling approach is better than another or that the President has greater support than other candidates running for office. The scientist will collect data and analyze it against a **null hypothesis**, which states that there is no difference in counseling strategies or no preferred Presidential candidate, and so on. Using the standard normal curve, the scientist is able to assess whether there is a **significant difference** allowing the acceptance or rejection of the null hypothesis. More advanced forms of analysis include regression analysis, modeling, and game theory.

Social scientists need to be concerned about **bias** in a sample. Bias can be caused by sample selection problems, ambiguous questions, or simply some people refusing to answer some or all of the questions. An **asymmetrical** distribution is one that is skewed either to the right or the left because of some factor in the distribution.

Social Scientists utilize a variety of ways to present data visually, including pie charts, bar charts, maps, scatter plots and tables, which present results from studies and surveys.

Skill 6.16 Know how to apply skills for resolving conflict, including persuasion, compromise, debate, and negotiation

Society has experienced **conflict** throughout history. This can be as simple as a difference of opinion or as complex as a divorce or a custody battle. Poorly-resolved conflict can lead to violence or frustration. Much of the work of the legal system deals with resolving conflicts through civil action filed in a court of law. Legal action is usually the most costly resolution option.

Two parties can choose to negotiate a conflict either between themselves or with the assistance of a third party. **Negotiation** provides the opportunity for issues to be debated and for both sides to attempt to persuade each other to reach a mutually agreeable decision. Often the best solutions are win-win solutions in which the solution leaves both parties better off, as opposed to the traditional win-lose (or "zero-sum") solution common to legal procedures. Often in a dispute, a **compromise** is reached in which at least one party agrees to a settlement that does not meet all of its desired criteria but is adequate to resolve the conflict.

Mediation provides a third party who acts as an intermediary voice, listening to both sides and attempting to negotiate a settlement of the dispute. When both parties agree to **arbitrate** a dispute, a third party hears the positions and issues an opinion, which may be binding on the parties.

Skill 6.17 Understand and use social studies terminology correctly

The social sciences, like other fields, utilize terms specific to their disciplines. Throughout this book, we have focused on identifying and defining terms specific to each particular discipline. Review each area in the social studies section and become comfortable with the terms used in that discipline.

COMPETENCY 7.0 SOCIAL STUDIES INSTRUCTION AND ASSESSMENT

Skill 7.1 Know state content and performance standards for social studies that comprise the Texas Essential Knowledge and Skills (TEKS)

The mission of the Texas Education Agency is to provide leadership, guidance, and resources to help schools meet the educational needs of all students. The Texas Essential Knowledge and Skills website contains the information needed for grade level to grade level for knowledge and skills. Please refer to www.tea.state.tx.us and for social studies specifics, and to www.tea.state.tx.us/rules/tac/chapter113/index.html for further details.

Skill 7.2 Understand the vertical alignment of the social sciences in the Texas Essential Knowledge and Skills (TEKS) from grade level to grade level, including prerequisite knowledge and skills

Please refer to http://www.tea.state.tx.us/rules/tac/chapter113/index.html for the vertical alignment of the social sciences for Texas Essential Knowledge and Skills from grade level to grade level.

Skill 7.3 Understand the implications of stages of child growth and development for designing and implementing effective learning experiences in the social sciences

The teacher has a broad knowledge and thorough understanding of the development that typically occurs during the students' current period of life. More importantly, the teacher understands how children learn best during each period of development. The most important premise of child development is that all domains of development (physical, social, and academic) are integrated. Development in each dimension is influenced by the other dimensions. More-over, today's educator must also have knowledge of exceptionalities and how they affect all domains of a child's development.

Social and behavioral theories look at students' social interactions in the class-room and instruct or impact learning opportunities in the classroom. The psycho-logical approaches behind both theories are subject to individual variables that are learned and applied either proactively or negatively in the classroom. The stimulus of the classroom can promote learning or evoke behavior that is counterproductive for both students and teachers. Students are social beings that normally gravitate to action in the classroom. Thus, teachers must be cognizant when planning classroom environments that provide both focus and engagement in maximizing learning opportunities.

Physical Development

It is important for the teacher to be aware of a child's physical stage of development and how physical growth and development affect a child's learning. Factors determined by the physical stage of development include: ability to sit and attend, the need for activity, the relationship between physical skills and self-esteem, and the degree to which physical involvement in an activity (as opposed to being able to understand an abstract concept) affects learning.

Cognitive (Academic) Development

Children go through patterns of learning, beginning with pre-operational thought processes and then move to concrete operational thoughts. Eventually they begin to acquire the mental capacity to think about and solve problems in their head because they can manipulate objects symbolically. Children of most ages can use symbols, such as words and numbers, to represent objects and relations, but they need concrete reference points. It is essential that children be encouraged to use and develop the thinking skills that they possess in solving problems that interest them. The content of the curriculum must be relevant, engaging, and meaningful to the students.

Social Development

Children progress through a variety of social stages, beginning with an awareness of peers but a lack of concern for their presence. Young children engage in "parallel" activities—i.e., playing alongside their peers without directly interacting with them. During the primary years, children develop an intense interest in their peers; they establish productive, positive social and working relationships with one another. This stage of social growth continues to increase in importance throughout the child's school years, including their intermediate, middle school, and high school years. It is necessary for the teacher to recognize the importance of developing positive peer group relationships. This, they must provide opportunities and support for cooperative small group projects that not only develop cognitive ability but also promote peer interaction. The ability to work and relate effectively with peers is of major importance and contributes greatly to the child's sense of competence.

To develop this sense of competence, children must acquire the knowledge and skills recognized by our culture as important, especially those skills which promote academic achievement. Elementary age children face many changes during their early school years, which may positively and/or negatively impact how learning occurs. Some cognitive developments (i.e., learning to read) may broaden their areas of interest as students realize the amount of information (i.e., novels, magazines, non-fiction books) that is out there. Conversely, a young student's limited comprehension may inhibit some of their confidence (emotional) or conflict with values taught at home (moral). Joke telling (linguistic) becomes popular with children age six or seven and children may use this newly discovered "talent" to gain friends or social "stature" in their class (social). For young students, learning within one domain often spills over into other areas.

When we say that development takes place within domains, we mean that different aspects of a human change. So, for example, physical changes take place (e.g., body growth, sexuality); cognitive changes take place (e.g., better ability to reason); linguistic changes take place (e.g., a child's vocabulary develops further); social changes take place (e.g., figuring out identity); emotional changes take place (e.g., a person grows more concerned about other people); and moral changes take place (e.g., a person challenges ethical, familiar, or legal limits).

Skill 7.4   Understand the appropriate use of technology as a tool for learning and communicating social studies concepts

The Internet and other research resources provide a wealth of information on thousands of interesting topics for students preparing presentations or projects. Using search engines such as Google, Yahoo, and reference databases such as Infotrac allow students to search multiple Internet resources or databases on one subject search. Students should have an outline of the purpose of a project or research presentation that includes:

- Purpose—identifies the reason for the research information
- Objective—having a clear goal for a project will allow the students to be specific on Internet searches
- Preparation—when using resources or collecting data, students should create folders for sorting through the information. Providing labels for the folders will create a system of organization that will make construction of the final project or presentation easier and less time consuming
- Procedure—organized folders and a procedural list of what the project or presentation should include will create A+ work for students and A+ grading for teachers
- Visuals or artifacts—choose data or visuals that are specific to the subject or presentation. Make sure that poster boards or Power Point presentations can be visually seen from all areas of the classroom. Teachers can provide lap-top computers for Power Point presentations.

Having the school's librarian or technology expert as a guest speaker in class-rooms provides another method of sharing and modeling proper presentation preparation using technology. Teachers can also appoint technology experts from the students in a classroom to work with students on projects and presentations. In high schools, technology classes provide students with upper-class teacher assistants who fill the role of technology assistants.

Skill 7.5 Select and use effective instructional practices, activities, technologies, and materials to promote students' knowledge and skills in the social sciences

The interdisciplinary curriculum planning approach to student learning creates a meaningful balance inclusive of curriculum depth and breadth. Take for instance the following scenario: Mrs. Jackson presents her 9A Language Arts class with an assignment for collaborative group work. She provides them with the birth date and death of the author Ernest Hemingway and asks them to figure how old he was when he died. She gives them five minutes as a group to work on the final answer. After five minutes, she asked each group for their answer and wrote the answers on the board. Each group gave a different answer. When Mrs. Jackson came to the last group, a female student stated, "Why do we have to do math in a Language Arts class?"

The application of knowledge learned from a basic math class would have problem-solved the Language Arts' question. Given the date of his birth and the date of his death, all students needed to do was subtract his birth from his death year to come up with a numerical answer (Hemingway's age when he died). Providing students with a constructivist modality of applying knowledge to problem-solve pertinent information for a language arts' class should be an integral part of instructional practice and learning in an interdisciplinary classroom.

Historically, previous centuries of educational research have shown a strong correlation between the need for interdisciplinary instruction and cognitive learning application. Understanding how students process information and create learning was the goal of earlier educators. Earlier researchers looked at how the brain connected information pieces into meaning and found that learning takes place along intricate neural pathways that formulate processing and meaning from data input into the brain. The implications for student learning are vast. Teachers can help students break down subject content area into bits of information that can be memorized and applied to a former learning experience. They can then be processed into independent resources of information.

Skill 7.6 Know how to promote students' use of social science skills, vocabulary, and research tools, including technological tools

Teachers should have a toolkit of instructional strategies, materials and technologies with which to encourage and teach students how to problem solve and think critically about subject content. With each curriculum chosen by a district for school implementation comes an expectation that students must reach bench-marks and standards of learning skills. In today's public classrooms, there is an established level of academic performance and proficiency that students are required to reach. Research of national and state standards indicate that there are additional benchmarks and learning objectives in at least a dozen subject areas.

They include science, foreign languages, English language arts, history, art, health, civics, economics, geography, physical education, mathematics, and social studies. Students are required to master all of these subjects in state assessments (Marzano & Kendall, 1996).

A critical thinking skill is a skill target that teachers help students develop to sustain learning in specific subject areas that can be applied within other subject areas. For example, when learning algebraic concepts in order to solve word problem's (e.g., how much fencing material is needed to build a fence around a backyard area that has an 8' x 12"), a math student must understand the order of numerical expression in how to simplify algebraic expressions. Teachers can impart strategies that teach students how to group the fencing measurements into an algebraic word problem. Then, with minor addition, subtraction and multiplication, the student can produce a simple number equal to the amount of fencing materials needed to build the fence.

Students use basic skills to understand things that are read, such as a reading passage or a math word problem or directions for a project. However, students apply additional thinking skills to what they read, how they might apply it to them-selves, or how to make comparisons or choices based on the information given. These higher-order thinking skills are called **critical thinking skills** as students think about thinking and teachers are instrumental in helping students use these skills in everyday activities.

There are many resources available for the teaching of social science concepts. The resources used should be appropriate to the learning objectives specified. The teacher wants to use different kinds of resources in order to make the subject matter more interesting to the student and to appeal to different learning styles. First of all, a good textbook is required. This gives students something to which they can refer to and something to study from. The use of audio-video aides is also beneficial in the classroom. Many people are visual learners and will retain information better when it is in visual form. Audio-visual presentations, such as movies, give them concepts in pictures that they will easily retain.

Library projects are also good for students. The library has an abundance of resources that students should become familiar with at an early age, so they learn to use the library throughout their education. There are books and magazines that they can look through and read to expand their knowledge beyond textbooks. Younger children, particularly, like to look at pictures. The computer also offers abundant opportunities as a teaching tool and resource. The Internet provides a wealth of information on all topics and something can be found that is suitable for any age group. Children like to play games, so presenting the material in a game-like format is also a good teaching tool. Making little puzzles for vocabulary or letting them present the information in the form of a story or even a play helps them learn and retain various concepts. Field trips, if possible, are also a good way to expose children to various aspects of social science. Trips to the state Capitol Building, history museums, or the Alamo are things children enjoy and remember. Today's world of technology offers myriad resources to the teacher. He or she should make use of as many of them as possible to keep the material more interesting for the student and to aide in its retention.

Skill 7.7   Know how to communicate the value of social studies education to students, parents/caregivers, colleagues, and the community

By involving parents, caregivers, colleagues and the community in students' social studies education, we are all benefiting by learning about what is going on in our world and how we interact with each other. By explaining how social studies content helps form students as responsible citizens and provides them with the knowledge that need to make informed decisions about interacting with the political, social, and economic world around them, teachers may help students, parents, caregivers, colleagues, and community members better understand the value of a social studies education.

Consider providing relevant, local details about events that are related to social studies to help make your explanation more interesting and persuasive. For example, being able to describe how knowing the way in which elections function can help citizens know when, where, and how to register to vote may help make civics education relevant to others.

See also Skill 6.3

Skill 7.8   Know how to provide instruction that relates skills, concepts, and ideas in different social science disciplines

Refer to Skill 6.2 and discussed throughout study guide

Skill 7.9   Provide instruction that makes connections between knowledge and methods in the social sciences and in other content areas

It is important for teachers to consider students' development and readiness when deciding instructional decisions. If an educational program is child-centered, then it will address the developmental abilities and needs of the students because it will take its cues from students' interests, concerns, and questions. Making an educational program child-centered involves building on the natural curiosity that children bring to school and asking them what they want to learn.

Teachers help students to identify their own questions, puzzles, and goals, and then structure for them widening circles of experience and investigation of those topics. Teachers manage to infuse all the skills, knowledge, and concepts that society mandates into a child-driven curriculum. This does not mean passive teachers who respond only to students' explicit cues. Teachers also draw on their understanding of children's individual needs and interests to design pro-grams that lead children into areas they might not choose, but that engage them and they enjoy. Teachers also bring their own interests and enthusiasms into the classroom to share and to use to motivate their students.

Implementing such a child-centered curriculum is the result of very careful and deliberate planning. Planning serves as a means of organizing instruction and it influences classroom teaching. Well thought-out planning includes specifying behavioral objectives, specifying students' entry behavior (knowledge and skills), selecting and sequencing learning activities so as to move students from entry behavior to objective, and evaluating the outcomes of instruction in order to improve planning.

Skill 7.10   Demonstrate knowledge of forms of assessment appropriate for evaluating students' progress and needs in the social sciences

See rest of Competency 7.0

Skill 7.11   Use multiple forms of assessment and knowledge of the Texas Essential Knowledge and Skills (TEKS) to determine students' progress and needs and to help plan instruction that addresses the strengths, needs, and interests of all students, including English Language Learners

Assessment methods are always important in teaching; they determine if the student has sufficiently learned the required material. There are different ways of accomplishing this. Assessment methods basically mean asking a question and receiving a response from the student, whether it is written or verbal. The test is the usual method where the student answers questions on the material he has studied. Tests, of course, can be written or verbal. Tests for younger children can be game-like. They can be asked to draw lines connecting various associated symbols or to pick a picture representing a concept. Other methods involve writing essays on various topics. They don't have to be long, but just long enough for the student to demonstrate that he has adequate knowledge of a subject. Oral reports can accomplish the same goal.

In evaluating school reform improvements for school communities, educators may implement and assess student academic performance using norm-referenced, criterion-referenced, and performance-based assessments. Effective classroom assessment can provide educators with a wealth of information on student performance and teacher instructional practices. Using student assessment can provide teachers with data in analyzing student academic performance and making inferences on student learning planning that can foster increased academic achievement and success for students.

Assessments

The process of collecting, quantifying and qualifying student performance data using multiple assessment information is called assessment. A comprehensive assessment system must include diverse assessment tools such as norm-referenced, criterion-referenced, performance-based options, or any student generated alternative assessments that can measure learning outcomes and goals for student achievement and success in school communities.

Norm-referenced Assessments

Norm-referenced tests (NRT) are used to classify student learners for homogenous groupings based on ability levels or basic skills into a ranking category. In many school communities, NRTs are used to place students into AP (Advanced Placement), honors, regular or remedial classes that can significantly impact student future educational opportunities or success.

NRTs are also used by national testing companies to test a national sample of students to norm against standard test-takers, Such standardized tests include the Iowa Test of Basic Skills (Riverside), the Florida Achievement Test (McGraw-Hill), the Texas Assessment of Knowledge and Skills (TAKS) by the Student Assessment Division and other major test publishers. Stiggins (1994) states "Norm-referenced tests (NRT) are designed to highlight achievement differences between and among students to produce a dependable rank order of students across a continuum of achievement from high achievers to low achievers."

Educators may select NRTs to focus on students with lower basic skills, which could limit the development of curriculum content that would otherwise provide students with content that would accelerate their skill levels from basic to higher skill applications in order to address the state assessments and core subject expectations. NRT ranking ranges from 1-99 with 25% of students scoring in the lower ranking of 1-25 and 25% of students scoring in the higher ranking of 76-99.

TAKS measures statewide curriculum in reading for Grades 3–9; writing for Grades 4 and 7; English Language Arts in Grades 10 and 11; mathematics for Grades 3–11; science for Grades 5, 10 and 11, and social studies for Grades 8, 10, and 11. The Spanish TAKS is given to Grades 3 through 6. Satisfactory performance on the TAKS at Grade 11 is prerequisite for a high school diploma.

Criterion-referenced Assessments

Criterion-referenced assessments look at specific student learning goals and performance compared to a norm group of student learners. According to Bond (1996), "Educators or policy makers may choose to use a Criterion-referenced test (CRT) when they wish to see how well students have learned the knowledge and skills which they are expected to have mastered." Many school districts and state legislation use CRTs to ascertain whether schools are meeting national and state learning standards. The latest national educational mandate of "No Child Left Behind" (NCLB) and Adequate Yearly Progress (AYP) use CRTs to measure student learning, school performance, and school improvement goals as structured accountability expectations in school communities. CRTs are generally used in learning environments to reflect the effectiveness of curriculum implementation and learning outcomes.

Performance-based Assessments
Performance-based assessments are currently being used in a number of state testing programs to measure the learning outcomes of individual students in subject content areas. Requiring the class of 2008 to pass the state assessment in order to graduate high school has created a high-stakes testing and educational accountability environment for both students and teachers. It has also challenged students and teachers, alike, to meet the expected skill based requirements for 10th grade students, who are now taking the test.

In today's classrooms, performance-based assessments in core subject areas must have established and specific performance criteria that start with pre-testing in a subject area and maintain daily or weekly testing to gauge student learning goals and objectives. To understand a student's learning is to understand how a student processes information. Effective performance assessments will show the gaps or holes in student learning, which allows for an intense concentration on providing fillers to bridge non-sequential learning gaps. Typical performance assessments include oral and written student work in the form of research papers, oral presentations, class projects, journals, student portfolio collections of work, and community service projects.

Summary
With today's emphasis on student learning accountability, the public's and the legislature's demands for school community accountability, both for effective teaching and the assessment of student learning outcomes, will remain a constant mandate of educational accountability. In 1994, thirty-one states use NRTs for student assessments, while thirty-three states use CRTs in assessing student learning outcomes (Bond, 1996). Performance-based assessments are being used exclusively for state testing of high school students in ascertaining student learning outcomes based on individual processing and presentation of academic learning. Before a state, district, or school community can determine which type of testing is the most effective, there must be a determination of testing outcome expectation; content learning outcome; and deciding effectiveness of the assessments in meeting the learning goals and objectives of the students.

ESOL

Teaching students who are learning English as a second language poses some unique challenges, particularly in a standards-based environment. The key is realizing that no matter how little English a student knows, the teacher should teach with the student's developmental level in mind. This means that instruction should not be "dumbed-down" for ESOL students. Different approaches should be used, however, to ensure that these students (1) get multiple opportunities to learn and practice English and (2) still learn content.

Many ESOL approaches are based on social learning methods. By being placed in mixed level groups or paired with a student of another ability level, students will get a chance to practice English in a natural, non-threatening environment. Students should not be pushed in these groups to use complex language or to experiment with words that are too difficult. They should simply get a chance to practice with simple words and phrases.

In teacher-directed instructional situations, visual aids, such as pictures, objects, and video are particularly effective at helping students connect words with items they are already familiar with.

ESOL students may need additional accommodations with assessments, assignments, and projects. For example, teachers may find that written tests provide little to no information about a student's understanding of the content. Therefore, an oral test may be better suited for ESOL students. When students are some-what comfortable and capable with written tests, a shortened test may actually be preferable; note that they will need extra time to translate.

From high school and college, most of us think that learning a language strictly involves drills, memorization, and tests. While this is a common method used (some people call it a structural, grammatical, or linguistic approach), and though it works for some students, it certainly does not work for all.

Although there are dozens of methods that have been developed to help people learn additional languages, the focus will be on some of the more common approaches used in today's K–12 classrooms. Cognitive approaches to language learning focus on concepts. While words and grammar are important, cognitive approaches focus on using language for conceptual purposes—rather than learning words and grammar for the sake of learning new words and grammatical structures. This approach focuses heavily on students' learning styles, and it cannot necessarily be pinned down as having specific techniques. Rather, it is more of a philosophy of instruction.

There are many approaches that are noted for their motivational purposes. Generally, when teachers work to motivate students to learn a language, they attempt to reduce fear and to assist students in identifying with native speakers of the target language. A very common method is often called the functional approach. In this approach, the teacher focuses on communicative elements. For example, a first grade ESOL teacher might help students learn phrases that will assist them in finding a restroom, asking for help on the playground, and so on. Many functionally based adult ESOL programs help learners with travel-related phrases and words.

Another common motivational approach is Total Physical Response. This is a kinesthetic approach that combines language learning and physical movement. Basically, students learn new vocabulary and grammar by responding with physical motion to verbal commands. Some say it is particularly effective because the physical actions create effective brain connections with the words.

In general, the best methods do not treat students as if they have a language disorder. Rather, the best methods build upon what students already know and help to instill the target language as a communicative process rather than as a list of vocabulary words that have to be memorized.

Please refer to www.tea.state.tx.us and for social studies specifics www.tea.state.tx.us/rules/tac/chapter113/index.html for further details.

Bibliography

Adams, James Truslow. (26.0). "The March of Democracy," Vol 1. "The Rise of the Union". New York: Charles Scribner's Sons, Publisher.

Barbini, John & Warshaw, Steven. (26.0). "The World Past and Present." New York: Harcourt, Brace, Jovanovich, Publishers.

Berthon, Simon & Robinson, Andrew. (26.0. "The Shape of the World." Chicago: Rand McNally, Publisher.

Bice, David A. (26.0). "A Panorama of Florida II". (Second Edition). Marceline, Missouri: Walsworth Publishing Co., Inc.

Bram, Leon (Vice-President and Editorial Director). (26.0). "Funk and Wagnalls New Encyclopedia." United States of America.

Burns, Edward McNall & Ralph, Philip Lee. (26.0. "World Civilizations Their History and Culture" (5th ed.). New York: W.W. Norton, Publishers.

Dauben, Joseph W. (26.0). "The World Book Encyclopedia." Chicago: World Book Inc. A Scott Fetzer Company, Publisher.

De Blij, H.J. & Muller, Peter O. (26.0). "Geography Regions and Concepts" (Sixth Edition). New York: John Wiley & Sons, Inc., Publisher.

Encyclopedia Americana. (26.0). Danbury, Connecticut: Grolier Incorporated, Publisher.

Encyclopedia Britannica.. 2010. Encyclopædia Britannica Online. Nov.–Dec. 2010. http://www.britannica.com.

Faragher, John Mack, et al. Out of Many. Upper Saddle River, New Jersey: Prentice Hall, 2005.

Heigh, Christopher (Editor). (26.0). "The Cambridge Historical Encyclopedia of Great Britain and Ireland." Cambridge: Cambridge University Press, Publisher.

Henderson, David, et al. Concise Encyclopedia of Economics. Dec. 2010. http://www.econlib.org/library/CEE.html.

Hunkins, Francis P. & Armstrong, David G. (26.0). "World Geography People and Places." Columbus, Ohio: Charles E. Merrill Publishing Co. A Bell & Howell Company, Publishers.

Jarolimek, John; Anderson, J. Hubert & Durand, Loyal, Jr. (26.0). "World Neighbors." New York: Macmillan Publishing Company. London: Collier Macmillan Publishers.

"Landmark Cases of the Supreme Court." Streetlaw.org. Dec. 2010. http://www.streetlaw.org/en/landmark.aspx.

Lone Star Junction: A Texas and Texas History Resource. Nov.–Dec. 2010. http://www.lsjunction.com/.

McConnell, Campbell R. (26.0). "Economics-Principles, Problems, and Policies" (Tenth Edition). New York: McGraw-Hill Book Company, Publisher.

Millard, Dr. Anne & Vanags, Patricia. (26.0). "The Usborne Book of World History." London: Usborne Publishing Ltd., Publisher.

Novosad, Charles (Executive Editor). (26.0). "The Nystrom Desk Atlas." Chicago: Nystrom Division of Herff Jones, Inc., Publisher.

Patton, Clyde P.; Rengert, Arlene C.; Saveland, Robert N.; Cooper, Kenneth S. & Cam, Patricia T. (26.0). "A World View." Morristown, N.J.: Silver Burdette Companion, Publisher.

Schwartz, Melvin & O'Connor, John R. (26.0). "Exploring A Changing World." New York: Globe Book Company, Publisher.

"The Annals of America: Selected Readings on Great Issues in American History 1620-1968." (26.0). United States of America: William Benton, Publisher.

Tindall, George Brown & Shi, David E. (26.0). "America—A Narrative History" (Fourth Edition). New York: W.W. Norton & Company, Publisher.

Todd, Lewis Paul & Curti, Merle. (26.0). "Rise of the American Nation" (Third Edition). New York: Harcourt, Brace, Jovanovich, Inc., Publishers.

Tyler, Jenny; Watts, Lisa; Bowyer, Carol; Trundle, Roma & Warrender, Annabelle (26.0) 'The Usborne Book of World Geography." London: Usborne Publishing Ltd., Publisher.

U.S. Census Bureau. United States Government. Dec. 12, 2010. http://www.census.gov/.

Willson, David H. (26.0). "A History of England." Hinsdale, Illinois: The Dryder Press, Inc. Publisher.

Sample Test

1. The period of intellectual and artistic rebirth in Europe was called:
(Easy) (Skill 1.1)

   A. Age of Exploration

   B. Colonialism

   C. Renaissance

   D. Imperialism

2. What year was Texas first admitted to the Union?
(Average) (Skill 1.1)

   A. 1836

   B. 1845

   C. 1861

   D. 1877

3. What was a major source of contention between American settlers in Texas and the Mexican government in the 1830s and 1840s?
(Rigorous) (Skill 1.2)

   A. The Americans wished to retain slavery, which had been outlawed in Mexico.

   B. The Americans had agreed to learn Spanish and become Roman Catholic, but failed to do so.

   C. The Americans retained ties to the United States, and Santa Ana feared the power of the United States.

   D. All of the above

4. Which of the following was not a leading a factor leading to the American Revolution?
(Rigorous) (Skill 1.3)

   A. The desire for an imperial state

   B. Belief in equality

   C. Belief in no taxation without representation

   D. The desire for freedom

5. **The first communities became settled because of: (Average) (Skill 1.4)**

A. the desire to trade

B. the emergence of agriculture

C. the creation of pottery

D. the development of mythology

6. **Chronology is closely related to all of the following skills except: (Average) (Skill 1.5)**

A. Sequencing

B. Cause and effect

C. Making connections

D. Drawing conclusions

7. **The significance of which of the following events is mostly likely to be interpreted differently depending on the interpreter's frame reference: (Rigorous) (Skill 1.6)**

A. the closing of a local factory

B. the effects of a major earthquake

C. the election of a new president

D. a declaration of war

8. **One tribe of Native Americans formed a representative government referred to as the _____ Confederacy. (Rigorous) (Skill 1.7)**

A. Cherokee

B. Seminole

C. Wampanoag

D. Iroquois

9.   Which one of the following is not a reason why Europeans came to the New World?
(Average) (Skill 1.8)

A.   To find resources in order to increase wealth

B.   To learn about native cultures

C.   To increase a ruler's power and importance

D.   To spread Christianity

10.   Collectively, the first ten Amendments to the Constitution are known as the: (Easy) (Skill 1.9)

A.   Articles of Confederation

B.   Mayflower Compact

C.   Bill of Rights

D.   Declaration of the Rights of Man

11.   The belief that the United States should expand all the way to the Pacific Ocean was called:
(Easy) (Skill 1.10)

A.   Monroe Doctrine

B.   Federalism

C.   Manifest Destiny

D.   Nationalism

12.   The tensions between the North and South before the Civil War mostly stemmed from:
(Rigorous) (Skill 1.11)

A.   political differences

B.   cultural differences

C.   economic differences

D.   historical differences

13.   The right of the states to declare invalid any act of Congress that they felt was unjust was known as:
(Average) (Skill 1.12)

A.   Declaration of Independence

B.   Missouri Compromise

C.   Monroe Doctrine

D.   Doctrine of Nullification

14.   The First and Second Great Awakenings refer to:
(Average)(Skill 1.13)

A.   religious movements

B.   political movements

C.   military movements

D.   industrialization

15. In 1900, a hurricane devastated the city of: (Average)(Skill 1.14)

   A. Houston

   B. Galveston

   C. Corpus Christi

   D. San Antonio

16. Stephen Austin led a movement to colonize Texas as: (Easy)(Skill 1.15)

   A. French

   B. Spanish

   C. Mexican

   D. American

17. During the early 1900s, millions of immigrants entered the United States at: (Easy) (Skill 1.16)

   A. South Padre Island

   B. California-Mexico border

   C. Port of Charleston

   D. Ellis Island

18. The basic unit of study in geography is: (Easy) (Skill 2.1)

   A. The region

   B. A country

   C. One mile

   D. A culture

19. Which of the following is not a region of Texas? (Rigorous) (Skill 2.2)

   A. Pineywoods

   B. the Gulf Coast

   C. Capital District

   D. Panhandle Plains

20. All of these are examples of human-environment interaction except: (Rigorous) (Skill 2.3)

   A. agriculture

   B. map-making

   C. mining

   D. building suburbs

21. The influence of physical characteristics of how people live is part of which theme of geography? (Rigorous) (Skill 2.4)

A. regions

B. location

C. movement

D. human-environment interaction

22. Absolute location is identified by: (Average) (Skill 2.5)

A. direction

B. latitude and longitude

C. city and state

D. regional characteristics

23. Erosion occurs as the result of (Easy) (Skill 2.6)

A. wind and water

B. plate tectonics

C. climate

D. subduction

24. Most people in the United States live in: (Average) (Skill 2.7)

A. rural areas

B. river deltas

C. cities

D. mountainous areas

25. Which river is the longest in the United States? (Average) (Skill 2.8)

A. Rio Grande

B. St. Lawrence

C. Mississippi

D. Colorado

26. What natural resource most influences Texas life and politics today? (Average) (Skill 2.9)

A. Cotton

B. Oil

C. Salt

D. Rice

27. **What technological development most influenced the growth of the American West? (Rigorous) (Skill 2.10)**

    A. the steamboat

    B. the cotton gin

    C. the telegraph

    D. the railroad

28. **Which of the following is not a basic need that must be met? (Average) (Skill 3.1)**

    A. food

    B. recreation

    C. clothing

    D. shelter

29. **Economics is best described as the study of: (Average) (Skill 3.2)**

    A. how money is used in different societies

    B. how different political systems produce goods and services

    C. how human beings use limited resources to supply their needs and wants

    D. how human beings have developed trading practices through the years

30. **Which of the following is not a significant influence within the free enterprise system? (Rigorous) (Skill 3.3)**

    A. government planning

    B. markets

    C. entrepreneurs

    D. innovation

31. **Savings most contributes to the growth of the economy by (Rigorous) (Skill 3.4)**

    A. decreasing consumer spending

    B. increasing the overall money supply

    C. providing funds for investment

    D. encouraging inflation

32. **The patterns of work in developing countries: (Rigorous)(Skill 3.5)**

    A. resemble those of the past

    B. are more efficient than those of industrialized nations

    C. are comparable to those of developed nations

    D. have changed greatly over the last two centuries

33. The free enterprise system of Texas is based on that of: (Easy) (Skill 3.6)

A. Spain

B. Mexico

C. France

D. the United States

34. Consumers most influence the economy by: (Average) (Skill 3.7)

A. creating demand

B. setting prices

C. determining supply

D. selling products

35. Perfect competition and monopolistic competition most differ in relation to: (Rigorous) (Skill 3.8)

A. type of product sold

B. use in the free enterprise system

C. number of competing producers

D. similarities among products

36. The interaction of supply and demand most affect: (Rigorous) (Skill 3.9)

A. scarcity

B. prices

C. production

D. entrepreneurship

37. The service industry includes: (Easy) (Skill 3.10)

A. farming

B. manufacturing

C. retail sales

D. health care

38. The _____ is a monetary measure of the economy's output during a specified time period and is used by all nations to measure and compare national production. (Average) (Skill 3.11)

A. Inflation Rate

B. Gross Domestic Product (GDP)

C. Unemployment Rate

D. National Output

39. Which of the following is not an economic indicator? (Rigorous) (Skill 3.11)

A. literacy rate

B. life expectancy

C. unemployment rate

D. free enterprise

40. Which of the following is not a result of the Industrial Revolution? (Average)(Skill 3.12)

A. Growth of cities

B. Increased productivity

C. Specialization and division of labor

D. Rise in religious tolerance

41. Increased _____ is both a cause and an effect of greater economic interdependence. (Rigorous) (Skill 3.13)

A. globalization

B. consumer demand

C. scarcity

D. unemployment

42. The stock market crash of 1929 directly contributed to the beginning of: (Easy) (Skill 3.14)

A. World War I

B. the Marshall Plan

C. the Great Depression

D. the Second Industrial Revolution

43. What is not a purpose of rules and laws? (Average) (Skill 4.1)

A. maintain order

B. catch criminals

C. keep people safe

D. establish guidelines for behavior

44. Which one of the following is not a function or responsibility of the U.S. political parties? (Average) (Skill 4.2)

A. Conducting elections or the voting process

B. Obtaining funds needed for election campaigns

C. Choosing candidates to run for public office

D. Making voters aware of issues and other public affairs information

45. Which of the following is a function of the executive branch? (Average) (Skill 4.2)

   A. make laws

   B. enforce laws

   C. interpret laws

   D. repeal laws

46. Which of the following is not a branch of government? (Easy) (Skill 4.2)

   A. executive branch

   B. federal branch

   C. legislative branch

   D. judicial branch

47. The principle of checks and balances refers to: (Average) (Skill 4.3)

   A. the ability of each branch of government to limit the actions of others

   B. the creation of a series of guaranteed rights

   C. the balance of power between the federal government and the states

   D. the recognition of minority rights alongside majority rule

48. The Republic of Texas had a constitution that did all of the following except: (Rigorous)(Skill 4.4)

   A. Provided for a government with three branches

   B. Provided for checks and balances

   C. Had a Bill of Rights

   D. Had Articles of Confederation

49. The head of state of a monarchy might be called a: (Easy) (Skill 4.6)

   A. president

   B. king

   C. prime minister

   D. dictator

50. Constitutions are formally changed by: (Average) (Skill 4.7)

   A. amendments

   B. court decisions

   C. laws

   D. referendums

51. **What Supreme Court ruling dealt with the issue of civil rights? (Average) (Skill 4.8)**

   A. Miranda *v* Arizona

   B. Mapp *v* Ohio

   C. Dred Scott *v* Sandford

   D. Marbury *v* Madison

52. **The basic building block of the democratic process is: (Average) (Skill 4.9)**

   A. legislation

   B. voting

   C. free speech

   D. judicial review

53. **The 50 stars on the U.S. flag stand for: (Easy) (Skill 4.10)**

   A. the number of U.S. senators

   B. 50 years of U.S. independence from Britain

   C. amendments to the U.S. Constitution

   D. the 50 U.S. states

54. **In a democratic society, the right to vote is closely tied to the responsibility of: (Rigorous) (Skill 4.11)**

   A. jury duty

   B. running for office

   C. being informed

   D. speaking freely

55. **What is not a way that Texans can fulfill their responsibilities to the state? (Rigorous) (Skill 4.12)**

   A. by voting in other states' elections

   B. by displaying respect for others when traveling

   C. by following state and national laws

   D. by participating in local government

56. **Citizenship in a European Union nation grants: (Rigorous) (Skill 4.13)**

   A. exactly the same citizenship rights in all other European Union nations

   B. special citizenship rights shared among European Union nations

   C. no additional citizenship rights in other European Union nations

   D. differing citizenship rights in different European Union nations

57. **The movement of cultural ideas or materials between populations is known as: (Rigorous)(Skill 5.1)**

   A. Adaptation

   B. Innovation

   C. Acculturalization

   D. Cultural diffusion

58. **Throughout history, families have filled all of the following types of roles except: (Rigorous) (Skill 5.3)**

   A. cultural

   B. political

   C. economic

   D. social

59. **All of the following are basic institutions around which societies are organized except: (Rigorous) (Skill 5.4)**

   A. education

   B. religion

   C. corporation

   D. family

60. **Historical Native Americans in Texas relied on _____ to pass on cultural information. (Average) (Skill 5.5)**

   A. sculpture

   B. written texts

   C. spirituals

   D. oral tradition

61. **Typically, an ethnic group is a subdivision of a: (Average) (Skill 5.7)**

   A. religious group

   B. political group

   C. racial group

   D. national group

62. The officially secular culture of the United States is least like that of: (Rigorous) (Skill 5.8)

    A. Iran

    B. Great Britain

    C. China

    D. Egypt

63. What has greatly contributed to American diversity? (Easy) (Skill 5.9)

    A. the Bill of Rights

    B. immigration

    C. federalism

    D. cultural unity

64. In recent decades, the social status of women in the United States have been: (Average) (Skill 5.10)

    A. increasing slightly

    B. increasing greatly

    C. decreasing noticeably

    D. staying about the same

65. Unlike today, children in the past often participated in the family's: (Rigorous) (Skill 5.11)

    A. personal practice

    B. economic practice

    C. educational practice

    D. religious practice

66. The concept of self is most defined by: (Easy) (Skill 5.12)

    A. a person's sense of identity

    B. a person's relations with social groups

    C. a person's religious beliefs

    D. a person's family role

67. What invention most contributed to high-tech development during the late twentieth century? (Average) (Skill 5.13)

    A. electricity

    B. microscope

    C. microchip

    D. Theory of Relativity

68. What was one social effect of the expansion of the railroad during the nineteenth century? (Rigorous) (Skill 5.14)

    A. increased immigration from Europe

    B. expanded trade between the eastern and western United States

    C. the decline of labor unions

    D. the establishment of standardized time zones

69. What was not an effect of the Agricultural Revolution? (Average) (Skill 5.15)

    A. the growth of cities

    B. greater reliance on scientific evidence

    C. increased food production

    D. the emergence of division of labor

70. The Industrial Revolution contributed directly to all of the following except: (Average) (Skill 5.16)

    A. decline of the agricultural economy

    B. urbanization

    C. economic growth

    D. the Civil War

71. In recent years, advances in biotechnology have led to debate over the ethics of using: (Easy) (Skill 5.17)

    A. nuclear energy

    B. fossil fuels

    C. human stem cells

    D. solar power

72. Social science researchers believe that they can perform all of the following actions except: (Average) (Skill 6.1)

    A. research human behavior

    B. quantify human behavior

    C. predict human behavior

    D. influence human behavior

73. Which of the following is typically studied as part of the social sciences? (Average) (Skill 6.2)

    A. Political science

    B. Geometry

    C. Physics

    D. Grammar

74. **What is the greatest benefit of a social studies education? (Rigorous) (Skill 6.3)**

   A. helping young people grow up into informed citizens

   B. teaching students to pass standardized tests

   C. making children trust the government

   D. preparing students to make a living as historians

75. **A primary source is written: (Easy) (Skill 6.5)**

   A. by a person who witnessed an event

   B. by a person who studied an event

   C. by a person who lived long after an event happened

   D. by a person who wanted to persuade others of something about an event

76. **A good research question is all of the following except: (Rigorous) (Skill 6.6)**

   A. relevant

   B. very broad

   C. researchable

   D. feasible

77. **Social scientists might present data in a: (Rigorous) (Skill 6.7)**

   A. chart

   B. photograph

   C. short story

   D. song

78. **Propaganda tries to: (Average) (Skill 6.8)**

   A. appeal to reason

   B. prove a hypothesis

   C. present quantifiable data

   D. persuade the viewer

79. **Frame of reference is most closely related to: (Rigorous) (Skill 6.9)**

   A. historical context

   B. research questions

   C. propaganda

   D. art history

80. Point of view may be influenced by all of the following except: (Rigorous) (Skill 6.9)

    A. gender

    B. socioeconomic class

    C. historical context

    D. demographic studies

81. What is an atlas? (Easy) (Skill 6.11)

    A. a research study

    B. a primary source

    C. a collection of maps

    D. a biased source

82. What is the first step in the problem solving process? (Average) (Skill 6.12)

    A. brainstorm solutions

    B. evaluate success

    C. identify the problem

    D. choose a solution

83. Which of the following is not a step in the decision making process: (Rigorous) (Skill 6.13)

    A. Identify situation requiring decisions

    B. Gather information

    C. Identify options

    D. Manufacture data to support

84. The study of spatial relationships and interaction would be used by people in the field of: (Easy) (Skill 6.14)

    A. Political Science

    B. Anthropology

    C. Geography

    D. Sociology

85. Demographics may relate to the study of all of the following except: (Average) (Skill 6.15)

    A. people's jobs

    B. people's education levels

    C. people's interaction with the natural environment

    D. people's relative health levels

86. **Which of the following is not useful in resolving conflict?**
(Average)(Skill 6.16)

    A. Persuasion

    B. Anger

    C. Compromise

    D. Negotiation

87. **A project or research presentation outline should include all of the following except:**
(Rigorous) (Skill 7.4)

    A. Student's opinion

    B. Purpose

    C. Procedure

    D. Objective

88. **The interdisciplinary curriculum approach does all but the following:**
(Rigorous) (Skill 7.5)

    A. Provide a meaningful balance with curriculum and depth

    B. Promote critical thinking

    C. Waste time

    D. Provide a constructive modality of applying knowledge to problem solving

89. **The social science teacher should:**
(Average) (Skill 7.9)

    A. Teach what he/she likes

    B. Skip difficult material

    C. Give students the option of selecting what they want to study

    D. Make connections between knowledge, methods in social science and other areas

90. **When teaching English as a Second Language, the teacher should:**
(Rigorous)(Skill 7.11)

    A. Teach with the student's developmental level in mind

    B. Have no standards and move with the flow

    C. Dumb down the instruction

    D. Use only one inflexible approach

Answer Key

1.	C	34.	A	67.	C
2.	B	35.	C	68.	D
3	D	36.	B	69.	B
4.	A	37.	D	70.	D
5.	B	38.	B	71.	C
6.	D	39.	D	72.	D
7.	A	40.	D	73.	A
8.	D	41.	A	74.	A
9.	B	42.	C	75.	A
10.	C	43.	B	76.	B
11.	C	44.	A	77.	A
12.	C	45.	B	78.	D
13.	D	46.	B	79.	A
14.	A	47.	A	80.	D
15.	B	48.	D	81.	C
16.	D	49.	B	82.	C
17.	D	50.	A	83.	D
18.	A	51.	C	84.	C
19.	C	52.	B	85.	C
20.	B	53.	D	86.	B
21.	D	54.	C	87.	A
22.	B	55.	A	88.	C
23.	A	56.	B	89.	D
24.	C	57.	D	90.	A
25.	C	58.	B		
26.	B	59.	C		
27.	D	60.	D		
28.	B	61.	C		
29.	C	62.	A		
30.	A	63.	B		
31.	C	64.	B		
32.	A	65.	B		
33.	D	66.	A		

Rigor Table

	Easy %20	Average Rigor %40	Rigorous %40
Question #	1, 10, 11, 16, 17, 18, 23, 33, 37, 42, 46, 49, 53, 63, 66, 71, 75, 81, 84	2, 5, 6, 9, 14, 15, 22, 24, 25, 26, 28, 29, 34, 38, 40, 43, 44, 45, 47, 50, 51, 52, 60, 61, 64, 67, 69, 70, 72, 73, 78, 82, 85, 86, 89	3, 4, 7, 8, 12, 19, 20, 21, 27, 30, 31, 32, 35, 36, 39, 41, 48, 54, 55, 56, 57, 58, 59, 62, 65, 68, 74, 76, 77, 79, 80, 83, 87, 88, 90

Rationales with Sample Questions

1. **The period of intellectual and artistic rebirth in Europe was called: (Easy) (Skill 1.1)**

A. Age of Exploration

B. Colonialism

C. Renaissance

D. Imperialism

Answer: C. Renaissance

The (A) Age of Exploration describes the time during which Europeans explored the New World. (B) Colonialism and (D) Imperialism are both types of foreign policy that dominated the world beginning during this time period, which was called the (C) Renaissance.

2. **What year was Texas first admitted to the Union? (Average) (Skill 1.1)**

A. 1836

B. 1845

C. 1861

D. 1870

Answer: B. 1845

Texas declared independence in (A) 1836. It was annexed to the United States and became a state in (B) 1845. It seceded in (C) 1861, but was readmitted to the Union in (D) 1870.

3. **What was a major source of contention between American settlers in Texas and the Mexican government in the 1830s and 1840s? (Rigorous) (Skill 1.2)**

A.   The Americans wished to retain slavery, which had been outlawed in Mexico.

B.   The Americans had agreed to learn Spanish and become Roman Catholic, but failed to do so.

C.   The Americans retained ties to the United States, and Santa Ana feared the power of the United States.

D.   All of the above

Answer: D. All of the above

The American settlers simply were not willing to assimilate into Mexican society but maintained their prior commitments to slave holding, the English language, Protestantism, and the United States government.

4. **Which of the following was not a leading factor to the American Revolution? (Rigorous) (Skill 1.3)**

A.   The desire for an imperial state

B.   Belief in equality

C.   Belief in no taxation without representation

D.   The desire for freedom

Answer: A. The desire for an imperial state

The colonists had no desire for an (A) imperial state. They wanted equality, a representative government and freedom.

5.   The first communities became settled because of:
      (Average) (Skill 1.4)

A.   the desire to trade

B.   the emergence of agriculture

C.   the creation of pottery

D.   the development of mythology

Answer: B. the emergence of agriculture

Early permanent settlements appeared as (B) the emergence of agriculture meant that people could stay in the same place rather than following food sources from place to place. Trade, pottery, and mythology all developed as a result of human settlement.

6.   Chronology is closely related to all of the following skills except:
      (Average) (Skill 1.5)

A.   Sequencing

B.   Cause and effect

C.   Making connections

D.   Drawing conclusions

Answer: D. Drawing conclusions

Using a time line or other aid to show chronology will show clear (A) sequence and help students determine (B) cause and effect and (C) make connections between events. It is not likely to directly allow students to (D) draw conclusions.

7.   The significance of which of the following events is mostly likely to be interpreted differently depending on the interpreter's frame reference: (Rigorous) (Skill 1.6)

A.   the closing of a local factory

B.   the effects of a major earthquake

C.   the election of a new president

D.   a declaration of war

Answer: A. the closing of a local factory

A person living in a town affected by (A) the closing of a local factory is likely to interpret that event far differently that a corporate executive living far away. Major events, such as (B) natural disasters, (C) elections, and (D) wars are less likely to be directly influenced by a person's frame of reference because they have more objective significance.

8.   One tribe of Indians formed a representative government referred to as the _____ Confederacy.
      (Rigorous) (Skill 1.7)

A.   Cherokee

B.   Seminole

C.   Wampanoag

D.   Iroquois

Answer: D. Iroquois

Five of the (D) Iroquois tribes formed a Confederacy, a shared form of government. Living in the Southeast were the (B) Seminoles and Creeks, a huge collection of people who are best known, however, for their struggle against Spanish and English settlers, especially led by the great Osceola. The (A) Cherokee also lived in the Southeast. They were one of the most advanced tribes, living in domed houses and wearing deerskin and rabbit fur. Accomplished hunters, farmers, and fishermen, the Cherokee were known the continent over for their intricate and beautiful basketry and clay pottery. They also played a game called lacrosse, which survives to this day in countries around the world. The (C) Wampanoag tribe was found mainly in Massachusetts.

9. **Which one of the following is not a reason why Europeans came to the New World? (Average) (Skill 1.8)**

A.   To find resources in order to increase wealth

B.   To learn about native cultures

C.   To increase a ruler's power and importance

D.   To spread Christianity

Answer: B. to learn about native cultures

European explorers hoped to (A) gain access to natural resources and wealth in order to (C) support the power of their ruler. Late missionaries came to (D) convert native peoples to Christianity. No one expressed interest in (B) learning about native cultures.

10. **Collectively, the first ten Amendments to the Constitution are known as the:**
     (Easy) (Skill 1.9)

A.   Articles of Confederation

B.   Mayflower Compact

C.   Bill of Rights

D.   Declaration of the Rights of Man

Answer: C. Bill of Rights

The (A) Articles of Confederation was the document under which the thirteen colonies of the American Revolution came together and was the first governing document of the United States. The (B) Mayflower Compact was an agreement signed by several of the pilgrims aboard the Mayflower before establishing their colony at Plymouth in 1620. The (D) Declaration of the Rights of Man was the French document adopted after the French Revolution in 1789. The first ten amendments of the US Constitution, spelling out the limitations of the federal government, are referred to as (C) the Bill of Rights.

11. **The belief that the United States should expand all the way to the Pacific Ocean was called:**
    (Easy) (Skill 1.10)

A.   Monroe Doctrine

B.   Federalism

C.   Manifest Destiny

D.   Nationalism

Answer: C. Manifest Destiny

The belief that the United States should control all of North America was called (C) Manifest Destiny. This idea fueled much of the violence and aggression towards those already occupying the lands such as the Native Americans. Manifest Destiny was certainly driven by sentiments of (D) nationalism and shared the expansionist ideals of (A) the Monroe Doctrine.

12. **The tensions between the North and South before the Civil War mostly stemmed from:**
    (Rigorous) (Skill 1.11)

A.   political differences

B.   cultural differences

C.   economic differences

D.   historical differences

Answer: C. economic differences

The (C) economies of the North and South diverged greatly during the early nineteenth century, as the North became more industrialized and the South relied more heavily on cash crops. These differences fueled greater divisions in politics, culture, and other factors over time.

13. **The right of the states to declare invalid any act of Congress that they felt was unjust was known as:**
    (Average) (Skill 1.12)

A.   Declaration of Independence

B.   Missouri Compromise

C.   Monroe Doctrine

D.   the Doctrine of Nullification

Answer: D. the Doctrine of Nullification

(A) The Declaration of Independence declared the colonists' independence from England. (B) The Missouri Compromise stated that Missouri's constitution could not deny the protections and privileges to citizens that were guaranteed by the U.S. Constitution. The acceptance in 1820 of this second compromise opened the way for Missouri's statehood. (C) The Monroe Doctrine banned European incursion into the Americas. (D) The Doctrine of Nullification states that the states have the right to "nullify" – declare invalid – any act of Congress they believed to be unjust or unconstitutional.

14. **The First and Second Great Awakenings refer to:**
(Rigorous)(Skill 1.13)

A. religious movements

B. political movements

C. military movements

D. industrialization

Answer: A. religious movements

Baptists have been present in Georgia since the first colonists arrived in 1733. At about that time, the Methodist denomination was developing in England and the American colonies during what is called the **First Great Awakening**. This protestant religious movement in the colonies emphasized a personal involvement in one's church and personal responsibility for sin and salvation. In Georgia, as elsewhere, protestant denominations gained in membership throughout the eighteenth century. **The Second Great Awakening** was a similar wave of religious zeal that moved through Georgia and the rest of the country in the early nineteenth century. Methodist and Baptist churches in particular saw huge growth. The Civil War cooled this revival in the North, but in the South, religious involvement was strengthened.

15. **In 1900, a hurricane devastated the city of:**
(Average)(Skill 1.14)

A. Houston

B. Galveston

C. Corpus Christi

D. San Antonio

Answer: B. Galveston

Although (A) Houston and (C) Corpus Christi are both located near the Gulf Coast, it was (B) Galveston that suffered from a devastating hurricane in 1900.

16. **Stephen Austin led a movement to colonize Texas as:**
    (Easy)(Skill 1.15)

A.   French

B.   Spanish

C.   Mexican

D.   American

American: D. American

Austin led a group of settlers that settled in Texas and wanted Texas to be colonized as American.

17. **During the early 1900s, millions of immigrants entered the United States at:**
    (Easy) (Skill 1.16)

A.   South Padre Island

B.   California-Mexico border

C.   Port of Charleston

D.   Ellis Island

Answer: D. Ellis Island

Ellis Island was the most significant entry point for European immigrants during the late 1800s and early 1900s. Comparably few immigrants entered the country through the (B) California-Mexico border or (C) the Port of Charleston.

18.   **The basic unit of study in geography is:**
      (Easy) (Skill 2.1)

A.   The region

B.   A country

C.   One mile

D.   A culture

Answer: A. The region

A basic unit of geographic study is the region, an area on the earth's surface that is defined by certain unifying characteristics. The unifying characteristics may be physical, human, or cultural. In addition to studying the unifying characteristics of a region, geographers study how a region changes over time.

19.   **Which of the following is not a region of Texas? (Rigorous) (Skill 2.2)**

A.   Pineywoods

B.   the Gulf Coast

C.   Capital District

D.   Panhandle Plains

Answer: C. Capital District

Texas is home to several regions, including the (A) Pineywoods region, (B) Gulf Coast, and (D) Panhandle Plains. It is not home to a (C) region called the Capital District.

20. **All of these are examples of human-environment interaction except: (Rigorous) (Skill 2.3)**

A. agriculture

B. map-making

C. mining

D. building suburbs

Answer: B. map-making

Human-environment interaction describes ways that people adapt to and use the land, such as (A) farming, (B) mining, and (D) building communities such as suburbs. (B) Map-making does not fall under this category.

21. **The influence of physical characteristics of how people live is part of which theme of geography? (Rigorous) (Skill 2.4)**

A. regions

B. location

C. movement

D. human-environment interaction

Answer: D. human-environment interaction

The five themes of geography describe places and people's interaction with those places in various ways. The concept of how the land influences people's lives is part of the theme of (D) human-environment interaction.

22.   **Absolute location is identified by: (Average) (Skill 2.5)**

A.   direction

B.   latitude and longitude

C.   city and state

D.   regional characteristics

Answer: B. latitude and longitude

Absolute location is the description of a place's geographic location using lines of (B) latitude and longitude. Relative location describes a place using (A) direction from other places, while a place's (c) city and state and (D) regional characteristics are still other ways to describe it geographically.

23.   **Erosion occurs as the result of (Easy) (Skill 2.6)**

A.   wind and water

B.   plate tectonics

C.   climate

D.   subduction

Answer: A. wind and water

Erosion is a natural process which changes the surface of Earth through the forces of (A) wind and water. (D) Subduction is part of the process of (B) plate tectonics, which describes how Earth's crust shifts over time. (C) Climate relates to weather.

24. **Most people in the United States live in: (Average) (Skill 2.7)**

A.   rural areas

B.   river deltas

C.   cities

D.   mountainous areas

Answer: C. cities

Since the time of the Industrial Revolution, the American population has steadily become urbanized, living in both large and small (C) cities.

25. **Which river is the longest in the United States? (Average) (Skill 2.7)**

A.   Rio Grande

B.   St. Lawrence

C.   Mississippi

D.   Colorado

Answer: C. Mississippi

The (C) Mississippi River is the longest river in the United States, extending from the U.S.-Canada border to the Gulf of Mexico, draining the Ohio River from the east and the Missouri River to the west. It is 2,320 miles long. Other significant rivers are the (B) St. Lawrence at 744 miles, which connects Lake Erie to the Atlantic Ocean, and the (A) Rio Grande, (1885 miles) forming most of the border between Mexico and the United States. The (D) Colorado River is in the southwestern United States and northwestern Mexico approximately 1,450 miles long.

26.   **What natural resource most influences Texas life and politics today? (Average) (Skill 2.9)**

A.   Cotton

B.   Oil

C.   Salt

D.   Rice

Answer: B. Oil

Since (B) oil was found in the early 1900s, it has played a significant role in livelihoods of Texans and influenced the state's goals and polities. (A) Cotton and (D) rice have also been important crops in the state, although their influence was largely in the past.

27.   **What technological development most influenced the growth of the American West? (Rigorous) (Skill 2.10)**

A.   the steamboat

B.   the cotton gin

C.   the telegraph

D.   the railroad

Answer: D. the railroad

The American West grew greatly after the expansion of the (D) railroad during the mid-nineteenth century. The (A) steamboat had been an important transit development and the (B) an important industrial invention closer to the turn of the nineteenth century. The (C) telegraph eased long-distance communication but did not encourage settlement.

28. **Which of the following is not a basic need that must be met?**
    (Average) (Skill 3.1)

A.   food

B.   recreation

C.   clothing

D.   shelter

Answer: B. recreation

Throughout history, human beings have found various ways to meet their basic needs of (A) food, (C) clothing, and (D) shelter. As those needs are met, people have time to develop (B) recreation.

29. **Economics is best described as the study of:**
    (Average) (Skill 3.2)

A.   how money is used in different societies

B.   how different political systems produce goods and services

C.   how human beings use limited resources to supply their needs and wants

D.   how human beings have developed trading practices through the years

Answer: C. The study of how human beings use limited resources to supply their needs and wants

(A) How money is used in different societies might be of interest to a sociologist or anthropologist. (B) The study of how different political systems produce goods and services is a topic of study that could be included under the field of political science. (D) The study of historical trading practices could fall under the study of history. Only (C) is the best general description of the social science of economics as a whole.

30. **Which of the following is not a significant influence within the free enterprise system? (Rigorous) (Skill 3.3)**

A. government planning

B. markets

C. entrepreneurs

D. innovation

Answer: A. government planning

The free enterprise system is driven by the demands of the free (B) market, and relies on the (D) innovations of (C) entrepreneurs. It has little involvement from (A) the government.

31. **Savings most contributes to the growth of the economy by (Rigorous) (Skill 3.4)**

A. decreasing consumer spending

B. increasing the overall money supply

C. providing funds for investment

D. encouraging inflation

Answer: C. providing funds for investment

By putting money in banks, people make it available for (C) further investment. The other options do not help cause economic growth.

32. **The patterns of work in developing countries: (Rigorous)(Skill 3.5)**

A.   resemble those of the past

B.   are more efficient than those of industrialized nations

C.   are comparable to those of developed nations

D.   have changed greatly over the last two centuries

Answer: A. resemble those of the past

Developing nations have economics that rely much more heavily on subsistence agriculture and other traditional economic activities, similar to (A) those of the past. Developed nations have economies that are more efficient and have (D) changed greatly over the past 200 years.

33. **The free enterprise system of Texas is based on that of: (Easy) (Skill 3.6)**

A.   Spain

B.   Mexico

C.   France

D.   the United States

Answer: D. the United States

Like (D) the United States, Texas uses the free enterprise economic system. The state models much of its economic and political practices after those of the nation as whole.

34. **Consumers most influence the economy by: (Average) (Skill 3.7)**

A. creating demand

B. setting prices

C. determining supply

D. selling products

Answer: A. creating demand

Consumers influence the marketplace by exercising their power to choose to buy or not buy certain goods and services, thus (A) creating more or less demand for these products. Producers (B) set prices, (C) determine supply, and (D) sell products to consumers.

35. **Perfect competition and monopolistic competition most differ in relation to: (Rigorous) (Skill 3.8)**

A. type of product sold

B. use in the free enterprise system

C. number of competing producers

D. similarities among products

Answer: C. number of competing producers

As (B) part of the free enterprise system, both perfect competition and monopolistic competition rely on the offering of (D) identical or nearly identical products. However, in a monopoly, only one producer offers these products, while in perfect competition (C) many do.

36. **The interaction of supply and demand most affect: (Rigorous) (Skill 3.9)**

A.   scarcity

B.   prices

C.   production

D.   entrepreneurship

Answer: B. prices

As levels of supply and demand diverge, (B) prices may rise or fall significantly until they reach equilibrium. Levels of supply are influenced by the relative (A) scarcity of the resources needed to provide a good or service and (C) the amount producers are willing to supply.

37. **The service industry includes: (Easy) (Skill 3.10)**

A.   farming

B.   manufacturing

C.   retail sales

D.   health care

Answer: D. health care

The economy has many sectors, including (A) agriculture, (B) manufacturing and (C) sales directly to consumers. The service industry provides intangible services, such as (D) health care.

38.   The _____ is a monetary measure of the economy's output during a specified time period and is used by all nations to measure and compare national production. **(Average) (Skill 3.11)**

A.   Inflation Rate

B.   Gross Domestic Product (GDP)

C.   Unemployment Rate

D.   National Output

Answer: B. Gross Domestic Product (GDP)

The GDP is a monetary measure of the economy's output during a specified time period and is used by all nations to measure and compare national production. Tabulating the economy's output can be measured in two ways, both of which give the same result: the expenditures approach and the incomes approach. Basically, what is spent on the national output by each sector of the economy is equal to what is earned producing the national output by each of the factors of production. The two methods have to be equal.

39.   **Which of the following is not an economic indicator? (Rigorous) (Skill 3.11)**

A.   literacy rate

B.   life expectancy

C.   unemployment rate

D.   free enterprise

Answer: D. free enterprise

Economic indicators provide information about the economy. The (A) literacy rate tells about the education of citizens of an economy, and (B) life expectancy provides information about their health. Both of these factors influence an economy's levels of productivity. The (C) unemployment rate tells about the overall health of an economy. (D) Free enterprise identifies a type of economic system.

40. **Which of the following is not a result of the Industrial Revolution? (Average)(Skill 3.12)**

A. Growth of cities

B. Increased productivity

C. Specialization and division of labor

D. Rise in religious tolerance

Answer: D. Rise in religious tolerance

The Industrial Revolution resulted in machinery and better production techniques which resulted in increased jobs and output. The increased output was due to (B) increased productivity and (C) the specialization and division of labor. This led to (A) the growth of cities and people migrated for better jobs. The Industrial Revolution had nothing to do with (D) a rise in religious tolerance.

41. **Increased _____ is both a cause and an effect of greater economic interdependence. (Rigorous) (Skill 3.13)**

A. globalization

B. consumer demand

C. scarcity

D. unemployment

Answer: A. globalization

As economies around the world become more interdependent, their relative on one another become increasingly linked. This (A) globalization both results from interdependence and makes it grew stronger.

42. **The stock market crash of 1929 directly contributed to the beginning of: (Easy) (Skill 3.14)**

A.   World War I

B.   the Marshall Plan

C.   the Great Depression

D.   the Second Industrial Revolution

Answer: C. the Great Depression

Along with increasing consumer debt, over-production, poor lending practices, and declining farm prices, the stock market crash of 1929 was one of the main factors leading the (C) Great Depression of the 1930s.

43. **What is not a purpose of rules and laws? (Average) (Skill 4.1)**

A.   maintain order

B.   catch criminals

C.   keep people safe

D.   establish guidelines for behavior

Answer: B. catch criminals

Rules and laws help establish (A) order and (D) guidelines for behavior that let people know how they should behave. This helps (C) keep people safe. When laws are broken, then law enforcement must (B) catch criminals, but the purpose of laws is not to create crime.

44. **Which one of the following is not a function or responsibility of the US political parties?**
   (Average) (Skill 4.2)

A. Conducting elections or the voting process

B. Obtaining funds needed for election campaigns

C. Choosing candidates to run for public office

D. Making voters aware of issues and other public affairs information

Answer: A. Conducting elections or the voting process

The US political parties have numerous functions and responsibilities. Among them are obtaining funds needed for election campaigns, choosing the candidates to run for office, and making voters aware of the issues. The political parties, however, do not conduct elections or the voting process, as that would be an obvious conflict of interest.

45. **Which of the following is a function of the executive branch?**
   (Average) (Skill 4.2)

A. make laws

B. enforce laws

C. interpret laws

D. repeal laws

Answer: B. enforce laws

The legislative branch is responsible for (A) making and (D) repealing laws. The judicial branch is charged with (C) interpreting the laws made by the legislative branch. The executive branch is responsible for (B) enforcing those laws.

46. **Which of the following is not a branch of government? (Easy) (Skill 4.2)**

A. executive branch

B. federal branch

C. legislative branch

D. judicial branch

Answer: B. federal branch

The three branches of U.S. government are (A) the executive branch, (C) the legislative branch, and (D) the judicial branch. The (B) federal government is a level of government, rather than a branch.

47. **The principle of checks and balances refers to: (Average) (Skill 4.3)**

A. the ability of each branch of government to limit the actions of others

B. the creation of a series of guaranteed rights

C. the balance of power between the federal government and the states

D. the recognition of minority rights alongside majority rule

Answer: A. the ability of each branch of government to limit the actions of others

The U.S. Constitution provides for limits of government power by creating three branches of government that have (A) the ability to limit each of the other branches. The Constitution also provides for a (B) Bill of Rights, (C) federalism, and (D) respect for minority rights.

48. **The Republic of Texas had a constitution that did all of the following except:**
(Rigorous)(Skill 4.4)

A.   Provided for a government with three branches

B.   Provided for checks and balances

C.   Had a Bill of Rights

D.   Had Articles of Confederation

Answer: D. Had Articles of Confederation

The Republic of Texas constitution provided for (A) a government with three branches, (B) checks and balances and (C) a bill of rights. The (D) Articles of Confederation was not a part of the Republic of Texas government.

49.   **The head of state of a monarchy might be called a: (Easy) (Skill 4.6)**

A.   president

B.   king

C.   prime minister

D.   dictator

Answer: B. king

A monarchy is a form of government headed by an absolute, hereditary ruler, such as a (B) king or queen. The presidential system is headed by (A) president, while the parliamentary system is typically led by a (C) prime minister. (D) Dictators rule over tyrannies and dictatorships.

50. **Constitutions are formally changed by: (Average) (Skill 4.7)**

A.   amendments

B.   court decisions

C.   laws

D.   referendums

Answer: A. amendments

Both the U.S. constitutions and state constitutions are formally changed, or amended, by (A) amendments. (B) Court decisions, (C) laws, and (D) referendums may informally influence how constitutions are interpreted.

51. **What Supreme Court ruling dealt with the issue of civil rights? (Average) (Skill 4.8)**

A.   Miranda *v* Arizona

B.   Mapp *v* Ohio

C.   Dred Scott *v* Sandford

D.   Marbury *v* Madison

Answer: C. Dred *v* Sandford

Although all of these decisions are considered landmark Supreme Court cases, only (C) Dred Scott *v* Sandford influenced civil rights in the United States. Both (A) Miranda *v* Arizona and (B) Mapp *v* Ohio related to rights of the accused, while (D) Marbury *v* Madison established the principle of judicial review.

52. **The basic building block of the democratic process is: (Average) (Skill 4.9)**

A. legislation

B. voting

C. free speech

D. judicial review

Answer: B. voting

The principles of democracy—literally translated from the Greek phrase "power of the people"—is the voting process. Only through democratic elections do the people establish procedures to (A) make laws, guarantee rights such as (B) free speech, and grant power to governments that may practice (D) judicial review.

53. **The 50 stars on the U.S. flag stand for: (Easy) (Skill 4.10)**

A. the number of U.S. senators

B. 50 years of U.S. independence from Britain

C. amendments to the U.S. Constitution

D. the 50 U.S. states

Answer: D the 50 U.S. states

The design of the familiar stars and stripes of the American flag have changed over the years, with a new star added for each (D) state admitted to the Union. The thirteen stripes represent the thirteen original colonies.

54. **In a democratic society, the right to vote is closely tied to the responsibility of: (Rigorous) (Skill 4.11)**

A.   jury duty

B.   running for office

C.   being informed

D.   speaking freely

Answer: C. being informed

In a democracy, rights come with attendant responsibilities. For example, in order to vote effectively in a democracy, citizens must fulfill the responsibility of (C) being information in order to make the best decision.

55. **What is not a way that Texans can fulfill their responsibilities to the state? (Rigorous) (Skill 4.12)**

A.   by voting in other states' elections

B.   by displaying respect for others when traveling

C.   by following state and national laws

D.   by participating in local government

Answer: by voting in other states' elections

Texans have duties to their state but as they have duties to the nation of the United States. For example, Texans should represent their state positively by (B) showing respect others when traveling outside of the state. They should also fulfill basic duties of citizens such as (C) following laws and (D) participating in government. They should not, however, (A) directly participate in other states' elections.

56. **Citizenship in a European Union nation grants: (Rigorous) (Skill 4.13)**

A. exactly the same citizenship rights in all other European Union nations

B. special citizenship rights shared among European Union nations

C. no additional citizenship rights in other European Union nations

D. differing citizenship rights in different European Union nations

Answer: B. special citizenship rights shared among European Union

Some affiliated groups of countries, such as the British Commonwealth and the European Union, offer special citizenship rights to citizens of all affiliated nations. These rights are not (A) exactly the same as those of native citizens, but offer at least some privileges.

57. **The movement of cultural ideas or materials between population is known as:**
    (Rigorous) (Skill 5.1)

A. Adaptation

B. Innovation

C. Acculturalization

D. Cultural diffusion

Answer: D. Cultural diffusion

(A) Adaptation is the process that individuals and societies go through in changing their behavior and organization to cope with social, economic and environmental pressures. (B) Innovation is the introduction of new ways of performing work or organizing societies, and can spur drastic changes in a culture. (C) Acculturation is an exchange or adoption of cultural features when two cultures come into regular direct contact. (D) Cultural diffusion is the movement of cultural ideas or materials between populations independent of the movement of those populations.

58. **Throughout history, families have filled all of the following types of roles except: (Rigorous) (Skill 5.3)**

A.   cultural

B.   political

C.   economic

D.   social

Answer: B

Today, families in the United States join together primarily as (D) social groups that pass along important (A) cultural values. In the past, many families—including children—often also functioned as (C) economic units, working family farms or running family businesses. However, families have little formal (B) political role.

59. **All of the following are basic institutions around which societies are organized except: (Rigorous) (Skill 5.4)**

A.   education

B.   religion

C.   corporation

D.   family

Answer: C. corporation

Sociologists have identified important institutions around which societies organize themselves, including (A) schools, (B) belief systems, and (D) family structure that share cultural and social values. Although economic institutions play important roles in societies, the (C) corporation is too narrow to qualify as a major institution on its own.

60. **Historical Native Americans in Texas relied on _____ to pass on cultural information. (Average) (Skill 5.5)**

A. sculpture

B. written texts

C. spirituals

D. oral tradition

Answer: D. oral tradition

Native Americans made many important cultural advances, but largely did not develop the written language needed to record information in (B) written texts. Native American art more often took the form of crafted goods than (A) sculptures, and (C) spirituals were cultural offerings of enslaved African Americans. However, Native Americans did rely on the (D) oral tradition to pass along information from person to person and generation to generation.

61. **Typically, an ethnic group is a subdivision of a: (Average) (Skill 5.7)**

A. religious group

B. political group

C. racial group

D. national group

Answer: C. racial group

Ethnic groups are groups of people who identify themselves along traditional commonalities, including but not limited to (A) religion and shared (D) national traits. Each (C) racial group may contain several distinct ethnic groups.

62. **The officially secular culture of the United States is least like that of: (Rigorous) (Skill 5.8)**

A.   Iran

B.   Great Britain

C.   China

D.   Egypt

Answer: A. Iran

Like (B) Great Britain, (C) China, and (D) Egypt, the United States is not ruled by a religious government or power. However, the nation of (A) Iran is formally a fundamentalist Islamic republic.

63. **What has greatly contributed to American diversity? (Easy) (Skill 5.9)**

A.   the Bill of Rights

B.   immigration

C.   federalism

D.   cultural unity

Answer: B. immigration

Throughout its history, the United States has been a nation of (B) immigrants from all over the world. This united culture thus displays diverse influences that have enriched its history and life.

64.   In recent decades, the social status of women in the United States have been: (Average) (Skill 5.10)

A.   increasing slightly

B.   increasing greatly

C.   decreasing noticeably

D.   staying about the same

Answer: B. increasing greatly

Since the beginning of the twentieth century, women have made immense political, social, and economic strides toward equality. Today, women are closing the pay gap and playing greater and greater roles in American government and cultural life.

65.   Unlike today, children in the past often participated in the family's: (Rigorous) (Skill 5.11)

A.   personal practice

B.   economic practice

C.   educational practice

D.   religious practice

Answer: B. economic practice

Until the twentieth century, even young children were vital most families' economic livelihoods. Children worked on farms, in factories, and in family businesses.

66.   **The concept of self is most defined by: (Easy) (Skill 5.12)**

A.   a person's sense of identity

B.   a person's relations with social groups

C.   a person's religious beliefs

D.   a person's family role

Answer: A. a person's sense of identity

According to social scientists, the self is determined by a person's own sense of identity. This then influence a person's other roles, as in social groups and institutions.

67.   **What invention most contributed to high-tech development during the late twentieth century? (Average) (Skill 5.13)**

A.   electricity

B.   microscope

C.   microchip

D.   Theory of Relativity

Answer: C. microchip

The development of the microchip in the mid-twentieth century kicked off an extended period of rapid technological development based on computer and electronics technology.

68. **What was one social effect of the expansion of the railroad during the nineteenth century? (Rigorous) (Skill 5.14)**

A. increased immigration from Europe

B. expanded trade between the eastern and western United States

C. the decline of labor unions

D. the establishment of standardized time zones

Answer: D. the establishment of standardized time zones

Technological developments can have significant social effects even as they shape economic and technological life. For example, the rise of the nationwide rail system during the late 1800s led to a shift from local time to large standardized time zones that permitted easier train scheduling.

69. **What was not an effect of the Agricultural Revolution? (Average) (Skill 5.15)**

A. the growth of cities

B. greater reliance on scientific evidence

C. increased food production

D. the emergence of division of labor

Answer: B. greater reliance on scientific evidence

The Agricultural Revolution had significant effects on the development of human civilization. However, the Scientific Revolution was responsible for (B) increased reliance on evidence, rather than belief.

70. **The Industrial Revolution contributed directly to all of the following except: (Average) (Skill 5.16)**

A.   decline of the agricultural economy

B.   urbanization

C.   economic growth

D.   the Civil War

Answer: D. the Civil War

Although economic differences between the North and South contributed to tensions that led to the outbreak of the Civil War, industrialization was not a direct factor in the conflict. It did, however, encourage a shift to a manufacturing economy, growth of cities, and higher economic output.

71. **In recent years, advances in biotechnology have led to debate over the ethics of using: (Easy) (Skill 5.17)**

A.   nuclear energy

B.   fossil fuels

C.   human stem cells

D.   solar power

Answer: C. human stem cells

Biotechnology, or the study of biological processes to develop new technology, has enabled people to perform experimentation on human stem cells and even clone animals. However, the ethical implications of such practices have been hotly debated.

72. **Social science researchers believe that they can perform all of the following actions except: (Average) (Skill 6.1)**

A.   research human behavior

B.   quantify human behavior

C.   predict human behavior

D.   influence human behavior

Answer: D. influence human behavior

At the heart of the social sciences is a belief that human behavior can be effectively (A) researched, (B) quantified, and eventually (C) predicted. However, researchers do not attempt to directly (D) influence human behavior.

73. **Which of the following is most reasonably studied under the social sciences?**
(Average) (Skill 6.2)

A.   Political science

B.   Geometry

C.   Physics

D.   Grammar

Answer: A. Political Science

(B) Geometry is one of the oldest sciences and is a part of the study of mathematics concerned with questions of size, shape and relative position of figures and with properties of space. (C) Physics is the science of matter and motion that deals with concepts such as force, energy, mass and charge, for example. (D) Grammar is the study of rules that governs the use of language. (A) Political science is primarily concerned with the political and governmental activities of societies.

74. **What is the greatest benefit of a social studies education? (Rigorous) (Skill 6.3)**

A.   helping young people grow up into informed citizens

B.   teaching students to pass standardized tests

C.   making children trust the government

D.   preparing students to make a living as historians

Answer: A. helping young people grow up into informed citizens

Democratic societies such as the United States function best when an informed, engaged citizenry actively participates in government. Educating students about the nation's history, society, and government allows them to fully participate in the nation's political system as adults.

75. **A primary source is written: (Easy) (Skill 6.5)**

A.   by a person who witnessed an event

B.   by a person who studied an event

C.   by a person who lived long after an event happened

D.   by a person who wanted to persuade others of something about an event

Answer: A. by a person who witnessed an event

Primary sources are created by people who (A) witnessed or took part in an event, and include letters, diaries, photographs, and other such documents.

76. **A good research question is all of the following except: (Rigorous) (Skill 6.6)**

A.   relevant

B.   very broad

C.   researchable

D.   feasible

Answer: B. very broad

A good research question is one that students can reasonably explore. In order to accomplish this, questions should be (A) relevant to the topic at hand, (C) have available research resources, and be (D) feasible to address. Topics that (B) very broad can be hard to research and write about succinctly.

77. **Social scientists might present data in a: (Rigorous) (Skill 6.7)**

A.   chart

B.   photograph

C.   short story

D.   song

Answer: A. chart

Social scientists—like any other type of scientist—present data in scientific, quantifiable forms, such as (A) charts, graphs, and tables. They are more likely to study (B) photographs, (C) stories, or (D) songs than to present data in them.

78.   **Propaganda tries to: (Average) (Skill 6.8)**

A.   appeal to reason

B.   prove a hypothesis

C.   present quantifiable data

D.   persuade the viewer

Answer: D. persuade the viewer

Propaganda may be used by governments or advertisers to (D) persuade viewers to unquestioningly accept its message. Propaganda appeals to emotion rather than reason, and typically makes broad, unprovable claims.

79.   **Frame of reference is most closely related to: (Rigorous) (Skill 6.9)**

A.   historical context

B.   research questions

C.   propaganda

D.   art history

Answer: A. historical context

Historians must consider frame of reference, or the influences and (A) historical context in which someone interpreted events, when studying historical events and writings.

80. **Point of view may be influenced by all of the following except: (Rigorous) (Skill 6.9)**

A.   gender

B.   socioeconomic class

C.   historical context

D.   demographic studies

Answer: D. demographic studies

Point of view is an individual's own personal perspective on events, and may be influenced by that person's (A) gender, (B) socioeconomic class, or (C) historical context. It is unlikely to be influenced by (D) demographic studies.

81. **What is an atlas? (Easy) (Skill 6.11)**

A.   a research study

B.   a primary source

C.   a collection of maps

D.   a biased source

Answer: C. a collection of maps

An atlas is a (C) bound collection of maps on a variety of topics. As such, it offers a basis for (A) study as an unbiased, factual secondary source.

82. **What is the first step in the problem solving process? (Average) (Skill 6.12)**

A.   brainstorm solutions

B.   evaluate success

C.   identify the problem

D.   choose a solution

Answer: C. identify the problem

In order to begin the six steps of the problem-solving process, one must first (C) clearly identify the problem to be solved. The other steps will follow logically from that point.

83. **Which of the following is not a step in the decision making process? (Rigorous) (Skill 6.13)**

A.   Identify situation requiring decisions

B.   Gather information

C.   Identify options

D.   Manufacture data to support your opinion

Answer: D. Manufacturing data to support your opinion

The decision making process consists of various steps that should be followed. (D) Manufacturing data to support your personal opinions if not one of those steps.

84. **The study of spatial relationships and interaction would be used by people in the field of:**
    (Easy) (Skill 6.14)

A. Political Science

B. Anthropology

C. Geography

D. Sociology

Answer: C. Geography

(C) Geography is the discipline within Social Science that most concerns itself with the study of "spatial relationships and interaction". (B) Anthropology is the study of human culture and the way in which people of different cultures live. The artifacts created by people of a certain culture can provide information about the behaviors and beliefs of that culture, making anthropology the best-fitting field of study for this field trip. (D) Sociology and (A) political science are more likely to study behaviors and institutions directly than through individual artifacts created by a specific culture.

85. **Demographics may relate to the study of all of the following except:**
    (Average) (Skill 6.15)

A. people's jobs

B. people's education levels

C. people's interaction with the natural environment

D. people's relative health levels

Answer: C. people's interaction with the natural environment

Demographics is the study of the characteristics of various populations. However, the interactions between those populations and their environments fall properly under the field of geography.

86. **Which of the following is not useful in resolving conflict?**
    (Average) (Skill 6.16)

A. Persuasion

B. Anger

C. Compromise

D. Negotiation

Answer: B. Anger

Conflict has been a part of history and if it isn't resolved, it can lead to violence. Resolving conflict involves using the skills of (A) persuasion, (C) compromise and (D) negotiation. (B) Anger is not useful in solving problems and resolving conflict.

87. **A project or research presentation outline should include all of the following except:**
    (Rigorous) (Skill 7.4)

A. Student's opinion

B. Purpose

C. Procedure

D. Objective

Answer: A. Student's opinion

Research projects should be objective and not based on (A) the student's opinion. (B) Purpose, presentation, (C) procedure and (D) objectivity should all be a part of the outline.

88. **The interdisciplinary curriculum approach does all but the following: (Rigorous) (Skill 7.5)**

A. Provide a meaningful balance with curriculum and depth

B. Promotes critical thinking

C. Is a waste of time

D. Provides a constructive modality of applying knowledge to problem solving

Answer: C. Is a waste of time

An interdisciplinary curriculum approach integrates the different aspects of the different disciplines. It is not (C) a waste of time. It (A) provides a meaningful balance with curriculum and depth, (B) promotes critical thinking and (D) provides a constructive modality of applying knowledge to problem solving

89. **The social science teacher should: (Average) (Skill 7.9)**

A. Teach what he/she likes

B. Skip difficult material

C. Give students the option of selecting what they want to study

D. Make connections between knowledge, methods in social science and other areas

Answer: D. Make connections between knowledge, methods in social science and other areas

Even though it is more pleasant to (A) teach what we like and to (B) skip difficult material this is not advisable. (C) Giving students the option of selecting what they want to study does not guarantee that the level of instruction meets the standards. The teacher should take the extra time and effort to (D) make connections between knowledge, methods in social science and other areas

90. **When teaching English as a Second Language, the teacher should: (Rigorous) (Skill 7.11)**

A.   Teach with the student's developmental level in mind

B.   Have no standards and move with the flow

C.   "Dumb-down" the instruction

D.   Use only one approach and be inflexible

Answer: A. Teach with the student's developmental level in mind

The teacher should always (A) teach with the student's developmental level in mind. The student's do not benefit if there are (B) no standards and the teacher (C) "dumbs-down" the instruction. (D) Inflexibility and using only one approach leads to less learning.

CPSIA information can be obtained
at www.ICGtesting.com
Printed in the USA
BVHW011519290719
PP10148500001B/1/P